Reconciling Violence and Kingship

Reconciling Violence and Kingship
A Study of Judges and 1 Samuel

MARTY ALAN MICHELSON

☙PICKWICK *Publications* · Eugene, Oregon

RECONCILING VIOLENCE AND KINGSHIP
A Study of Judges and 1 Samuel

Copyright © 2011 Marty Alan Michelson. All rights reserved. Except for brief quotations in critical publications or reviews, no part of this book may be reproduced in any manner without prior written permission from the publisher. Write: Permissions, Wipf and Stock Publishers, 199 W. 8th Ave., Suite 3, Eugene, OR 97401.

Pickwick Publications
An Imprint of Wipf and Stock Publishers
199 W. 8th Ave., Suite 3
Eugene, OR 97401

www.wipfandstock.com

ISBN 13: 978-1-60899-338-3

Cataloguing-in-Publication data:

Michelson, Marty Alan.

    Reconciling violence and kingship : a study of Judges and 1 Samuel / Marty Alan Michelson.

    x + 230 pp. ; 23 cm. Includes bibliographical references and indices.

    ISBN 13: 978-1-60899-338-3

    1. Bible. O.T. Judges—Criticism, interpretation, etc. 2. Bible. O.T. Samuel, 1st—Criticism, interpretation, etc. 3. Violence in the Bible. 4. Kings and rulers—Biblical teaching. I. Title.

BS1325.2. M20 2011

Manufactured in the U.S.A.

Contents

Abbreviations / vi

1 Thesis and Scope of Study / 1
2 Composition and Kingship in the Deuteronomistic History / 15
3 Abimelech / 41
4 Micah, the Levite, and the Concubine / 71
5 Saul and Kingship / 113
6 Assessing a Girardian Hermeneutic within This Study / 153
7 Summary and Conclusions / 198

Bibliography / 203
Subject Index / 225
Scripture Index / 229

Abbreviations

AB	Anchor Bible
AbrN	*Abr-Nahrain*
ASCE	*Annual of the Society of Christian Ethics*
AThR	*Anglican Theological Review*
BAIAS	*Bulletin of the Anglo-Israel Archaeological Society*
BASOR	*Bulletin of the American Schools of Oriental Research*
BBB	Bonner biblische Beiträge
BETL	Bibliotheca Ephemeridum theologicarum Lovaniensium
Bib	*Biblica*
BibInt	*Biblical Interpretation*
BibRev	*Bible Review*
BIOSCS	Bulletin of the International Organization for Septuagint and Cognate Studies
BJS	Brown Judaic Studies
BN	Biblische Notizen
BMiq	*Beit Miqra*
BSac	*Bibliotheca sacra*
BT	*Bible Translator*
BTB	*Biblical Theology Bulletin*
BZ	*Biblische Zeitschrift*
BZAW	Beihefte zur Zeitschrift für die alttestamentliche Wissenschaft
CBC	Cambridge Bible Commenary
CBQ	*Catholic Biblical Quarterly*
CC	*Cross Currents*
ChrCent	*Christian Century*
CJVMC	*Contagion: Journal of Violence, Mimesis, and Culture*
Com	Commentary
ConBOT	Coniectanea Biblica: Old Testament Series
CSF	Christen im Streit um den Frieden
Cur	*Currents*
CurTM	*Currents in Theology and Mission*
EB	Echter Bibel
EcRev	*Ecumenical Review*
ETL	*Ephemerides Theologicae Lovanienses*
ET	*Expository Times*

FRLANT	Forschungen zur Religon und Literatur des Alten und Neuen Testaments
HAR	Hebrew Annual Review
HTR	Harvard Theological Review
HUCA	Hebrew Union College Annual
IEJ	Israel Exploration Journal
Imm	Immanuel
Int	Interpretation
ISBS	International Symposium for Biblical Studies
ITC	International Theological Commentary
JBQ	Jewish Biblical Quarterly
JETS	Journal of the Evangelical Theological Society
JITC	Journal of the Interdenominational Theological Center
JJS	Journal of Jewish Studies
JNES	Journal of Near Eastern Studies
JQR	Jewish Quarterly Review
JRT	Journal of Religious Thought
JSOT	Journal for the Study of the Old Testament
JSOTSup	Journal for the Study of the Old Testament Supplement Series
JTS	Journal of Theological Studies
Jud	Judaism
KAT	Kommentar zum Alten Testament
LBS	Library of Biblical Studies
LitB	Literature and Belief
LT	Literature and Theology
MB	Modern Believing
ModT	Modern Theology
MGWJ	Monatschrift fur Geschichte und Wissenschaft des Judentums
NIDOTTE	New International Dictionary of Old Testament Theology & Exegesis
NIBC	New International Biblical Commentaries
OBO	Orbis biblicus et orientalis
OBT	Overtures to Biblical Theology
Or	Orientalia
OTG	Old Testament Guides
OTL	Old Testament Library
OtSt	Oudtestamentische Studien
OTWSA	Die Ou Testamentiese Werkgemeenskap Suid-Afrika
Pers	Perspectives
PT	Poetics Today
RB	Revue Biblique
RevExp	Review and Expositor
RSSSR	Research in the Social Scientific Study of Religion
RTR	Reformed Theological Review

SBJT	*Southwestern Baptist Journal of Theology*
SBLDS	Society of Biblical Literature Dissertation Series
SBLSP	Society of Biblical Literature Seminar Papers
Scrip	*Scriptura*
SJOT	*Scandinavian Journal of Theology*
SJT	*Scottish Journal of Theology*
SK	*Skirf en Kerk*
SSN	Studia semitica neerlandica
SQHSS	*Salmagundi: A Quarterly of the Humanities and Social Sciences*
ST	*Studia Theologica*
TynB	*Tyndale Bulletin*
TW	Theologische Wissenschaft
TZ	*Theologische Zeitschrift*
VT	*Vetus Testamentum*
VTSup	Vetus Testamentum Supplement
WBC	Word Biblical Commentary
WMANT	Wissenschaftliche Monographien zum Alten und Neuen Testament
WTJ	*Westminster Theological Journal*
ZAW	*Zeitschrift für die alttestamentlische Wissenschaft*

1

Thesis and Scope of Study

ACTS OF VIOLENCE CULMINATING in human death pepper the stories found in the Deuteronomistic History. Particularly gruesome outbreaks of violence mar the book of Judges. The violence includes warfare between tribal groups, nations on the battlefield, regicide within the king's inner chamber, child sacrifice, arson, rape, fratricide, and dismemberment. The violence in Judges and early in 1 Samuel set the stage for configuring the monarchy within ancient Israel. In this study I will argue that these outbreaks of violence are not arbitrarily narrated events. These stories of violence connect with one another to establish sanctioned violence in kingship. That this violence is "sanctioned" does not make it any less violent. That is, there is a means by which a "permitted" violence curbs chaotic outbreaks of violence. Girardian theory will help us to see the function of this violence which, stemming from mimetic rivalry, culminates in the scapegoating mechanism. Girardian theory will also help us to see how one form of this institutionalized scapegoating mechanism might result in "sacral kingship."[1] In the local King Abimelech, in the Levite stories associated with the dismemberment of a concubine, and in the first act of Saul as king, monarchy is more than a political institution to be "like all the nations" (1 Sam 8:20); monarchy is a form of sacred violence, perpetuated for the sake of dissipating outbreaks of violence. The violence associated with monarchy that dissipates violence is the crucial hermeneutic this study will attempt to demonstrate. George Pattison writes about this in relation to warfare texts in Joshua; "maleficent violence is replaced by beneficent violence, violence drives out violence, and the victim who was initially blamed for

---

1. Girard, *Things Hidden*. The work of Simon Simonse in this century with regard to monarchy and kingship in Africa certainly applies here. Simonse, *Kings of Disaster*.

the violence is now hailed as the one who delivers the community from its own self-destructive tendencies."[2]

The escalating violence in the book of Judges sets the foundation for a new societal organization established through the monarchy in 1 and 2 Samuel. This story of emergent societal identity, integral to the "sacred" story of the Bible, operates in what appears to be categorically profane ways.[3] Why do "sacred" narratives tell such a story? In this study we will demonstrate that in the storied movement toward monarchy, the chaotic violence becomes controlled violence that prevents its further escalation. Through the monarch, violence is transformed into an event that, while violent, reconciles conflict that might otherwise lead to chaos, dissolution, or anarchy. This transformation of violence and conflict into an event of resolution and unification makes it sacred, because violence that does not dissolve communities and instead unites them is sacred. The full scope of this study will explicate this process. "The sacred is the sum of human assumptions resulting from collective transferences focused on a reconciliatory victim at the conclusion of a mimetic crisis."[4]

METHODOLOGICAL APPROACH

Using a close reading of the literary construction of this text as my primary methodology, I will argue in this study that there is a literary connection between Judg 8:29—9:56; Judg 17:1—21:25; and 1 Sam 9:1—11:15. This literary reading will be informed by the work of René Girard and his unique understanding of the textual interplay of desire, mimesis, rivalry, and scapegoating.

Girardian theory emerged out of literature studies that moved towards anthropological understanding. Girard himself was first a scholar of history, then literature, and finally of culture/anthropology. These three passages are part of a larger textual story referred to by scholars as the Deuteronomistic History. This history tells the story of the development of Israel from the end of her wilderness wandering to the Exile in Babylon. The Deuteronomistic History, according to Martin Noth,

---

2. Pattison, "Violence," 136.

3. I do not intend to use the categories of sacred and profane as found, for example, in the works of Mircea Eliade, Mary Douglas, et al. I use the categories here only in so far as they set the stage for understanding the kind of hermeneutic that a Girardian informed literary reading will provide.

4. Girard, *Things Hidden*, 42.

was believed to be the work of one author who redacted stories into a composite whole, from Joshua to the end of 2 Kings. Scholarly opinion of Noth's analysis has led to different conceptions and interpretations of Joshua through 2 Kings, but the idea of a coherent literary work across these now separate books remains.[5]

One of the core issues involved in the early dispute over Noth's theory had to do with the reason for writing this history. That is, was it composed from a "pessimistic" or "optimistic" perspective, and what was the view of the monarchy that was so central to this entire history? A close reading of texts within the Deuteronomistic History suggests that there might be sources that favored monarchy (pro-monarchial texts) and others that denounced monarchy (anti-monarchial texts).[6] The fact that, since Noth, opinion has not settled on this issue of pro-monarchial set against anti-monarchial texts is important for this study. I will argue that textual ambivalence with regard to monarchy is decisive in the final form of the literary text. These texts remain ambivalent to kingship regardless of its social acceptance or practice in the history of Israel. A literary reading of these texts will demonstrate that the specific texts under review function within the larger Deuteronomistic History to make the reader uneasy and unsettled about the positive or negative import of monarchy. The story is unsettled about the monarchy because monarchy participates in the same enactment of violence that could lead to dissolution of the community.[7]

It should be obvious that it is not only in these biblical texts that we encounter the idea of monarchy in Israel. Canonically speaking, the biblical texts are aware of the idea of kingship as a system of government in the texts of Genesis. Again, canonically speaking, it is clear that the ways of monarchy are introduced in Deuteronomy. And, certainly the

---

5. A presentation of the variant views of authorship for the Deuteronomistic History is not the focus here, but majority opinions separate along what might be called the Cross and Smend schools. Brief review of these issues can be found in multiple works. A single, accessible review was published by Campbell, "Martin Noth," 31–62.

6. The work of scholars related to this pro versus anti-monarchial source-critical method will be detailed in the opening section of the study.

7. In this study we will begin with Abimelech, noting how violence metes out rivalry and death, but we will end with Saul, noting how violence is redistributed such that rivalry is unraveled and death is impeded. With Antony Campbell we note that between the stories of Abimelech and Saul we have the first stories of monarchy in Israel. "As an institution, monarchy was new in Israel. The one previous attempt had been a failure, Abimelech (Judg 9)." Campbell, *1 Samuel*, 85.

texts that extend into 2 Samuel and 1 and 2 Kings deal explicitly with issues of kingship. The rationale for the reading of the texts proposed in this study apart from other texts that deal with the idea or institution of monarchy is twofold.

This study will demonstrate that these particular texts connect with issues of kingship in several unique ways. First, the presentation of Abimelech, whose name uses the idea of kingship in a story that immediately follows his father's refusal to become a king, will narrate explicit monarchial themes in the book of Judges. Second, because the texts found between Judges 17 and Judges 21 have the explicit references to kingship in the biblical text that "there was no king in Israel," we are dealing with explicit monarchial themes. Third, while the focus of our reading will proceed as a close literary reading, it is also within the frame of the uniquely Girardian reading of this literature that the aim of this study will make proposals regarding the historical reality of the start of kingship in Israel. Of importance to us, then, is the opinion of some scholars that within these chapters on the start of kingship in Israel we have the oldest strata of historical record.[8] Fourth, since the time of Martin Noth it has become characteristic of scholarship to note the editorial insertions and speeches of the Deuteronomist.[9] Therefore, 1 Samuel 9–11 form part of the corpus of material about the start of kingship in Israel specifically with Israel's first king, Saul. Additionally, 1 Samuel 9–11 are framed by two chapters, 1 Samuel 8 and 1 Samuel 12, that have been recognized as being the work of the Deuteronomist's anti-monarchial hand in both chapters,[10] And finally, this study will nar-

---

8. It should be noted that that does not necessarily mean that all scholars view all of the material from this period to have been old, and certainly it is the case within redactional studies of this material that scholars have argued for various strands of traditions. The redactional layers of this material will be reviewed in chapter 2 of this study. The claim of this statement notes that within this section we have genuinely old historical material. With respect to 1 Samuel 9 specifically, Isaac Mendelsohn demonstrated a historical strata for this material in the comparative literature with Alalakh and Ugarit from as early as the eighteenth to thirteenth centuries BCE. Mendelsohn, "Samuel's Denunciation," 17–22. With respect to 1 Samuel 11 and the Ammonite incident, Klein writes that this is "usually considered to be one of the oldest and most authentic about Saul." Klein, *1 Samuel*, 104.

9. The work of Martin Noth will be more fully explained and detailed in the history of scholarship that will be presented in chapter 2 of this study.

10. "The redaction of the chapter [1 Samuel 8] is to be attributed to Dtr. Note the historian's characteristic vocabulary: 'reject,' v 7; 'abandon,' 'worshiping other gods,' v 8;

row the focus on kinship to the 1 Samuel 9–11 that are part of a section broadly accepted to narrate the start of kingship. That is, a review of the literature of 1 Samuel demonstrates that since the time of Wellhausen scholars have understood the narrative section between 1 Samuel 7 and 1 Samuel 15 to form a cohesive unit about the beginning of kingship in the person of Saul.[11] As has been recently noted by David Howard, "The usual starting point for studies on biblical attitudes toward Israelite kingship is in 1 Samuel 7–12."[12] About these texts in 1 Samuel, Bruce Birch stated, "Scholars have long recognized that the Book of 1 Samuel is crucial for our understanding of the development of the Israelite kingship. It is virtually our only written source for the transition period from tribal league to monarchy . . . This is especially true of those chapters dealing directly with the establishment of Saul as the first king of Israel (7–15). It is here that the greatest historical and theological interest has focused, and it is here that scholars have most often searched for the key to the composition of the book."[13]

'cry out,' 'you chose,' and 'Yahweh will not answer,' v 18. In addition there are a number of close ties to such passages as . . . 1 Sam 12 . . . whose ascription to the historian is generally conceded." Klein, *1 Samuel*, 74. See also Birch, *The Rise*, 26–27. See also Veijola, *Das Königtum*, 84–91. This position is not without its detractors. With respect to 1 Samuel 12 Klein writes, "This chapter was used by the Deuteronomistic historian to sum up his interpretation of the rise of kingship" (114). Steven L. McKenzie postulates a position that maintains the integrity of 1 Samuel 8 through 12, and that rejects the work of those who see chapters 8 and 12 as later editorial redactions. McKenzie, "The Trouble," 301–7.

11. The contribution of Wellhausen includes Wellhausen, *Der Text*. Wellhausen, *Prolegomena*.

12. Howard, "The Case," 103. Howard's article provides a solid review of the work of Gerald Gerbrandt's dissertation and later book titled *Kingship according to the Deuteronomistic History*. Howard also notes that references to kingship occur in 1 Samuel prior to chapter 9, which is the starting point for this study. He writes, "The first reference in Samuel to kinship occurs in the Song of Hannah. Here, in 2:10—as well as in words of the man of God in 2:35—YHWH's king and anointed one are referred to. Their occurrence here reinforces the view that kingship is viewed positively in the Deuteronomistic History. They function proleptically, since there was still no king at this juncture in the book, and they serve to signal at the outset the book's interest in the chosen king" (111). This reference to kingship, then, is important in the scope of the entire story of kingship found in 1 Samuel, and, as Howard notes, in 1 and 2 Samuel taken together. That these references point to the kingship is sure, but they will not frame the focus of this study for the reasons detailed in this chapter. See also the work of Gerbrandt that will be detailed in this study (Gerbrandt, *Kingship*).

13. Birch, *The Rise*, xi.

It is granted that scholars have varied opinions on these chapters, and the focus and the work of these scholars will be incorporated throughout this study.[14] The principal reason for narrowing the focus of this study to 1 Samuel chapters 9–11 within the larger narrative unit dealing with the start of kingship in Israel has to do with the fact that chapters 9–11 exclusively and uniquely treat the introduction and acclamation and inauguration of Saul as king principally apart from the activity of Samuel.[15] Further, in the three chapters—9, 10, and 11—scholars have characterized a threefold pattern of introducing us to Saul in private (principally in chapter 9), in public (principally in chapter 10), and in a public re-affirmation or renewal (principally in chapter 11).[16] The argument of this study will demonstrate that the first two private and public acknowledgements of Saul's kingship only point to his status as "prince" and set the stage for but not the reality of inauguration of kingship, which only occurs in chapter 11.

It has been stated that the rationale for the reading of the texts proposed in this study, separate from other texts that deal with the idea or

---

14. Two examples, supplementary to that of Bruce Birch, who hold to 1 Samuel 7–15 as forming a cohesive unit are demonstrated in the following works. Hertzberg, *1 & 2 Samuel*. Also, Klein, *1 Samuel*, 62ff. Hertzberg writes, "With ch. 7 we begin a new complex of the Books of Samuel, which, while not having the relative compactness of such sections as I. 1–3 and 4–6, nevertheless shows a certain unity of subject. It describes the rise of the first king and his achievements" (Hertzberg, *1 & 2 Samuel*, 65). An example of a scholar who works with these same chapters with regard to their import for kingship, but delimits the chapters to 1 Samuel 7–12, see Campbell, *1 Samuel*. At focus in Campbell's study of these chapters is the role of Samuel as the "kingmaker," which, we will suggest in this study, is not the principal focus, particularly in chapters 9–11. We note here the work of Gerald Eddie Gerbrandt, who has contributed a significant and unique study on kingship insofar he specifically does not begin with these chapters to study the issue of kingship, but comes back to them only after having studied more uniquely 2 Kings 18–23. Gerbrandt notes the focus of his study is an "*attempt to describe the Deuteronomist's view of kingship as reflected in the whole Deuteronomistic History*," (Gerbrandt, *Kingship*, 38; italics original).

15. When Samuel is first introduced in these chapters, 9–11, he is an anonymous seer. After his being named, even Saul downplays the nature of what the seer had done for him in his conversation with his uncle. And, it is only after the fact of Saul's rescuing Jabesh Gilead in chapter 11 that Samuel shows up with Saul.

16. One scholar who builds upon the implication of the three separate narratives, but who discounts their historical importance, is Volkmar Fritz. Though this study will demonstrate that we disagree with his assessment, we state here where he writes, "none of the three narratives goes back to actual historical events, so I Sam 9–11 cannot serve as a source for the history of the origin of the monarchy." Fritz, "Die Deûtungen," 362.

institution of monarchy is twofold. First, this study will demonstrate that the story line, characters, and characterization of persons and violence will share internal connections through a literary reading. Our literary reading of these texts will follow a synchronic approach similar to Robert Alter in *The Art of Biblical Narrative*.[17] We will demonstrate by our close reading of these texts that they exhibit "intimate connections through motif and theme" and the function of the connections is to demonstrate "explicit parallels and contrasts" for the start of kingship in Israel's history.[18] Like Alter, we will discover in these stories correspondences of language and thematic matter in which an "intricately interconnected unity" coheres. We argue that this intricate interconnection operates to help us discern and explain the core roots of the emergence of monarchy in Israel's history.[19]

Second, within this study, the literary reading of the specific texts mentioned above will be made with attention to the work of René Girard.[20] Girardian theory enables a reading that understands why institutionalized violence does not lead to social dissolution. Other theories of violence might be used to understand emerging monarchy and even rituals associated with sacrifice in Israel. Violence can and has been studied in several ways in Hebrew Bible texts, particularly institutionalized violence in ritual and sacrifice. Works by Catherine Bell, Clifford Geertz, Claude Lévi-Strauss, and Victor Turner are important and could be cited, alongside others.[21] The work of these scholars, however, does

17. Alter, *The Art*.

18. Ibid., 3–11.

19. Ibid. Unlike Alter's, our purpose will not simply be to examine the literary text for its interconnections, though that will be our first aim. We will also aim to see how these interconnections might point us to some narrated history for Israel which can be discerned in Girardian categories.

20. In order to be aware of the dialogue regarding the viability of a Girardian hermeneutic, one should note *Semeia 33* (1985), the theme of which is "René Girard and Biblical Studies." Girard's theory has been applied in numerous ways to both the Old and New Testament texts. In fact, Girardian theorists have established new literary readings from the Deuteronomistic History within the last few years. Articles and books continue to be developed by René Girard and by those who use his hypothesis. Most proximate to my work are several articles published since 2000. See especially Swartley, *Violence Renounced*. Girard himself continues to write and maintain a dialogue with both those who embrace his positions and those who disagree with them. Girard gave a response to *Violence Renounced* that is published within the book.

21. Select representative works of these scholars include Golsan, *René Girard*; Bell, *Ritual*; Geertz, *The Interpretation*; Levi-Strauss, *Totemism*; Turner, *The Ritual Process*.

not emerge from and read *texts* in ways that directly contribute to a literary reading. For this study, the theory of René Girard helps explore violence in text and story, thereby enabling me to maintain a literary focus in my study. Other biblical scholars have used Girard's theory to examine the Deuteronomistic History,[22] the book of Joshua,[23] and how desire, rivalry, and mimesis function in the Succession Narrative within the Deuteronomistic History.[24] Thus, Girard's unique understanding of violence and culture as "texted" and "storied" bolsters the focus of this study whose focus is on narratives about texted violence and emergent kingship.

Girard's theory of mimesis is founded in his theory of myth, in which he argues that myths "reflect a contagious process of disorder that culminates with the death or expulsion of a victim."[25] Girard theorizes that it is the myths of culture that are the primary means by which mimesis is made evident in culture. As a result, while Girardian theory has much to say about how mimesis leads to scapegoating and resolution, his hypothesis for scapegoating and resolution is based in the literary analysis of texts that exemplify stereotypes of persecution and the scapegoat myth.[26] Girard has demonstrated that the myths of culture, through stories that are texted, are a means to understanding the social genesis of ritual, specifically rituals of sacrifice.

Girard's theory of institutionalized violence and how it leads to social stability is a central claim of this study. Many aspects of Girardian

---

22. Mabee, "Text as Peacemaker," 70–84.
23. Matties, "Can Girard," 85–102.
24. Jensen, "Desire," 39–59.
25. Golsan, *René Girard*, 151.

26. Girard is careful to note that his work is a "hypothesis." Further, while Girard's work has been used in a variety of disciplines, his hypothesis is not without its detractors. Girard speaks of his detractors in his published works, *Things Hidden*, and in numerous interviews. Scholars who employ Girard don't necessarily agree with everything his hypothesis embraces. For example, see Wink, *Engaging the Powers*, 140–55. The central critique against Girard concerns the universality of his hypothesis. Essentially he is critiqued for too simply unifying a theory of culture and religion in the idea that the sacred is violence. All communities deny the horror of their fratricide by sacrilizing cultural mechanisms that allow victimization, sacrifice, and scapegoating. See the comments of Jonathan Z. Smith, Walter Burkert, and René Girard, in Hammerton-Kelly, ed., *Violent Origins*, 136. These objections to the Girardian hypothesis are important but should not negate the contribution that Girard's hypothesis can make to this literary reading of these texts.

theory play into the development of this crisis, including mimesis and mimetic rivalry, the merging of boundaries (or) lack of distinctions, and enacted violence. *Mimesis* is Girard's preferred term for the imitative kinds of acts or desires that happen between persons. Girard argues that rivals imitate each other because they seek the same object, goal, or agenda. The imitation of each other escalates as mimetic rivalry between the persons grows. As the rivalry continues, there emerges a sense of oneness of opinion or desire mutually held by the rivals. The reality that both persons want the same goal, object, or agenda creates a loss of distinction between the persons. While they are clearly not the "same" person, their plans and perspectives are the same. This imitative rivalry, compounded by a sense of lost self to the other's goals, creates an irresolvable conflict. One or the other rival must be removed. Girard hypothesizes (based on the work of various cultural myths) that it is at the point of irresolvable conflict that an alternative emerges. The alternative does not "free" the tension of rivalry and conflict; it redirects it. The redirection of this violence is against a separate victim, the scapegoat. Violence is enacted against an outside entity, but not arbitrarily. Girard demonstrates that the violence perpetrated upon the victim/scapegoat brings a resolution to the rivalry through enacted violence. Further, the "achievement" of the scapegoat to appease the rivalrous conflict causes the victim to be perceived anew. While the scapegoat is still victim, the scapegoat becomes, in one and the same act, the "god" who rescues from the crisis. Girard's theory holds that the office of king emerged from the event of the victim/scapegoat newly seen as "god." The king is the community's scapegoat. Hence, Girardian theory calls kingship "sacral" because of the distinction it brings. Sacral kingship begins for a society as a result of the mimetic rivalry that leads to the sacrificial crisis.

Girard's theory informs the story we read in Judges 9 and 17–21, and in 1 Samuel 9–11. Emergent rivalries (particularly featuring characters like Abimelech) rise to the point of dissolution and chaotic sacrifice (the dismembered concubine) where kingship emerges to resolve the conflict (even when Saul enacts the same kinds of violence by dismembering a yoke of oxen.) It is precisely in the end of the narrative of Judges where kingship seems to be introduced as a necessary office (Judg 19:1; 21:25). And yet when it comes, the people (and God!) are ambivalent toward it, even while they respond to the sanctioned violence Saul uses to enact it. Girard notes that prior to monarchy, there are only spontaneous victims as a result of spontaneous crises. Monarchy becomes the institutionalized scapegoat to prevent crisis. The unsanctioned spontaneous sacrifice(s) that bring(s) resolution in the Abimelech and Levite's concubine narratives find sanction with the monarch. As a result, monarchy is viewed as sacred and good for what it brings, but it is also seen as victimized and despised.[27] This is the antipathy present in the story of emerging monarchy in Judges and 1 Samuel.

SIGNIFICANCE AND CONTRIBUTION

This study will, using literary and Girardian theory, explain the ambivalence toward kingship in Judg 8:29—9:56; 17:1—21:25; and 1 Samuel 9:1—11:15.[28] This study will do a literary analysis of the texts associated with the character of Abimelech in Judges 9, the literary framing of Judges 17-21 with the note that "there was no king in Israel," and the connections these two narratives have and continue with the establishment of Saul's kingship, specifically in 1 Samuel 11. In Judges 9 we are introduced for the first time in the Deuteronomistic History to kingship's arriving in Israel. The text will show us clearly that kingship is the issue. In Judges 17-21 we have stories that are clearly framed in the context of kingship, even though no king actually appears. While no agent acts as king, the narrative four times repeats the refrain that there is no king. This demonstrates the narrative presence of kingship as a repeated theme. The content of 1 Samuel 9-11 is sometimes viewed as three stories that culminate in Saul's kingship. Our analysis will demonstrate that there is only one inauguration scene of kingship. But the texts will clearly demonstrate the arrival of kingship in Israel. Obviously in our analysis we will be passing over texts between our chapters. The justification for passing over these texts is deliberate. The principal characters of Jephthah and Samson in Judges have nothing to do with kingship. And,

---

27. Girard writes specifically, "At first there is neither kingship nor any institution. There is only the spontaneous reconciliation over and against the victim who is a 'true scapegoat'... Like any human institution, monarchy is at first nothing but the will to reproduce the reconciliatory mechanism" (Girard, *Things Hidden*, 51).

28. The ambivalence associated with kingship is not only in these stories where kingship emerges in Israel. After kingship is established, David enacts, participates in, and is the victim of violence. The final words of the Deuteronomistic History regarding Jehoiachin, a possible king, are elusive about the future kingship. The office of King, it seems, is never "all good" or "all bad" in the entire presentation of the Deuteronomistic History.

Thesis and Scope of Study

while Hannah and Samuel and Eli's household are connected to issues of the priesthood in Israel, and while texts related to these figures do include references that point toward the future of the monarchy in Israel, the stories do not deal with a person in the office of the king. As David M. Howard notes with respect to these texts in the song of Hannah and the words of the man of God, "They function proleptically, since there was still no king at this juncture in the book, and they serve to signal at the outset the *book's interest* in the chosen king."[29] In 1 Samuel, the person of Samuel is designated as a judge and the anticipated person who will anoint the king but only Saul emerges as a king.

Further, our study will demonstrate significant intertextual connections in Judges 9 and 17–21, and 1 Samuel 9–11, demonstrating their thematic coherence and textual symmetry. These texts understand a crisis associated with desire, rivalry, and mimesis that culminates in kingship.[30] Girard's work allows us to see beyond source-critical assumptions and perceive a unique literary and anthropological dis-ease[31] with kingship.

OUTLINE

Chapter 2: Composition and Kingship in the Deuteronomistic History

This section of the study will give me space to recognize the claims that have been made about texts related to kingship in ancient Israel. This section will include a review of some of the source critical works that make claims supporting pro-monarchial over against anti-monarchial texts within Judges and 1 Samuel. The purpose of this review will be to set the groundwork for viewing the strengths of a literary and anthropologically informed Girardian reading of these texts. By the end of this

---

29. Howard, "The Case," 111 (italics mine). In the framing of the larger story of 1 and 2 Samuel, this story of Hannah's prayer plays a larger role.

30. About the culmination of kingship in 1 Samuel 11 David Jobling writes, "In these chapters, kingship arrives in Israel. Indeed it arrives several times over, in the various anointings and kingmakings [sic]... it is a kingship nobody wants" (Jobling *1 Samuel*, 60). His analysis that nobody wants kingship is amiss in so far as the people do ask for it and do support it when it achieves a release from the kinds of violence that could break out in their midst apart from a king.

31. The hyphenated word is intentional. I intend by it to communicate the uneasiness or instability associated with kingship. I also use it to communicate the "sickness" of kingship that continues with it in spite of the seeming stability it might bring, at least for a time.

study, we will see that "pro-" versus "anti-" monarchial issues can be set aside as a result of this literary reading.

Chapter 3: Abimelech: Judges 8:29—9:56

I will apply literary criticism to discern how violence has functioned within the narrative structure of each set of texts. This particular text demonstrates an ambivalence toward kingship and the violence associated with Abimelech. A close reading will allow us to see how symbols function within the narrative and to see how violence inspired by desire and rivalry leads to the destruction of Shechem and Thebez.[32] The main character himself—not truly a king, but recognized as a sort of local regent and with a curious name[33]—will meet a violent death. As a result of this death, new order and peace is established. Abimelech's relationship as insider-outsider to the family line of Gideon (Jerubbaal) and to the inhabitants of Shechem also lends itself to Girardian perspectives for interpretation.[34]

Chapter 4: Micah, the Levite, and the Concubine: Judges 17–21

The full interplay of the story in Judges 17–21 extends beyond the scope of the individuals who begin this section; the Levite and the Levite's concubine. This full story is framed by an important redacted statement regarding the violent reprisals that can happen in a time when "there is no king in Israel." A close reading of these texts will demonstrate the complex workings of violence and sacrificial crisis that emerge when there is no king. Additionally, this section will review the fact that there are many persons who make up the story narrated in Judges 17–21, but their anonymity within the narrative will be demonstrated to be significant regarding the characterization of persons in a time when there is no

---

32. Wolfgang Richter notes with the incorporation of Thebez in the story of Abimelech we have material found in the narrative of important "historical interest," (translation mine). Richter, *Traditionsgeschichtliche*, 273.

33. In Hebrew, Abimelech means "My Father (is) King." Yet, his father, Gideon/Jerubbaal, is said to have refused kingship. But Gideon/Jerubbaal also set up a shrine and did not refuse a sort of worship directed toward his house/family name. Hence, even the name *Abimelech* suggests emergent kingship, without the full status of monarchy in Israel.

34. Girard suggests that the "marginal" role of persons is important for sacrificial victims who also bring/mediate peace/resolution. Girard writes, "This marginal quality is crucial to the proper functioning of sacrifice" (Girard, *Violence and the Sacred*, 269).

king in Israel. Rivalry between father-in-law and Levite, and the mimetic activity of the tribes of Israel will be detailed in a literary reading bolstered by Girardian perspectives.[35]

Chapter 5: Saul and Kingship: 1 Samuel 9–11

This textual unit is not the first to introduce the specific office of king, nor is it the first to tell us about the person of Saul associated with kingship in Israel. However, this textual unit functions in the narrative to tell the event Saul accomplishes that inspires the people willingly to inaugurate him as king.[36] The rescue of Jabesh-Gilead is not simply important in the life of Saul, it connects in several important literary ways with the kind of kingship associated with Abimelech and most specifically with the place (Jabesh-Gilead) and kinds of activities that take place when a tribe is threatened in Israel. Here Saul, the acting regent, dismembers his oxen, sending the parts throughout the land in an imitative act of the Levite of Judges. Here, with the "king," this "same" violence does not bring rivalrous fratricide, but achieves the people's "unanimous" inauguration of the office of king!

Chapter 6: Assessing a Girardian Hermeneutic within this Study

I will summarize my work to argue that a literary reading of these texts demonstrates a deep rooted, textually intentional ambivalence toward the office of king or monarch. I will demonstrate that Girard helps us look at and understand the formation of kingship in Israel's history, without necessarily telling us that this is definitively "the way" that kingship emerged in Israel's history. While my work will be removed from the original purposes of Girard, I will show that Girard's hypothesis can

---

35. About this text in particular Pattison suggests Girardian analysis when he writes, "In the resolution of this crisis, as we have seen, projection and substitution are everything. The key text that sums up this view of Early Israel must, of course, be Jdg 21:25: 'In those days there was no king in Israel and every man did what was right in his own eyes'" (Pattison, "Violence," 137).

36. Diana Edelman notes, with reference to P. Dhorme, that it is only in 1 Samuel 11 that the Hebrew verb is used in associated with "inauguration," in verses 14–15. The translation for "inauguration" will be important as distinct from the "renewal" of kingship and will be detailed explicitly in this study. This study will demonstrate that in chapter 11, kingship begins and the acts of violence associated with its inauguration mirror and echo literary strategies in Judges 9 and 19–21 (Edelman, "Saul's Rescue," 199).

be applied in particular ways for interpretive value and meaning in the Deuteronomistic History.

Chapter 7: Summary and Conclusions

This chapter will assess the value of this study both in its close reading of the texts that have been examined and in its application of a Girardian perspective. I will offer some remarks on the fruitfulness of this study and how it might contribute to other readings of the Deuteronomistic History.

2

Composition and Kingship in the Deuteronomistic History

To understand the nature and focus of this study, we will need to come to terms with the specific narrative units outlined in chapter 1. We will give attention to how a Girardian perspective will inform each of these narrative units individually. But the aim of this study is not simply to understand the narrative units individually or through a Girardian lens individually. We will discern how Girardian theory can help us understand what is going on behind the texts. Taken together, the texts tell us how the people of Israel moved from chaos to conciliation through the violent act of Saul's sacrifice, thus inaugurating and heralding his kingship. If this is the case, we must first examine how issues of kingship have been understood and studied in these biblical texts, specifically the Deuteronomistic History.

This study has focused on several broad categories. We begin by understanding what is at stake in the work called the Deuteronomistic History since the time of Martin Noth. We proceed to understand the various responses to Noth's work. The work of each of these scholars demonstrates their perspectives on what event/history preceded the formal piece of writing we have known as the Deuteronomistic History. We note here that which may either be completely obvious, or so obvious that it is forgotten. We do not know the "real" history behind the Deuteronomistic History. We do not know "when" the history took place, "who" wrote it, or what portion(s) of its story or history is fact or fiction. Clearly there are places and times and events from within the Deuteronomistic History that can be validated in one of many ways—notably by archeology or by the recovery of other texts that validate certain stories.[1] This fact is important as a prelude to this chapter, because it serves to remind us that the application of this study has merit and value within the field of scholarship regarding the existence of monarchy in Israel's history. While I will read the Biblical text in such a way as to understand Saul as Israel's legitimate first king—at least in so far as he is Israel's first literary-narrated king—the fact of the matter is that even these stories, shaped by certain redactional histories we will explore in this chapter, remain only stories of some "real" version of history that we can never know. A historical-critical reading of the texts attempts to understand the history but does so through the presuppositions of the writers and the redactional theories they espouse. A Girardian analysis of these texts will approach the possible history embedded in the story. Girard will bypass the redactional issues, per se, and help us to attempt to understand what goes on "before" the text in the mythic history hidden in how the text narrates the creation of sacrifice and kingship for us.

AUTHORSHIP AND REDACTION OF THE DEUTERONOMISTIC HISTORY

Source-critical studies in the Pentateuch paved the way for source-critical work extending into other literature, leading to discussion of a Hexateuch or Tetrateuch. These issues in themselves have been worked on by a host of authors in various monographs, books, articles, and publications, so our review of the issues will be brief. In short, prior to the work of Martin Noth who names "an author" for the Deuteronomistic History, scholarship was dominated by a traditions-history approach and a source-critical approach to the biblical story.[2] The traditions wanted to talk about what history and traditions lay behind the stories. The source-critical approach wanted to deal with where these stories came from and how they reached their "final form." This source-critical analysis spilled over beyond the first five books of the Bible. Scholars began to look for sources extending into books beyond the Pentateuch,

---

1. A chief example of a story we can validate with a real history is much later in the historical matrix, but to be used here as an example, the events associated with Sennacherib and Hezekiah in 2 Kings 18–19. Not only is this particular story narrated here and elsewhere in the Bible text in Isaiah 36–37; it is also narrated to us in tablets found at Nineveh. Of course, the "spin" on the event is different depending on which king's version is read, but it seems evident that the event took place in real history.

2. Noth, *Überlieferungsgeschichtliche Studien*.

into the book of Joshua, for example. If the sources extended beyond the fifth book of the Pentateuch, scholars began to posit a six-book collection, the Hexateuch.

A major reaction against this position of seeing a Hexateuch of books through sources emerged later, as the nineteenth century ended, with the work of Julius Wellhausen and A. Kuenen.[3] It was W. M. L. de Wette who first suggested a connection between the book of Deuteronomy and the reform of Josiah, and it was Wellhausen and Kuenen who noted independent stories and possible layers of redactional history that would later become known as the Deuteronomistic History, independent that is of the seeming "sources" that carried over from the Torah.[4] Kari Latvus summarizes well the situation prior to the work of Martin Noth when she writes that two major assumptions were shared widely by scholars. "First, the texts of the former prophets were recognized to be more or less non-logical [sic] and fragmentary in their literary character; and second, those texts were understood to contain some Deuteronomistic material."[5]

It was Martin Noth whose review of these books began to take note of certain "tones" that resided in the books themselves that interest us.[6] Noth believed that the redactor of this body of literature acted more as a collector (*Sammler*) of texted tradition that already existed. This texted tradition was shaped by the organization of the collector to tell a particular kind of story with a discernible plot from beginning to end.

3. Wellhausen, *Die Composition*.

4. Others who have reviewed this same history review the scholarship differently. Kari Latvus, for example, addresses the scholarship of I. Benzinger, R. Kittel, and particularly C. Steuernagel. See Latvus, *God, Anger and Ideology*. Her review, like that of other more recent reviews, offers detail that goes beyond the needs of this study as we are not arguing here that there were not traditions or redactional layers. We assume that, and trust the work of the scholars. Our assessment is to look at the texts as they stand and then use Girard to move us to a possible time before the text. See also Smend, *Die Entstehung*. See also Hayes, *An Introduction*. For another perspective on the same framework of scholarship I will review in the course of this study, consult O'Brien, "Judges and the Deuteronomistic History," 235–59.

5. Latvus, *God, Anger and Ideology*, 14.

6. The tone of the final editor is particularly noted in speeches that Noth believed were constructed to reflect the editor's perspective. Graeme Auld writes about this: "In Noth's classic thesis, the Deuteronomistic History was shaped and informed by a series of chapters penned by the historian himself: some ostensibly his own editorial comment (Josh. 12; Judg. 2; 2 Kgs 17), some in the form of speeches put in the mouths of the leader of the time (Josh 23; 1 Sam. 12; 1 Kgs 8.)." Auld, "Reading Joshua" (172).

Within Noth's perspective, he argued that the one final edition of this completed work was created for and written with attention to frame a pessimistic view of history for people of Judah. This author, Noth argued, created the Deuteronomistic History, defined as Joshua, Judges, Samuel, and Kings. The book of Deuteronomy served as the theological introduction to stories of the Deuteronomistic History. Noth's hypothesis regarding the compositional formation of the Deuteronomistic History charted the way for virtually all scholars who have followed, even though other scholars clearly had other opinions on the matter. Noth's dominance prevailed and, to a large degree, even this study responds to his original thesis. While there had been important arguments made for redactional levels and independent literary history prior to Noth, it took several decades for the scholarship to begin to focus again on the layers and editorial work that operates in the Deuteronomistic History to be rekindled.[7]

Very important to this study is Noth's opinion regarding the purpose or intention for writing the Deuteronomistic History. In essence, Noth argued that a pessimistic view prevailed in this narrative compilation of stories. He believed that the stories were told in order to explain or to justify why it was the case that at the end of the story Israel was wiped out by the Assyrians and Judah was exiled by the Babylonians. Thus, his view contained kernel ideas that while at times there were good kings (often introduced in a stylistic fashion in the Deuteronomistic History), and while there were some pro-monarchial claims made with certain kings at certain times, the prevailing theme of the Deuteronomistic History was anti-monarchial. While Noth argued that the history was written to show the negative reasons why Judah was in Exile, one of the strands of scholarly reply to Noth is to disagree with his pessimistic view of Israel/Judah's history.

---

7. In her review of Noth for discussion of his theory as it applies to the book of Joshua, Lori Rowlett notes the four basic categories outlined in Noth's work for a unified work in the Deuteronomistic History. Those four are: (1) chronology, (2) style, (3) arrangement, and (4) "theological unity in interpretation of history, particularly the writer's concern with God's 'retributive activity' when the people fail to heed demands that God has made upon their conduct" (Rowlett, *Joshua and the Rhetoric of Violence*, 31–32).

RESPONSES TO MARTIN NOTH

While we will, in brief, cover some of the important specific responses of scholars to Noth, we can summarize their basic disagreement with Noth in this rhetorical question to be asked of Noth's thesis: "If it is true that the Deuteronomistic History is pessimistic and anti-monarchial, why would someone go to all the trouble to write all this history for such a pessimistic purpose?"

It seems that no scholar attempts to argue that the Deuteronomistic History is entirely optimistic about Israel/Judah or about the positive import of the monarchy. This study demonstrates another response to Noth's original thesis. We will argue that the Deuteronomistic History is neither pessimistic nor optimistic about Israel's history. Neither is the Deuteronomistic History pro-monarchial or anti-monarchial.[8] Robert Boling writes in concert with our study that the stories are neither pro- nor anti-monarchial, but instead "they must be essentially pre-monarchial ... compiled early in the monarchy as a help in understanding the new and alien political arrangements within the Yahwist state."[9] This study will argue with Boling that the texts are neither pro- nor anti-monarchial. Contra Boling, we will argue that they are not truly pre-monarchial but instead speak to the moment of monarchy's inauguration. Understood

---

8. Lyle Eslinger comments on one section of the biblical narrative that this study will explore: 1 Samuel 9–11. About the section Eslinger writes, "Unfortunately, the presence of pro- and anti-monarchic opinions in 1 Samuel 8–12 is incapable of supporting the analytical weight that Wellhausen and others have placed on it" (Eslinger, "Viewpoints," 65). Eslinger goes on to focus on the omniscient narrator. About the significance of the narrator Eslinger writes: "It should come as no surprise that those adventurous readers who attempt to get through without the narrator's guidance are quickly bewildered. Lost in diverse details and opinions, such readers find themselves on the same plane as the characters in the narrative. Instead of standing outside the narrated events with the narrator, they jump inside with the characters. On that level of the narrative various opinions, multiple perspectives, and missing logical connections are natural and characteristic of human existence. When a reader chooses to view with the characters, he cannot expect anything else. If, on the other hand, he seeks meaning and order, the reader must submit to the creator of such things, the omniscient narrator" (69). About this narrator with such seeming power Eslinger also states, "The narrator of 1 Samuel 8–12 appears to maintain a steadfast neutrality towards the subject of monarchy" (68). Here we disagree with Eslinger without discounting the significance of the narrator. Our review seeks to demonstrate that the narrator's specific construction of these events will be specific about the significance of emergent monarchy in Israel's life. See also Steven L. McKenzie, who sees the stories in 1 Samuel as "not the decidedly anti-monarchial stance that so many scholars have tried to make it" (McKenzie, "The Trouble," 308).

9. Boling, "In Those Days," 36.

in Girardian categories that will be seen on exploration of this thesis, the Deuteronomistic History narrates Israel's story and the fact that monarchy did emerge. Its telling of this cultural reality in Israel's life is narrated to us in such a way that what is not important for us is the "event" or historical "fact"—but the way the story narrates mimetic rivalry channeled to a scapegoat, away from Israel itself, thus saving persons from fratricidal genocide and thus marking the one who brings about the scapegoat mechanism as one to be heralded/inaugurated as king, Saul.

Important responses to Noth's work came in the work of Hans Walter Wolff, then through redactional trajectories through Frank Cross and Rudolf Smend and others. While Noth gave significant attention to the negative implications of the Deuteronomistic History, stating essentially that it was written to explain to Judah why they went into Exile without any explicit theme of return for them. Several scholars reacted in opposition to his work. Several important speeches in the writing of the Deuteronomistic History are attributed to the author of Noth's Deuteronomistic History. If the speech sections were created by a redactor to pull the Deuteronomistic History together, then the speeches themselves and their contribution to the final form of the Deuteronomistic History are key to the compositional history of the Deuteronomistic History.

A primary major response to this came through Hans Walter Wolff.[10] It was Wolff who noted the basic theme of the book of Judges as the greater theme of the Deuteronomistic History as a whole, that theme that notes the apostasy and destruction that came for Israelite people, until they called on God and he rescued and redeemed them.[11] Said more simply, Wolff pointed to the "classic formula" of Judges articulated in the biblical text of Judges chapter 2 as the actual, intentional pattern of the Deuteronomistic History. It was neither specifically anti-monarchial nor pro-monarchial; it was rather attentive to apostasy from God. This allowed Wolff to note the positive themes of the Deuteronomistic History when and where moments of return to God were operative for Israel's history. It also allowed Wolff to see the conclusion of the Deuteronomistic History as positive and pro-monarchial in so far as a king was still alive,

---

10. Wolff's work was originally published in 1961 in *ZAW*, but reference in this study is made to the 1975 translation. "The Kerygma," 83–100.

11. Wolff's work builds upon the "catchword *shûb*" as part of "almost all of the important passages which enable us to recognize DtrH's intention" (ibid., 90).

even if alive in Babylon. For Wolff, the monarchy could continue and so too could Israel/Judah's existence as a people. Though the people were nearly wiped out by their apostasy, God could still, using the basic pattern and frame of the Judges matrix that informed Wolff's work, raise up a deliverer to lead them into a new epoch of God's history for them.

Following Wolff, several scholars gave attention to the writer(s) or the redactional layer(s) of the Deuteronomistic History. Setting the stage for several reactions were Frank Moore Cross and Rudolf Smend.[12]

Frank Moore Cross and His School

Cross and those who followed his proposed revision of Noth's work argued essentially for two redactional levels to the Deuteronomistic History, with the first one serving the purpose of justifying the final king (accepting his historical level) who was Josiah.[13] The function of the first edition would then be to justify Josiah's program of political and religious reform. This first redactional level sought to speak a message to the Northern nation of Israel (or those remaining in the North after Assyrian domination) that God was still in and with Judah and their extant hope in Judah. Cross's work then takes note of the sins of Jeroboam, which are countered by the good things done by the house of David and by promises made to his house, culminating in Josiah. The second redactional level of the Deuteronomistic History for Cross was framed in a period when Israel needed to repent for the things they had done wrong; these things had resulted in the Exile by the Babylonians. The work of Cross thus posits that Israel's history can be divided into two major epochs: an early age at the time of the judges, when there were no kings, and people followed the dictates of their own consciences; and an era during which the kings ruled. For Cross, neither stage of the tradition reflects the apex that Wellhausen had postulated.

Richard Nelson and Iain Provan push the work of Cross forward in important ways with the theories of redaction that affect and shape the Deuteronomistic History.[14] We hope to read the text as it stands and to

---

12. Cross, *Canaanite Myth*; Smend, "Das Gesetz", 494–509; Page, "Boundaries," 37–55, especially 39ff.

13. Cross, brings together his understanding of the two strands in the Deuteronomistic History especially here, *Canaanite Myth*, 274–90. Additionally, Cross deals with Saul, central in the research of this study, and his "limited monarchy," beginning on 219.

14. Nelson, *The Double Redaction*. In *The Double Redaction* Nelson details the work

examine how Girard might help us understand these stories as narrative and myth, not through their redactional traditions.[15]

Richard Nelson's analysis picks up the understanding of a Josianic edition operative in the Deuteronomistic History. Nelson begins with this understanding, then extends the argument to connect Josiah with Joshua in the context of the book of Joshua in the Deuteronomistic History.[16]

Nelson believes that the Deuteronomist inherited traditions that he preserved, "but this does not imply that he simply copied older material out of some antiquarian interest, without intending to integrate it into the overall unity of his work."[17] Nelson postulates that if we recognize Josiah as the person who is behind the task of Deuteronomistic Joshua, we will have a deeper insight into the method of redaction. In fact, we discover that this editorial perspective shapes the entire theological history. This shaping of his editorial method, says Nelson, shows up in his descriptions of figures other than Joshua as well. Both Moses and Samuel are pictured as holy-war leaders (Deut 31:9–13; 1 Sam 7:3–6), reminding us once more of Josiah. Finally, Nelson states: "Understanding the figure of Joshua in this way gives support to those who believe that the primary edition of Dtr was produced during the reign of Josiah as support for the Davidic kingship, as a call to faithfulness to the newly-discovered book of the law, as a challenge to reoccupy Israel *irredenta*, and as a way to interpret the old traditions for a new age."[18]

---

of Smend and Cross on pp. 19ff. and then demonstrates on pages 29ff how the "regnal formulae" will frame the basis of his approach. See also the focus of Nelson on the centrality of Josiah's role in the redaction, Nelson, "Josiah," 531–40. Provan, *Hezekiah*. Central to Provan's thesis is the book of 1and 2 Kings and the person of Hezekiah. For Provan, the Deuteronomistic History "underwent a major revision during the exile, and thereafter attracted isolated additions" (*Hezekiah*, 72). Provan in other writings addresses the issue of Israel's history, which is important to our study. See Provan, "Ideologies," 283ff.

15. The work of Provan, as distinct from Nelson's work, is particularly concerned with redaction at the time of Hezekiah. In either case it is worthy of note for our thesis that it was kings who created the proposed editorial shifts in the Deuteronomistic History, and it is kings who would have an interest in telling the story of kingship that we are examining here.

16. Nelson, "Josiah," 531–33.

17. Ibid., 536.

18. Ibid.

Standing apart from the editorial claims made for Josiah by Cross is the work of Iain Provan in *Hezekiah and the Books of Kings: A Contribution to the Debate about the Composition of the Deuteronomistic History*. Provan's work focuses the editorial layer of the early work of the Deuteronomist to a full century earlier than Cross, not with Josiah but with Hezekiah. Provan establishes in his literature review that the positions thus far maintained are entirely unsatisfactory.[19] His focus on Hezekiah pays particular attention to Hezekiah's connection to David and to his activity with the High Places in Israel. Provan argues that in the period of Hezekiah (2 Kings 18) we find a turning point in the evaluation of both King David and the High Places. Provan's argument suggests that the pre-exilic edition of the Deuteronomistic History concluded with the reign of Hezekiah, which of course pre-dates the Josianic edition.

Rudolf Smend and His School

Rudolf Smend's seminal response to Wolff and the scholars who follow the trajectories of Israel's narrated history in his hypothesis take a slightly different redactional trajectory from those already reviewed.[20] Smend argued that there were different redactions that resembled certain sources of documents: a DtrG (for base source) and a DtrN (for nomistic source). The work of Smend was largely focused on Joshua and Judges and how the "law" source created an intentional "revision" to the work whose "motive" was the law.[21]

Walter Dietrich is one who picked up and expanded the work of Smend. His thesis is that to the base source (DtrG) a prophetic source (DtrP) inserted unique speeches and fulfillment patterns alongside other prophetic material. For Dietrich, the "law" source (DtrN) added his material at the end of the process with the release of Jehoiachin.[22] Extensions of this work on redaction in the Deuteronomistic History,

---

19. Provan, *Hezekiah*, 22.

20. Smend, *Die Entstehung*. In the edition used for this study, published a decade after the original, Smend gave an overview of the "Smend school" that built upon his work. See 110–25.

21. Smend, "Das Gesetz," 509.

22. Dietrich, *Prophetie und Geschichte*. The close linguistic use of DtrP and DtrG is detailed especially between pages 88 and 95. In his work, Timo Veijola builds his understanding of kingship on DtrG, DtrP, and DtrN (Veijola, *Das Königtum*).

and in particular in 1 Samuel are found in P. Kyle McCarter. McCarter contends that there is a significant prophetic source—a specifically Northern focus—in the work of the Deuteronomistic History.[23]

Timo Veijola also fits within the Smend school, but his work will be reviewed in a few pages removed from this section, where his focus will be demonstrated more specifically to central issues in this study on kingship.

Mark O'Brien has made an effort to work with the various strands of traditions isolated by the Cross and Smend schools in a unique way in *The Deuteronomistic History Hypothesis: A Reassessment*.[24] O'Brien critiques Noth for failing to recognize later Deuteronomistic editing. He more emphatically criticizes the Smend school for not having "satisfactorily addressed the question of the nature and extent of the history (DtrH) that remains once the layers of later redaction are removed"[25]

O'Brien essentially agrees with Frank Moore Cross, but he criticizes Cross's proposal for failing to "accurately identifying the text, structure and conceptual plan of the Josianic History."[26] For O'Brien, the structure of the DtrH is organized around three different leadership models. The DtrH is essentially a history of Israel's leaders: Moses and Joshua (Deuteronomy through Judges 2:10); the judges (Judg 2:11—1 Sam 11:15); prophets and kings (1 Sam 13:1—2 Kgs 23:23).

LITERATURE AND HISTORY IN THE DEUTERONOMISTIC HISTORY

We have laid out these basic positions with regard to authorship and redactional levels in the Deuteronomistic History in order that we might comment here on the historical nature of this material. Scholars dispute the historical reliability of the text's stories. In broad categories, they want to either minimize or maximize the historical content of this material.[27]

---

23. McCarter, *1 Samuel*, 12–23.
24. O'Brien, *The Deuteronomistic History*. See also O'Brien, "Judges," 235–59.
25. O'Brien, *The Deuteronomistic History*, 10.
26. Ibid., 12.

27. The issues of history will not be central in this study, though they will play a part. Our argument proceeds on the basis that we believe some history is narrated in the biblical story. How the "exact" history was finally shaped is not clear, and for that issue this study will create a framework for understanding that history. Some history is evident, and kingship did arise in Israel. William Dever recognizes some

Composition and Kingship in the Deuteronomistic History

John Van Seters argues that what we have in the work of the Deuteronomistic History is a work of history wherein the author sought to given an account of Israel's position and status for historical purposes. It sought to explain (or at least account for) the history. About this Van Seters writes that he must set up the "continuities" between Samuel and Kings, then between Joshua and Judges, stating, "This is not a trivial issue. It goes to the very heart of what history meant in ancient Israel."[28]

David Gunn deals with the same literature and history as that of Van Seters but with a decidedly different methodology, that is attentive in particular to the literary shape of the text. Of course Gunn is only one example of response to the historical value or historical fact of the narratives that comprise the Deuteronomistic History and here we note his work in both the books of Samuel and Kings.[29] Gunn argues that this portion of the Deuteronomistic History is not history at all but is rather a full-fledged literary piece written for entertainment.[30]

We do know that monarchy emerged in Israel. We can discern the facts of the monarchy at certain times in the history of Israel based on extra-biblical witness. For example, it is clear that there was a king in Israel's history known as Hezekiah because we read about him in the records of the Assyrian King Sennacherib. For some, though, the history of the Deuteronomistic History becomes a question of when the monarchy emerged and how and why the monarchy emerged. As we will see in the latter section of this study, there is the possibility that the monarchy emerged out of a sacred murder, a scapegoating event. Girardian theory will help us read back through texts to a potential real historical event, now masked in myth.

---

historical reality when he writes generally about the fact of a people known as Israel: "Furthermore, the actual term 'Israelite' is attested in contemporary sources, as is well known. The Merneptah stele proves beyond doubt that shortly before 1200 BCE Egyptian intelligence knew of an inimical 'Israel' somewhere in Palestine; and that location can hardly be the Egyptian-held coastal plain, Shephelah or Jezreel Valley" (Dever, "The Identity," 17). This study will not argue that we have proof of the actual start of kingship in Judges and 1 Samuel, but that there is beyond a doubt some evidence of its origin narrated for us.

28. Van Seters, *In Search of History*, 248.

29. Gunn, *The Story of King David*. See also Gunn, *The Fate of King Saul*.

30. One need read only the first sentence of Gunn's work on Saul, where he states, "It is my belief that much of the Old Testament narrative belongs naturally to the life-sphere of art and entertainment" (Gunn, *The Fate of King Saul*, 11).

THE JUDGES AND MONARCHY IN THE DEUTERONOMISTIC HISTORY

Albrecht Alt argued in 1934 for the existence of a central judicial authority in Israel that preceded the monarchy.[31] Noth viewed the central role of the judges differently in the history of Israel, adapting the work of Alt to fit the Amphictyony theory he had postulated.[32] About this idea Noth writes, "The fact that this information was recorded officially and transmitted to posterity can probably only be explained by the fact that in the earliest period of Israel's history dates were based on the period of the judges' years of office. If that is so, it follows that this was the central office in the Israelites' twelve-tribe association."[33] The work of Noth, itself a continuation of Alt's work, was picked up importantly in the works of D. A. McKenzie.

While the idea of the Amphictyony held sway with some, it clearly did not with others. Barnabas Lindars, for example, discredits the idea of the Amphictyony completely saying that any credit for "inventing the system [of rule] must go, first, to those in the time of David and Solomon who were responsible for the national cult, for the army, and for secular administration, and who thus crystallized the actual state of the tribes at the time"[34] In a series of published articles and books, Niels Peter Lemche discredits the notion of the Amphictyony as the model of Israelite society noting several incongruities, notably that "there was only one Amphictyony, that of Delphi, and . . . the technical term was only used at a later date by the Greek and Roman authors to denote other leagues" after the eighth century BCE and thus could not have been used for twelfth- or eleventh-century Israel.[35] In another article, expressing the same dissent from the model of Amphictyony, Lemche concludes with a challenge: "The result is that Old Testament scholarship is now confronted with a very demanding but undoubtedly rewarding task to look for new explanations to the tangle which is the consequence of the demise of the Amphictyony."[36] We suggest that our study will untangle

---

31. Alt, "The Origins," 88–103.
32. Noth, *The History of Israel*.
33. Ibid., 102.
34. Lindars, "The Israelite Tribes," 112.
35. Lemche, "The Greek 'Amphictyony,'" 48.
36. Lemche, "Israel in the Period," 22.

the story of emergent monarchy in Israel as we explore a new explanation rooted in the Biblical texts, but understood in Girardian categories.

THE PLACE AND POSITION OF THE JUDGES

The views expounded in the widening field of study, though with some dissent, viewed the institution of monarchy in ancient Israel as a practice of jurisprudence wherein the king took over the role of interpreting law for Israel. About this J. Salmon writes that not only "was the Judge tradition one of the main roots from which the Israelite monarchy grew, but the assumption of the office of 'Judge of Israel' by the king was without doubt a calculated move made by the early monarchy in order to acquire the authority which resided in the amphictyonic office."[37] The assumption of Salmon here is massive. It assumes that a person could have taken a juridical role and made that role into a sovereign role as monarch. It is precisely this kind of way of thinking about kingship that this study seeks to undermine.

With respect to the nature of the Judges themselves, who they were and how we determine a context for understanding the role of the judge in Ancient Israel, Keith Whitelam has given a clear analysis in his book, *The Just King: Monarchial Judicial Authority in Ancient Israel*.[38] Whitelam's conclusion, though not without its merit, will be demonstrated to be at odds with the point that this study seeks to articulate. His point is that monarchy emerged in Israel as the function of a sort of natural process from the rule of the Judges. After his solid historical review, Whitelam states that kingship emerges in ancient Israel as "simply the gradual development of 'forces already present within Israelite society.'"[39] Part of the basis for Whitelam's argument is, as he proposes, that "a closer examination of royal jurisdiction during the reign of Saul will reveal that the extent of royal judicial authority was largely undefined and rather ambiguous. Such a situation is consistent with the view

---

37. Salmon, "Judicial Authority," 247.

38. Whitelam, *The Just King*, 51–69.

39. Here Whitelam is quoting himself. The earlier quote from which Whitelam draws is, "In the same way, it is feasible that monarchial judicial authority was a development of elements already present in the pre-monarchial period" (Whitelam, *The Just King*, 68–69).

that a remarkable degree of consistency existed between the monarchy and the preceding period."[40]

While it is not our place to mark out the whole of Whitelam's argument or the basis of scholarship upon which it is built, along with others we suggest his argument is weak and allows for the possibility of a Girardian reading of these same texts.[41] As with any argument going back to ancient texts and archaeological evidence we must state here for Whitelam's argument and for our own, that we cannot know 'for sure' what happened in Israel's history and we cannot know 'as fact' how kingship emerged. That being the case, part of the failure of Whitelam's argument that we would point out here stems from the last quote where he ties "judicial authority" with the rather "ambiguous" period of the judges. The argument supposes that kings, like judges, offered interpretation of law for the persons presided over. The judge Deborah is one of the few judges who is said to hold court (Judg 4:5) and the kings in Israel are hardly ever narrated as interpreting law. That being the case, we will argue that the reason that there is so little existence of "royal jurisdiction" is because the royal reality in Israel was not based in "jurisdiction" of law. Instead, the new form of rule called kingship was inaugurated on the basis of the person who scapegoated violence for Israel thus saving Israel. Saul, we will argue, was not the "gradual development" of natural forces in Israel, but was inaugurated on the basis of the new thing he did for Israel by means of attending to participation in and removal of violence through sacrificial victimage. We side here with A. D. H. Mayes who writes, "It must now be abundantly clear that it is a distortion of the nature of Israel in the pre-monarchic period to think of it in terms of a society steadily progressing towards the establishment of monarchy . . . However, in the end Israel did introduce the monarchic institution, and one is entitled to search for possible roots for this change in the nature of pre-monarchic Israelite society."[42]

This search is central to our thesis.

---

40. Whitelam, *The Just King*, 69. See also Whitelam's conclusion, where he echoes the same refrain (ibid., 220).

41. In particular, Iain Provan critiques the work of Whitelam. A response to Whitelam marks the opening pages of a biblical account of history edited by Provan (Provan, *A Biblical History*, 3–10). See also Provan, "Ideologies," 283ff.

42. Mayes, *Judges*, 87–88.

Whitelam's proposal is important. It sheds light on significant factors of "judicial law" and its relationship to kingship in Israel and in its surrounding environs. This study, however, will argue that the basis of kingship is not found with a "just" king, hence his title. Rather, we argue that kingship arises with a person who participates in but also curbs violence among brothers through sacrifice.

We also want to make reference here to the work of Robert R. Wilson. In his review of the judicial system of Israel in the pre-exilic period he recounts Joshua 7 and Judges 19–21 as the "only two texts [which] are clearly relevant to the subject" of the "shape of Israel's judicial system before the rise of the monarchy."[43] About these two texts that we will read for their "lot casting" episodes later, Wilson says they are "difficult to discern because of uncertainties about the reliability of the Biblical sources."[44] In his presentation, though, Wilson will go on to argue quite categorically that "it should be noted that Israel did not make an abrupt transition from lineage organization to kingship."[45] Of note for us in the characterization that Wilson makes is the uncertainties of the sources we receive. And, within these uncertainties come variant interpretive options. This study will suggest a variant interpretive option for the emergence of kingship in Israel as having come into existence in an abrupt moment of casting lots and scapegoating a crisis that kingship did emerge not with a whimper but with a bang.

The Place and Position of the Kings and Kingship

Numerous studies by various scholars deal with kings and kingship in the biblical context, both in the context of literary texts like the documents of the biblical story and in social contexts chiefly with comparison to kingship manifest in other places in Ancient Near East. The focus of the literature review on kingship presented here will attempt to focus more narrowly on issues of kingship within Israel proximate to the literature in the Deuteronomistic History.[46]

---

43. Wilson, "Israel's Judicial System," 229–48.
44. Ibid., 231.
45. Ibid, 240.
46. Further, the literature reviewed here will focus attention on monographs and not on several articles published during this time. Only a few of recently published articles will be reviewed here. It should be noted here that the delimitations of the biblical texts in each scholar's study is unique to that scholar. Most of the scholarly focus has been

WELLHAUSEN AND FRANKFORT AS AN ENTRY POINT INTO THE STUDY OF KINGSHIP IN THE DEUTERONOMISTIC HISTORY

As early as 1883, Julius Wellhausen focused the attention of Biblical scholars on issues of kingship by emphasizing that in the monarchy Israel's history reached its apex. For Wellhausen, kingship brought Israel into "the shelter of civil-order" as an organized social entity that emerged out of the "period of unrest and affliction, when every man did what was right in his own eyes, and the enemies of Israel accordingly got everything their own way."[47] With respect to the central texts wherein Samuel anoints Saul as Israel's first king, Wellhausen viewed the texts to reflect different foci. 1 Samuel 7:2—8:22 and 1 Samuel 10:17ff. were the product of a later hand in the Deuteronomistic history that expressed anti-monarchic sentiment into the more favorable story of monarchy found in 1 Sam 9:1—10:26, which Wellhausen linked with the Ammonite incident of 1 Sam 11:1–15.[48] In 1 Sam 9:1—10:16 Saul is only king de jure; he becomes king de facto when he proves himself in 1 Samuel 11.[49] What remains of chapters 8–12 is the anti-monarchic account in 10:17-27, which is linked with the other anti-monarchic material in chapters 7–8 and 12.

Wellhausen's work would be published and republished numerous times into the middle of the twentieth century where this study notes the work of Henri Frankfort in 1947. Frankfort's work applies more specifically in some direct ways with the comparative study of Israel's monarchy with monarchies in the Ancient Near East. Because his work has something to say about the cultic function of monarchy that will be important in this study and its focus on priestly and sacrificial understandings associated with the start of kingship, we mention its import.

In Frankfort's comparison between the Israelite monarchy and those elsewhere in the Ancient Near East, he believed that the institu-

---

on texts in 1 Samuel, as will be demonstrated. In the works of Gerbrandt and Becker in particular, we will see an expanded look at texts about monarchy in 2 Kings and Judges respectively (Gerbrandt, *Kingship*; Becker, *Richterzeit und Königtum*).

47. Wellhausen, *Prolegomena*.

48. Wellhausen. *Die Composition*, 243; Wellhausen, *History of Israel*, 247ff. The history of the criticism of these chapters since Wellhausen is reviewed by Langlamet, "Les récits," 161-200.

49. Wellhausen, *Prolegomena*.

tion in Israel was unique and only bore external comparisons to other forms of kingship. The central basis for this claim by Frankfort lies in his belief that Israel's unique status was not bound up with kingship or the covenants of kings like David but with the covenant at Sinai and the person of Moses. For Frankfort, Israel's identity did not find its apex in the monarchy but emerged prior to the monarchy in the exodus and at Sinai.[50] Frankfort claimed that the "Hebrew king normally functioned in the profane sphere, not in the sacred sphere ... He was emphatically not the leader of the cult."[51] Frankfort's approach takes for granted the canonical construction of the texts of the bible to present their correct chronological order in real historical fact and this is one of its weaknesses. His claim, though, that the Hebrew king operated apart from areas of the sacred arena are important for our study because we shall demonstrate in this study that the sacred redirection of violence is precisely what inaugurates kingship in Israel with Saul.

For each decade—the 1960s, 70s, and 80s—several works moved forward issues of kingship in the Deuteronomistic History.

Scholarship on Kingship in the Deuteronomistic History

SCHOLARSHIP IN THE 1960S

Artur Weiser reexamined the separate documents associated with kingship that Wellhausen had engaged. Weiser pointed out that neither of Wellhausen's literary strands exhibits a consistent point of view, whether pro- or anti-monarchic. Taking the so called anti-monarchic strand as an example, Weiser demonstrated that chapter 7 exhibits nothing of an anti-monarchic point of view whilst chapter 8 is critical only of what he views as a non-Israelite model of kingship proposed by the people, and not of kingship per se.[52] Separate from this, in chapter 10, verses 17–27a presents the election of Saul as God's will and differs from chapter 8 in the representation of the setting and reason for the request.[53]

In a separate publication Weiser notes that the complex diversity of perspectives in these stories led him to see several literary compilations,

---

50. Frankfort, *Kingship and the Gods*, 339–40.
51. Ibid., 342.
52. Weiser, *Samuel*, 27.
53. Ibid., 62.

incorporating traditions from diverse times and places.[54] The contrary points of view expressed in 1 Samuel 8–12 resulted from a literary compilation in which traditions "are not so much intermingled with each other as strung after each other, partly on a very loose thread."[55] Finally from Weiser, "In view of the diversity of motives and points of view in the passages [1 Samuel 8–12] under discussion we must on the contrary take into account a many –stranded process of utilizing and shaping the traditions which developed over a long period and set at different points and different times."[56]

Still in the 1960s, Alberto Soggin wrote concerning the history of Israelite monarchy primarily as a social and political institution in *Das Königtum in Israel*.[57] Soggin argued that the focus on kingship in Israel in particular emphasis on its charismatic quality, which plays into 1 Samuel 11 in this study. With respect to the charismatic focus on Saul's kingship, in particular, he notes the three separate traditions which have already been demarcated in the work of other scholars as understood in a variety of so-called anti-monarchial and pro-monarchial categories. Soggin maintains that the tradition about the circumstances of Saul's becoming king is historically reliable and maintains a pro-monarchial position.[58]

Continued work on issues of kingship in the 1960s came in Hans Boecker's work, *Die Beurteilung der Anfänge des Königtums in den deuteronomistischen Abschnitten des I Samuelbuches*.[59] Boecker's work on issues of kingship and its perception in the final document of the biblical text is important because, in his analysis, the anti-monarchial tones the chapters of 1 Samuel, while being anti-monarchial, frame certain qualifications to their anti-monarchial tone. For Boecker, and similar to Weiser, the concern of 1 Samuel 8 in particular is a qualified anti-monarchial tone with respect to the nature of the kingship requested by the people and not simply about the choice of Saul as the first king.[60] The Deuteronomistic History is not particularly concerned about Saul

54. Weiser, *The Old Testament*, 159–61.
55. Ibid., 162.
56. Ibid., 161.
57. Soggin, *Das Königtum*.
58. Ibid., 41ff.
59. Boecker, *Die Beurteilung*.
60. Ibid., 60.

Composition and Kingship in the Deuteronomistic History

as a person, it is concerned with kingship and Saul first brings kingship to Israel.[61] For Boecker then, the understanding of kingship in 1 Samuel 8–12, as a whole has positive affirmations when understood as deriving from the oracle of God associated with the scenes including Samuel receiving said oracle.[62]

Scholarship in the 1970s

In the early part of the 1970s several important works on the Deuteronomistic History were written which have already been detailed. The focus on kingship articulated in an article by Dennis J. McCarthy is cited here because of its connection with history and history writing in 1 Samuel 8–12.[63] With respect to 1 Samuel 8–12 he writes, "the passage is a unity which tries to give a coherent account and explanation of the inauguration of kingship in Israel. That is, it is history writing."[64] McCarthy is careful to delimit what kind of history writing this is (or is not) in 1 Samuel. That this is history writing does not mean it is factual in detail, only that "as a literary phenomenon it conforms to the definition of history: a record and analysis of past events."[65] One of the reasons to cite McCarthy's work as part of the literature review for this study is that we hope to draw out and draw upon the historical events that lie behind the narratives we read in Girardian terms. But, with McCarthy's work we should be reminded that the historian has a point of view, as do we as interpreters of the historians work.

Two significant monographs were published in 1976 with a focus on kingship, though from different perspectives in the works of Tryggve N. D. Mettinger and Bruce C. Birch.[66]

Mettinger's perspective on kingship is focused more principally on David, and even examines the use of Psalms in setting up categories of kingship. Mettinger's focus narrows on the "History of David's Rise to Power" and the "Succession Narrative" and then the Psalms. With respect to issues in 1 Samuel more proximate to this study specifically, Mettinger viewed 1 Samuel 7–8 and 1 Samuel 12 as framing the Deuteronomist's

---

61. Ibid., 57.
62. Ibid., 35 and 61.
63. McCarthy, "The Inauguration."
64. Ibid., 404.
65. Ibid.
66. Mettinger. *King and Messiah.*

negative attitude towards the investiture of Saul as king at Mizpah in 10:17ff.[67]

The title of Bruce Birch's text clearly demonstrates the focus of his concern for understanding kingship: *The Rise of the Israelite Monarchy; The Growth and Development of 1 Samuel 7–15*. The opening sentence of Birch's re-evaluation of 1 Samuel 7–15 exhibited matter-of-factly his concern: "Any careful examination of the doublets, tensions and varying points of view in 1 Samuel will lead to the conclusion that it is not a literary unit."[68]

Birch's analysis focuses exclusively on 1 Samuel 7–15, as his title indicates, and Birch moves forward in a way similar to the intended focus of this study. Birch states that he wants offer a "careful analysis of the individual units of [the] tradition [in 1 Samuel 7–15]" in order to "escape the necessity of presupposing theories of composition."[69] Birch proceeds by offering numerous summaries along the way where, after each section of verses he writes: "To summarize our conclusions on [verses]"[70] Birch's conclusion summarizes his analysis for a rich variety of independent traditions only being shaped by a prophetic pre-Deuteronomistic editor. Even where and when the prophetic editor has shaped the story, though, it has only been slight.[71]

In nearly consecutive years in the 1970s, Timo Veijola published two monographs specific to issues of redaction in the Deuteronomistic History and kingship, in particular in his second work. His first text, *Die ewige Dynastie: David und die Entstehung seiner Dynastie nach der deuteronomistischen Darstellung*, is more specific to the reign of David and how his reign had been characterized in the editorial process. While important as a monograph, its focus is not specific to the texts of this study.[72] His second text, *Das Königtum in der Beurteilung der deuteronomistischen Historiographie: Eine redaktionsgeschichtliche Untersuchung* has more intentional focus on the issues of kingship with respect to the texts in Judges and 1 Samuel. In Veijola's assessment, the base source in the Deuteronomistic History (DtrG, following the Smend school of

---

67. Ibid., 80.
68. Birch, *The Rise*, 1.
69. Ibid., 8.
70. Ibid., 20, 28, 42, 53, etc.
71. Ibid., 153–54.
72. Veijola, *Die ewige Dynastie*.

which he is part) had a positive view of kingship, including the editorial assertions to the need for a king found in Judges 17–21. Viejola viewed the scene of casting lots in 1 Samuel 10 as also being from DtrG and having a decidedly positive cast.[73] For Veijola, it was a later editor, DtrN whose opposition to monarchy was so great as to want no human king.[74]

Scholarship in the 1980s

Eslinger wrote concerning kingship in his book titled *Kingship of God in Crisis: A Close Reading of 1 Samuel 1–12*.[75] In this text, Eslinger reads across the texts of 1 Samuel with respect to the inauguration as Saul as king, but Eslinger begins with chapter 1 and his reading includes the Hannah/Eli/Ark narratives, where most scholars excises these stories in discerning issues specific to Saul's ascent to kingship. Eslinger's focus is across 1 Samuel 1–12 in order to trace Israel's transition from that of a theocracy to a monarchy subordinated to theocracy.

Demonstrating the literary coherence across the chapters that have been understood in different strata, Eslinger focuses on the role of the final product and against the "serious deficiencies in the segmentation of the text according to pro- and anti-monarchic viewpoints."[76] Eslinger asserts that "in every scene [of the texts found in 1 Samuel 8–12] both pro- and anti-monarchic attitudes are expressed or displayed by a variety of characters."[77] Eslinger has much to say about the narratives continuity and focuses, in particular, on the role of the narrator in the final product. With respect to 1 Samuel 8–12, specifically, Eslinger writes that the narrator "appears to maintain a steadfast neutrality towards the subject of monarchy ... He looks back on these events with a balanced view – pro- and anti-monarchic sentiments are seen in perspective as oppositions that result in a new synthesis ..."[78]

Gerald Eddie Gerbrandt wrote his *Kingship according to the Deuteronomistic History* in the 1980s. In it, he argues that the texts of the Deuteronomistic history reflect "a unified concept of kingship"

---

73. Veijola, *Das Königtum*, 39–52. This study will maintain a different interpretation for this "lot-casting" scene.
74. Ibid., 122.
75. Eslinger, *Kingship of God*.
76. Eslinger, "Viewpoints," 66.
77. Ibid.
78. Ibid., 68.

that is essentially pro-kingship.[79] Gerbrandt continues to question the issues of kingship raised by others when he wrote: "The correct question with which to confront the Deuteronomist . . . is not whether he was anti-kingship or pro-kingship. Rather, we need to ask what kind of kingship he saw as ideal for Israel, or what role kingship was expected to play for Israel."[80]

Essentially, Gerbrandt accepted the popular two-redaction theory as defended by Richard Nelson. With regard to Abimelech, Gerbrandt's thesis is important for framing this study. For Gerbrandt, the purpose of Judges 9 is not to condemn the institution of monarchy but rather to "indict Abimelech and the citizens of Shechem."[81] The issue is not that kingship "is a crime, but that when kingship is based on crime and the abuse of force, . . . then the inevitable outcome of such kingship will be destruction."[82]

Scholarship in the 1990s and in the Twenty-first Century

In 1990, David M. Howard rearticulated and advanced the work of Gerbrandt.[83] In his extended review of Gerbrandt's work, both summarizing and praising it. The only problem Howard notes as missing in Gerbrandt's project is Gerbrandt's failure to offer more research in a comparative study of various ancient Near Eastern conceptions of kingship. Howard writes in his final paragraph,

> Despite this problem [Gerbrandt's failure to include comparative literature], Gerbrandt's work remains invaluable in pointing us to a way between the Scylla of sing incompatible, contradictory 'sources' within the biblical texts and the Charybdis of seeing a rich theology of kingship . . . being built upon a concept that was anathema to God from the beginning. Rather, we should see that God's plan *throughout* Israel's history included the monarchy as a means of accomplishing his purposes for humanity, and nothing in the Deuteronomistic History contradicts this point. We are indebted to Gerbrandt for clarifying how it is that this corpus speaks to the issue.[84]

79. Gerbrandt *Kingship*, 192.
80. Ibid.
81. Ibid., 131.
82. Ibid., 132.
83. Howard, "The Case."
84. Ibid., 115 (italics original).

Becker and Levinson as Responses to Wellhausen and Frankfort: Entry Points to the Contributions of this Study

The work of Uwe Becker in *Richterzeit und Königtum: Redaktionsgeschichtliche Studien zum Richterbuch*, dealing with issues of kingship and proximate to the time of this writing, is an important work with respect to this study because of the specific way he engages the book of Judges in his review of kingship. As the title indicates, it considers the intersection of two fundamental issues in Judges; the books redaction and its attitude toward kingship. For Becker, issues of kingship are not confined to chapters 8–9 and 17–21 where it is explicitly mentioned, but rather is a fundamental issue throughout the book. The history of the period, in Becker's analysis, frames a theological critique of kingship where the period of the Judges was the ideal time.[85] Importantly, then, as we near the end of this literature review, Becker's analysis stands opposed to Wellhausen.

Becker's work, like the intention of this study, reads across stories with an effort to better understand contradictory evaluations of kingship. Important to this study is the significant review given by Becker of Judges 6–9 and Judges 17–21, meriting nearly 150 pages of analysis.[86]

And finally, bringing to a close this review of kingship texts in the Deuteronomistic History, we cite the work of Bernard M. Levinson in an article about re-conceptualizing kingship.[87]

In the work of Uwe Becker just reviewed, we noted how we return to the framework of Wellhausen, but in an opposing perspective. With Levinson, we return to the framework of Frankfort that has been cited, also in an opposing perspective.

With Levinson, we return to the concern with kingship that included sacerdotal claims which will be important to this study, in particular. Levinson himself cites Frankfort and declares his opposing perspective: "There is no reason to believe that ancient Israel differed from any other ancient Near Eastern state in its view of the king. Quite the contrary. Even

---

85. Becker summarizes his positions for the judges and their relationship to kingship in his *Ergebnis*. Becker, *Richterzeit*, 300–306.

86. In fact, Becker's analysis of Judges 6–9 is the largest section of his entire work, with particular attention to Abimelech meriting twenty pages of review. Taking nearly as much textual space is his review of Judges 17–21. See chapters 9 and 12 of Becker's work (ibid., 140–208 and 221–96).

87. Levinson, "The Reconceptualization," 511–30.

taking into account the institutional differences between the monarchies of the northern and southern kingdoms of Samaria and Judah, far more would have been shared with the broader Near Eastern royal ideology as regards the authority, role, prestige, and power of the monarch."[88]

In the specific focus of Levinson's analysis, kings in Israel and the Ancient Near East saw themselves as "defenders and patrons of the cult."[89] Levinson notes: David's dynastic oracle follows his proposal to build the temple (2 Samuel 7); Solomon plans, undertakes and completes its construction (1 Kings 1–8); Hezekiah takes steps to purify the cult (2 Kgs 18: 1–8); and Josiah both repairs the temple and purifies the cult while also centralizing it (2 Kings 22–23).[90] Notably then, the concerns of Levinson make every effort to tie the patterns of Israelite monarchy to other Ancient Near Eastern contexts specifically with respect to issues of the cult. The focus of this study will have an affinity with that of Levinson, though distinct from it. Where Levinson connects the monarchy to institutionalized cult and the practices of the temple in her later kings, this study will connect the monarchy to practices of the cult in sacrifice in her first king.

THE CONTRIBUTIONS OF THIS STUDY: A NEW UNDERSTANDING OF KINGSHIP IN THE DEUTERONOMISTIC HISTORY

As has been demonstrated by the foregoing, there are no easy answers to many questions regarding the compositional character or the 'real' history of the judges or kings in the narratives we have in the Deuteronomistic History. The fact that this study moves in a different direction than these efforts is not to discount the significance of this work. Marc Bloch is quoted by Gillian Feeley-Harnik in an article that attempts to use historical anthropology with application to biblical texts. In that article, Feeley-Harnik writes that historical data from Biblical texts is indeed limited, but "As Marc Bloch once said, 'A document is a witness; and like most witnesses, it does not say much except under cross-examination. The real difficulty lies in putting the right questions."[91] I intend for this

---

88. Ibid., 511.

89. Ibid., 517.

90. Ibid.

91. Quoted in Feeley-Harnik "Is Historical Anthropology Possible?" 98, quoting Bloch, *Land and Work in Mediaeval Europe*, 48.

study to put new questions to the texts with the hope of cross-examining them in a new way.

We propose to read back through certain particular literary connections that appear in three of these texts that are now separated in the final form of the text. Our analysis will demonstrate that there is a historical and literary coherence that connects these texts. It is possible that this historical and literary coherence points to a reality not yet understood that Girard might help us to understand. The historical issue that lies behind our texts is the issue and emergence of Kingship in Israel.

We have laid out the positions of numerous scholars in this review of literature. This study seeks to assert an awareness and affirmation of the positive value of the work of these scholars. In articulating these various positions, we state now that this study is unique from and yet participates with the work of these scholars. In this study, we want to in a sense, go back to the earlier concern of Martin Noth concerning the pro- or anti-monarchial cast of these narratives. The two-sidedness of these narratives—incorporating both pro-monarchial traditions and anti-monarchial traditions is now woven together as a literary whole. Our purposeful reading of these texts using the hypothesis of René Girard will help us discern pro and anti-monarchial readings in a new way connected to what might be called sacerdotal concerns, specifically issues of sacrifice. The Deuteronomistic History is ambivalent about the explicitly negative or explicitly positive import of kingship because kingship sacralizes violence in order to bring about reconciliation.

The primary task of this study will be to see if we can read the texts taken together as a whole and, if Girard's insight allows us to see how kingship emerges as, to use his term, *sacred monarchy*.[92] For Girard, the idea of sacred monarchy is:

> much too complex to have been the invention of power-hungry individuals; it would be necessary to attribute to them a literally immeasurable intelligence and strength, which would only amount to sacrilizing them. The king is not a glorified gang-leader, supported by pomp and decorum, capable of dissimulating his origin with deft propaganda concerning "divine right." Even if human beings had discovered the centrality of an at once immanent and transcendent power by looking within themselves or

---

92. Girard, *Things Hidden*, 54 (italics original).

outward to the world around them, even if they were capable of completely inventing it, one would still not be able to understand how they could have established such power among themselves, imposed it on the whole of society, and transformed it into the concrete institution and mechanism of government.[93]

Monarchy comes for Israel not with the forced rule of Abimelech. Instead, heralded by the symbolic link between "sovereignty and sacrifice that exists everywhere" kingship comes with Saul in 1 Samuel 11.[94]

---

93. Ibid.
94. Ibid, 55.

3

Abimelech

ABIMELECH'S PREDECESSORS: THE ROLES OF JOSHUA AND GIDEON

THE STORIES OF THE book of Judges move forward from the book of Joshua. Joshua as a book is dominated by the person named Joshua. Joshua's leadership hearkens into the opening chapters of the book of Judges. As a character, Joshua is one of the most dominant, over-arching characters of the entire Deuteronomistic History. The textual space given to him is surpassed by David, but arguably by no other character in the Deuteronomistic History.[1]

Once we move beyond Joshua, though, we meet a host of characters, principally those who led Israel and are known as judges. The title "judge," though, is rarely used in the specific narratives associated with the individual Judges.[2] The characters and persons within the narratives, both those who "judge" and others are worthy of study, though they will not be our focus here. We note that several of the characters are fully developed as persons in relationships and completing specific actions within the narratives. We meet Deborah, who engages in conversation, acts decisively, and who goes into battle. Ehud works with some measure

---

1. Many scholars have noted the resemblance of Joshua's actions to those of Josiah. If the Deuteronomistic History was "originally" drafted during Josiah's reign, or if it found any editorial work in that period, it would not be unlike a monarch to shape a narrative around hero figures that resemble himself. The first evidence of "spin doctors" did not emerge with modern journalism.

2. Note here that the verb we translate as "judge" is from שפט. This verb is used at the opening of the book of judges, in its formulaic description, to describe how God would raise up a "judge" to deliver the people. The construction appears in Judg 2:16–19. Nowhere in the rest of the book, though is any person called a "judge" though some of them are associated with "having judged" in the verbal construction.

of stealth to kill King Eglon of Moab. These characters are fully developed within the narrative, but about their historical reality we can be less certain. Sean M. Warner, in fact, suggests that the "individuals and events of the period of the judges seem to have been in a historical vacuum."[3] And, "concerning the date of the beginning of the period of the judges . . . The one certain result to emerge from our investigation is that certainty about this issue is impossible."[4]

As we move through these characters towards our principal character, Abimelech, we start with Abimelech's father, Gideon/Jerubbaal as a character within the narrative. The significance of Gideon is important to this study because it is within the Gideon narrative the idea of kingship for Israel first emerges in the narrative progression that is the Deuteronomistic History. While our emphasis will be on the narrative that continues and follows the Gideon narrative, we note with A. Graeme Auld that the story of Gideon, and the story we will see of Abimelech, is such "a well-connected story [that it] must be close to the centre [theme or focus or agenda] of the Old Testament."[5]

Much could be said about who Gideon is and what happens with him; a full three chapters of the twenty-one to be found in the book of Judges is devoted to him, Judges 6–8. He is fully developed and he acts in ways that allow him to "deliver" Israel from the threat of the Midianites. We meet Gideon when he has a conversation that begins with "an angel of the Lord" but concludes directly with YHWH. Indeed, if a character's significance is associated with their proximity to YHWH, Gideon is more significance than even Joshua in the narrative. If a person's greatness is distinguished by his conversation with YHWH, Gideon is the most important character of the entire Deuteronomistic History to this point in the narrative of the Deuteronomistic History.[6]

---

3. Warner, "The Dating of the Period of Judges," 457.

4. Ibid, 462–63.

5. Auld, "Gideon: Hacking at the Heart of the Old Testament," 257. The subtitle of Auld's article comes from the derivation of Gideon's name itself. *Gideon* means "hacker" or "chopper." It will be his son, though, who "hacks" up the family in order to place himself in leadership.

6. In his article Emerton suggests, "The most plausible reason suggested to explain why one man may have been called both Gideon and Jerubbaal is that one of the names was regal, but it must be admitted that the book of Judges does not explain the names thus, and the explanation is acceptable only if it is believed that Gideon-Jerubbaal became king" ("Gideon and Jerubbaal," 309–10). At the end of the same paragraph he

Abimelech

After Gideon's military victory over the Midianites, the narrator records for us how Gideon returned to the cities of Penuel and Succoth to punish them for not supporting his leadership, "tearing down the tower and killing the townspeople" (Judg 8:17). An act of similar destruction, but carried out differently, will be enacted by his son Abimelech in the narrative we now explore.

After the violent defeat of the Midianites, the destruction of the towers of the cities, and sword slaying of the kings, the "men of Israel" come to Gideon and speaking in the imperative say, "Rule over us (מְשָׁל־בָּנוּ), you, your son (text is singular with בִּנְךָ), and your grandson (בֶּן־בִּנְךָ)" (Judg 8:22). Gideon proclaims in direct discourse that he will not "rule" over the people, nor shall his son. YHWH alone shall rule over them. For our purposes in this study, we note that the text is clearly making statements about kingship. The text is explicit. With Barnabas Lindars we concur that these verses "hold a key place in any account of the origins of the Israelite monarchy."[7] We maintain though that Gideon does not become king in any direct sense here, nor is he understood to become king in the later narrative and we take this position contra the claims of others.[8] It should be noted alongside this that the use of מֶלֶךְ seems to be avoided in the text itself.

---

writes, "It seems best to continue to work with the hypothesis that the names belonged to the same person, even though we cannot be certain why Gideon was also called Jerubbaal" (ibid., 310).

7. Lindars, "Gideon and Kingship," 315.

8. See G. Henton Davies, who believes the evidence of similar passages and contexts "lead me to reject the view that Gideon's words are a refusal of kingship. Gideon's words are not a refusal: they are rather a protestation: a protestation of the kind of kingship he would exercise, an avowal that his kingship and that of his family will be so conducted as to eliminate any personal and tyrannical element, and to permit of the manifestation [sic] of the divine rule through his own" (Davies, "Judges 8:22–23," 157). Davies has argued that there was an office of kingship that existed, and that Gideon was the first to take it. This study argues that Abimelech is the first to be understood as a type of king, but as a king who fails to use the scapegoat mechanism to inaugurate his kingship. Davies believes Jotham was the "third claimant to Gideon's office," subsequent to the seventy sons generally and then Abimelech. Davies writes, "Three possible claimants for office point strongly to the fact that there was an office to claim" (ibid., 156). We reject the view that there was an "office" of kingship to claim, while maintaining the view that there was violent rivalry over issues of mimesis operating within the story. The fact that there were claimants to anything is not so much about an office that existed as much as it was about rivalrous imitation of the kind of sway that Gideon was allowed to have, which others wanted to possess upon his death.

After the speech, Gideon accepts gold captured as booty and builds an ephod. In the narrative we do not know what this ephod is or how it functions, and it will not appear again as an object until we meet the Levite in the final chapters of Judges, chapters we shall come back to in this study. We are only told here that an ephod is a "snare" to Gideon and his household in Ophrah. How and why it is a snare is not stipulated. This one who talks with YHWH leaves the land in tranquility for 40 years (Judg 8:28).

This fully developed character is requested to "rule" after defeating the kings of the Midianites. He draws his sword, he builds an ephod and he tears down towers. These themes will recycle in different ways in the narrative we are about to explore, but they set the important stage for the "kingship" that Abimelech will attempt to bring about. Curiously, as we turn to his story we note that for all the proximity Gideon had with YHWH, YHWH is not a character in the entire narrative of Abimelech—only Elohim is there.[9]

INTRODUCING ABIMELECH

Knowing Gideon/Jerubbaal is a necessary starting point for knowing Abimelech. It is impossible to read or hear the name Abimelech and not wonder about his father since his name quite plainly in Hebrew means "My Father is King." [10] Ironically, of course, with the introduction to Gideon we have just examined, we know that Gideon would not "rule" over Israel, neither would his sons, nor his grandsons. Gideon would not be king, so the narrative tells us plainly. Eugene Maly says about the narrative we will explore, "It is unlikely, given the natural tendencies of certain leaders to concentrate power in their hands, that some attempt at kingship, however feeble or unsuccessful, would not have been made.

---

9. While the inclusion of *YHWH* in the stories of Judges 6–8 is obvious, and the name change to *Elohim* and that alone in Judges 9 is also obvious in the text, I am not the first to note this issue. See also Emerton, "Gideon and Jerubbaal," 289.

10. We here reject the idea of Jan P. Fokkelman that the reference to "father" in Abimelech's names refers to God. He reads the naming of Abimelech as follows, "My father [i.e., God] is king." There seems to be no theophoric appellation in the naming of Abimelech at all, and to insert it clumsily here seems to miss the point. Further, in this entire narrative, only *Elohim* appears, and if the writer would have needed Abimelech to have a name connected to El, that name could have been provided with a double name like the one Gideon-Jerubbaal had (see Fokkelman, "Structural Remarks on Judges 9 and 19," 33).

Israelite tradition has left us the record of one such attempt. It is the account of Abimelech's revolution."[11]

We should note from the start of this narrative, particularly as it will apply to our Girardian reading later, how Abimelech is an outsider to it. Abimelech creates and does not quell violence. His rivalry with characters within the narrative leads to total devastation – of rivalrous enemies, of cities of support, of other cities, of towers, and finally, of Abimelech.

As the narrative turns away from Gideon and toward the ambivalent future of Israel, we read of Gideon in his house with his 70 sons. No doubt the tenfold use of the perfect number seven seeks to tell us something of the perfection of this telos in Gideon's life. Seventy sons, "of his own thigh, because many were his wives" the narrative tells us at 8:30. The construction is unique in Hebrew, and only appears here in the Deuteronomistic History.[12] We do not know the names of the sons, we do not know the names of the wives, we simply know that there are perfectly 70 of them. We expect this to be the *telos*, the end of his prodigious offspring given the construction in the text, but it is not.

In what follows we will argue that the roots of kingship, though they are not fully realized with Abimelech as king, are grounded in this narrative in Israel's history. Sam Dragga calls Abimelech "Israel's unanointed king," and we will explore this idea of his kingship as we continue, though for us he will never become king and will remain unanointed and un-inaugurated.[13] There are some who would argue that Abimelech was not a king at all. A. D. H. Mayes says the narrative about Abimelech "cannot be held to represent a tendency towards monarchism within tribal Israel. As far as the development of Israelite monarchy is concerned, Abimelech's kingship was probably a quite irrelevant episode."[14] This study argues against Mayes here suggesting that the story of Abimelech is intimately relevant to the emergence of

---

11. Maly, "The Jotham Fable," 299.

12. The construction with reference to offspring occurs only one other time in the Hebrew Bible, at Gen 46:26 with respect to the offspring of Jacob as they journey to meet Joseph in Egypt.

13. Dragga, "In the Shadow of the Judges," 43. In this study we shall compare Saul with Abimelech. Curiously Dragga compares Saul to Gideon, Jepthah, and Samson but fails to note any of our comparisons to Abimelech, who, we will argue, is most central.

14. Mayes, *Judges*, 88.

monarchy here, and in the inter-textual connections we will follow in Judges 17–21 and 1 Samuel 9–11.

Before we note the interconnections of this narrative with Judges 17–21 and 1 Samuel 9–11 we might note that there is some dispute over the narrative unity of Judges 9 itself. Volkmar Fritz has pointed out narrative contradictions in Judges 9 that he suggests can only be resolved by recognizing three separate traditions within the narrative.[15] T. A. Boogart, however, has demonstrated convincingly the narrative connections that point to the inherit weaknesses in Fritz's argument. Boogart writes that a unified narrative is found in Judges 9, and the "narrator has organized the incidents to illustrate dramatically the efficacy of what for Israel was a fundamental principle of reality: retribution."[16] While our focus will not be on "retribution" in the same way that Boogart examines it, it is important to note that the retribution of violence is what Saul will cleanse Israel from as he emerges as king, as we shall see later.

ABIMELECH'S MOTHER AND THE SHECHEMITES

A son, a single-other son, was born to Gideon/Jerubbaal by his concubine in Shechem.[17] A. D. Crown notes that the city of Shechem is mentioned two times in the book of Joshua and in "both cases the city appears as the site of an altar."[18] That the city of Shechem has a history connected to places of sacrifice will be significant for our story for we shall see that in the story; the would-be king Abimelech is unable to effect the kind of scapegoating sacrifice that Girard postulates, and as a result, is essentially violently sacrificed himself.[19]

15. Fritz, "Abimelech und Sichem in Jdc. 9," 129–44.

16. Boogart, "Stone for Stone," 47.

17. The specific location and geographical place of Shechem is not at issue in this study. It does appear, though, that Shechem was a significant center of trade and commerce in the ancient world. Joseph A. Callaway notes this city that it appears to have been "the center of a larger city-state. During the Amarna period, the ruler of Shechem extended his power as far north as Megiddo, controlling a larger territory of villages that must have reached as far south as Shiloh" (Callaway, "The Settlement in Canaan," 58). The idea that Shechem would have been a base for large geographical and economic control will become clear in the narrative we will read about Abimelech in what continues.

18. Crown, "A Reinterpretation," 92.

19. Reviv notes the connection of Shechem with developing systems of government in the second half of the second millennium. Among other things in his article he notes that Shechem "submitted itself to rulers from abroad, whose military power was com-

Shechem is also significant for understanding Abimelech's mother, the concubine in this narrative. We need to understand and explicate the status of this unnamed person by virtue of what we know of the Hebrew language by determining the "position" of a concubine. For reasons that will be clear in the next chapter of this study, we will leave a more detailed explanation of the concubine until then. For now we state simply that in Hebrew the word we translate here as concubine is פילגש. *Pilegesh* is the simple way that Mieke Bal uses the term in her renderings of stories with a "concubine";[20] "A concubine was a woman whose continued presence within the family was not dependent upon economic arrangements. Typically, a concubine was a secondary wife, whose involvement with the husband represented a secondary union, both in terms of being an additional wife and of having a lower status than the legal wife. Her function was to provide sexual enjoyment in a situation when the man already had offspring by his primary wife. If he did not have a child by his primary wife, a man could take a secondary wife to produce a child."[21]

We shall return to the character of "concubine" when we encounter more textual data and story associated with the concubine of Judges 19–21.[22]

The text narrates to us that this single son of this concubine was named "Abimelech." The construction in Hebrew (8:31) does not read exactly as we might expect; a translation might be "and he

---

posed of aliens." Therefore, an insider/outsider like Abimelech might have made sense to this community (Reviv, "The Government of Shechem," 254).

20. Mieke Bal does a superlative assessment of the nature and history of interpretive complexity involved with the *pilegesh* in Judges: her analysis centers on the *pilegesh* of Judges 19. See Mieke Bal, *Death and Dissymmetry*. I am opting to use the more conventional translation here of "concubine" even though I recognize it fails to fully explicate the complexities that Bal so clearly discerns. I do not believe using *pilegesh* as nomenclature solves our problems of understanding the nature and role of this person in our narratives, even though it does highlight the fact that every time we encounter a concubine, we ought to reflect on the fact that we truly do not know who this person was in Israel's history. For us, the readers of these narratives so far removed from the history of Israel, the concubine is an outsider who may remain forever outside our ability to discern.

21. Sternberg, "Social Scientific Criticism," 51.

22. Here in Judges 9, this unnamed woman is named for us by Josephus as Druma, but we will proceed with her textual anonymity. Josephus amplifies the text by calling Abimelech a "bastard" and probably deriving his mother's name from the place Arumah in 9:41 (Begg, "Abimelech," 147).

put to his name Abimelech." In the standard convention for naming in the Hebrew text, in the Deuteronomistic History and elsewhere in the Hebrew Bible, when a person or city is named, the verb used is one of being "called" (קרא)—here, the name is "set" upon Abimelech. Given the unique verb used here, I suggest that the name of Abimelech was not given him by Gideon but instead becomes a kind of nickname or moniker, "and it was given to him the name Abimelech" (גם־היא בן וישם את־שמו אבימלך, Judg 8:31).

The first person to name Abimelech is the narrator at 9:6 when the narrator in threefold pattern writes almost literally, "the kings the son of the king to be king." The first time a king appears in Israel's boundaries as king we are not to miss the point. If that is not enough, the second time Abimelech is named king in the narrative, a point to which we shall describe further in this chapter, occurs when after bitingly criticizing the lords of Shechem, Jotham describes the "kingship of my father is king" (9:16).[23] Though Gideon had numerous sons, not all his sons had "correct mothers."[24]

After introducing this outsider son and his concubine mother, the narrative turns for a moment back to the father (Judg 8:23). Gideon dies, is buried in ripe old age.[25] The narrative tells us something of the covenantal ideology of the day. We might recall Joshua 24 earlier in the Deuteronomistic History. At the end of Joshua's life, the people renew the covenant at Shechem (Joshua 24), and here in Judges just before we encounter Abimelech and his experiences in Shechem, we read that after Gideon's death the sons of Israel follow the "Baal of the Covenant" as god. It is interesting that the narrative moves to the Baal of the Covenant

---

23. The irony is biting. The only surviving son of the perfect seventy critiques the citizens of Shechem for making king a non-king and replacing his father, who would have been and could have been a better king. And in the narrative, we recognize the outsider status of Abimelech so that the title "my father is king" more aptly fits Abimelech himself than the one to whom Jotham sardonically applies it.

24. Steinberg, "Social Scientific Criticism," 58. Steinberg goes on to say, "Abimelech's mother is on a lower rung of the socio-economic hierarchy than Gideon's other wives, and the story is about the legitimate kinship structure for the organization of society." Her position is different from that of this study, where she argues for issues of organization based on kinship and we argue for it based on patterns of ritual scapegoating. But, it is true and important that the issues of Abimelech's insider/outsider relationship be explicated fully and Steinberg helps us do that.

25. A rare construction for "fine old age" used here, and in Ps 92:15 to describe the righteous.

and to the "god," because as the story proceeds YHWH recedes from any place in the story (8:33). It is important for this anti-king as presented in the narrative that his leadership is not Yahwistic. It does not reflect the ascension to real kingship that I will argue happens only in later with Saul. The sons of Israel fail to remember YHWH, and they fail to show חסד to the house of Jerubbaal-Gideon for all the good he had done with respect to Israel (8:35).[26]

When Gideon acts against the Baal cult of his day, narrated in 6:32, the text tells us that the one who had been Gideon was "called on that day Jerubbaal." At 7:1 we are told "Jerubbaal he (that is) Gideon rose . . ." In the only two preceding narratives where Gideon and Jerubbaal are constructed for us, the explanation is clear. There are numerous places within the story where either the name Jerubbaal or the name Gideon is used. But here, just as we turn to a new character in the story, we read in 8:35 the simple construction that no חסד was demonstrated to the house of "Jerubbaal-Gideon." Using the clear naming distinctions in this story, someone might go back and investigate the narrative traditions, the sources, that may have been used to create this complete story. But our concern with the final narrative should note the intentional, unambiguous back and forth usage of the names that takes place here. A final editor could have easily glossed over the contradictions and used only one name to configure the stories for us here, but that has not been done.

ABIMELECH AND DESIRE TO RULE

Having noted already the outside status of Abimelech in this narrative, we must stop to recognize that he is not "just" an outsider. He is, after all, the son of Jerubbaal-Gideon. And, he is from this important city where covenants had been established: Shechem. For all his outsider status, he is not so removed as to be somehow "alien" to the narrative. The insider/outsider ambivalence of Abimelech in this narrative is important, and we shall see a similar set of insider-outsider relations in the other narratives this study seeks to explore, particularly as we meet new characters in our narratives. But having noted his proximity to Shechem and to

---

26. The construction that is used for Israel is not "sons of Israel" or "men of Israel" as is typical in this narrative. Instead, the final word of 8:35 is simply "with Israel," which seems to recognize a governmental or state entity distinct from the members themselves, who inhabit this reality.

Jerubbaal in the narrative, the story continues to highlight for us the outsider status of Abimelech.

We are told that "Abimelech son of Jerubbaal" goes to his mother's brothers in Shechem.[27] He is at once the son of Jerubbaal, and not just separate from his brothers as we have seen before, but here, separate from any brothers. He seemingly has no brothers to participate with in life, so he must retreat to his mother's brothers. If we missed it, in the same verse the author notes for us a second time that it is not to his own brothers that he returns, but to his "mother's family" (אל־אחי אמו, Judg 9:1). This Abimelech, it seems, is one who certainly derives from a father and mother, and who has a family, but who is presented in ways that separate him out from his family status as one who is distinct and even different from others within his family. His distance from the family and from the inhabitants of Shechem will be heightened for us in the direct discourse that follows. "Putting it mildly, Abimelech is not very happy with such a position as an outsider, and he is dominated by a ruthless craving to change his marginal existence."[28]

"Which is better for you, to be ruled by seventy men—by all the sons of Jerubbaal—or to be ruled by one man? And remember, I am your own bone and flesh" (Judg 9:2). In these first words of speech we hear in the narrative (and these from Abimelech) there is much more revealed than might appear upon quick review. The statement involves concepts of "rule," the seventy "perfect" sons, the sonship status, the need for one to rule, and the call to recall "bone and flesh." We have our first glimpse into how Girard will help us read this narrative and the narratives that follow. Here we have the basis for rivalry and for greed (over rule), and the clear hints of mimesis in "bone and flesh." Later in this study we will see the application of a Girardian analysis of this chapter.

About this speech, Fokkelman notes, "The irony and the son's hatred of the father are to be found in the text, where Abimelech takes over a key word from his father. In 8:23 Gideon had used the combination משל בכם as many times in three clauses when turning down a position as ruler. In the electoral speech which we hear in 9:2 and which consists

---

27. We will discover soon enough that he goes there to become "king." It is beyond the scope of this study, but another "new" king will emerge after Solomon: Rehoboam will also go to Shechem to become king in I Kgs 12:1. Shechem has multiple connections with kingship that only begin here in our narrative.

28. Fokkelman, "Structural Remarks on Judges 9 and 19," 34.

of four lines, the very same combination is central as an ironical copy (twice in v. 2cd)."[29]

Robert Alter notes of this speech that it is one of the few stories in the Bible that begins "not with the report of an action but of speech."[30] And in terms of "thematic composition, chapter nine forms the centerpiece of the central block of stories in Judges."[31]

The last time we heard the idea of "rule" in the narrative was when the people came to Gideon and asked him to rule, but he stated that not he, nor his son, nor his grandsons would rule. But here, Abimelech seems to imply that someone would rule them and thus, the people should choose one over the seventy, for they are the same and not the same. We might wonder if "rule" must be the only option. There is no suggestion in the narrative of an outside threat that moves the people to seek a ruler. "Note that Abimelech's brief speech includes two grounds of persuasion: the numerical argument for the Shechemites and the familial one for his mother's kinsmen."[32]

Only with Abimelech does the need for a ruler emerge. Abimelech, in his discourse, recognizes and acknowledges that just as the seventy sons of Gideon/Jerubbal could rule, so Abimelech is like them in this sense . . . But he is not like them and he could be the "one" to rule over them. The speech of Abimelech recognizes and recharacterizes for us what we have already come to know in the narrative: Abimelech is like and unlike the others. Abimelech recognizes a situation of rivalry that might exist. And, Abimelech goes from the house of his father at Ophrah to another location, to his mother's brothers to remind them that he is their "bone and flesh" (וזכרתם כי־עצמכם ובשרכם אני).

Abimelech's need to remind them that he is their bone and flesh is curious. The use of "bone and flesh" as a means of recognizing brotherly relations is attributed in the Biblical text, as for example when Laban recognizes Jacob in Gen 29:14. But more than recognition of brotherhood and family ties, the earliest use of the idea in the Old Testament on goes back to the creation of woman from man, Gen 2:23. In that text, to recognize that the woman is "bone of my bones and flesh of my flesh" is to recognize the base imitative model of the man. When Abimelech

29. Ibid, 34.
30. Alter, *Language as Theme*, 6.
31. Ibid.
32. Ibid, 7.

chooses to speak in this way to his mother's brothers, he has to remind them that he is not an "other." He uses this powerful terminology to suggest he is a perfect copy, an exact replica, a base imitation of who they themselves are. To this point in the narrative while Abimelech has been an outsider to us in the story, if anything he had been connected to Gideon-Jerubbaal's house. It seems odd that the one whose name means "my father is king" would not turn to the role of his father as the basis for his seeking rule. Abimelech is part of both houses, and yet not part of either house. But his self-identity is bound up in his sameness with these others, that he wants to extend as being different as he seeks rule.

In addition to the fact that this "bone" and "flesh" language has implications for identifying Abimelech within certain familial structures, the terminology is elsewhere used to recognize monarchial connections. Uwe Becker notes the implication of the use of "daß ich euer Bein und Fleisch bin" here in 9:2–3 and in the traditions of David's rule as he establishes himself in Hebron in 2 Samuel 5:1.[33]

ABIMELECH AS INSIDER AND OUTSIDER

So that we do not forget the nature of Abimelech's relation to the persons in Shechem, we are told a third time that it is his "mother's brothers" who speak next in the narrative. They speak, the narrator tells us, by going to the "citizens" of Shechem (כל־בעלי שכם, Judg 9:2). Some translate the "citizens" here as "lords" of Shechem, and we note here that the term is sympathetic to the rule in religion and politics that is in Canaan. It is to the "baals" of Shechem that Abimelech's "mother's brothers" speak.[34] The narrative reads that the "hearts" of the people were moved towards Abimelech. We learn in this narrative that when "hearts" are affected, social and political situations begin to be shaped.[35] The lords of Shechem,

---

33. Becker, *Richterzeit*, 186–87. Naturally the occurrence in a story associated with David is not central to our focus in this study on Abimelech, Judges 17–21, or Saul. But because our concern is with the start of kingship, and Hebron is associated with the start of David's kingship, there are implications for wanting to be "bone" and "flesh" as part of mimetic issues that drive the start of kingship.

34. There might be irony here in the narrative that is not the focus of our work. Speaking to the baal is nothing more than speaking to persons, the baal is no god at all. But since our focus is not expressly theological in this study, we shall have to pursue this at another time.

35. Readers of this study should be prepared here to recognize the use of "hearts" and "heart" changes that will operate not only here but in the other narratives we will

with their change of heart, welcome this Abimelech because, though he has been to this point an outsider in the narrative, here someone finally claims him when his mother's brothers assert "he is our brother" (Judg 9:3). David Daube says about the Shechemites here that "they were persuaded and helped him to become king—yes, king, in Canaanite fashion, not simply another Judge."[36] It is not important to our narrative reading whether the kingship is after the "fashion" of the Canaanites or any other people per se except that Daube recognizes correctly that this is the attempt at kingship, not just something like another judge/*shophet* for Israel. Jan P. Fokkelman refers to Abimelech as simply "this tyrant of Shechem."[37] Dennis J. McCarthy characterizes the kind of rule that Abimelech provides as a "compact" or "treaty" for "dividing the spoils," but there seems no mention of treasure seeking or sacking of cities operative in the narrative itself.[38]

Important to our narrative, it is Abimelech who introduces the need for "rule" in the narrative. In our last narrative about Gideon we read that he would not accept rule. No one in this narrative seems to be asking for it; no one seems to need it; it is Abimelech who introduces the

---

read. For it is in the night when the old man and the unnamed Levite "hearts" are merry that violence breaks out (Judg 19:22) It is after his private anointing that the heart of Saul as נגיד changes, and signs of new leadership "begin to be fulfilled" in Israel (1 Sam 10:9).

36. Daube, "One from among Your Bretheren Shall You Set King Over You," 480. Daube's reading of the Judges 9 narrative here is in line with the explanation for kingship found in Deut 17:15. Daube's reading characterizes Saul as "native" and Abimelech as "foreigner" in his attempt to understand the legal provision for kings, which probably emerged later and is found in Deuteronomy 17. In Daube's article, then, he writes, "Surely, when Deut 17:15 reserves the kingship for 'one from among your brethren,' and debars 'a stranger who is not your brother,' it alludes to this earliest installment of a brother of foreigners: an aberration emphatically rejected" (Daube, "One from among" 481). It should be noted that the text never states that Abimelech is Israelite or non-Israelite per se. As a son of Gideon, Abimelech is an Israelite. But the lack of specific reference to Abimelech as Gideon's son will be one part of several that will demonstrate how Abimelech is like and unlike those with whom he lives and over whom he will rule. See also Brettler, "The Book of Judges," 406ff. Abraham Malamat points to an interesting possible precursor to kingship in Shechem at the time of the Habiru. He writes, "Thus, it appears that Lab'ayu, Shechem's aggressive ruler in the Amarna period, was an outsider who reigned supported by the Habiru bands in the area" (Malamat, "The Period of the Judges," 149).

37. Fokkelman, "Structural Remarks on Judges 9 and 19," 33.
38. McCarthy, "Compact and Kingship," 78.

possibilities and complexities that might emerge with rivalry and greed and imitation if someone to "rule" is not chosen.

This fringe character has used the "bone" and "flesh" language to garner his support. The support he receives is "perfect" as the Lords of Shechem give him 70 shekels from the house (temple) treasury of Baal-Berith (Lord of the Covenant). Robert Alter points out that while Gideon took gold to make an ephod, here Abimelech takes silver to hire worthless fellows. In his note Alter comments that "gold and silver are frequently paired terms in biblical idiom," and since we know what happened with the Israelites' being "snared" with the gold of Gideon, the reader should be aware that something of a new snare is being set with Abimelech.[39] With this perfect allotment, Abimelech hires men "empty and wanton." The exact construction for the types of persons Abimelech hires is unique to this narrative but we will meet characters like them again in our stories. The "bone and flesh" Abimelech now has "vain and empty" characters following him.[40]

From the house of Baal, the only "house" that specifically connects itself to Abimelech, this "bone-and-flesh" character with the "vain and empty" followers goes to the house of his father in Ophrah and there kills "his brothers" (Judg 9:5). In the narrative structure of Hebrew, we have moved only a few short words away from his being "hired" (for he is not king or ruler; he is simply a hired man here) to his act of fratricide.

To this point in the story, the narrator has never called Abimelech "brother" with respect to the seventy, nor have they referred to him as "brother." They were all "sons of" and related to their father Gideon/Jerubbaal. Once Abimelech is recognized as "brother" to his mother's brothers, though, and once he is empowered (and hired) by the baals of Shechem, the narrator causes us to see anew the social relationship that exists between Abimelech and these men. Certainly we know they are in a way his brothers, but to this point in the narrative the author has highlighted Abimelech's distinction from them as an-other son of Gideon, of a concubine. Even in Abimelech's speech to his mother's brothers he

---

39. Alter, *Language as Theme*, 8.

40. I suggest further a connection here with the situation of Saul's public inauguration. He returns there with "warriors" following him in 1 Sam 10:26 after his public anointing, but "all the people" follow him after his scapegoating at 1 Sam 11:15. The verb translated here as "follows" is the same in each of these narratives. The difference, of course, is in the type of action the following brings for Israel, which will become clearer for us as we proceed.

refers to the seventy as simply other "men" who might rule. Here, now, in the act of murder we see break down the separation or distinction the narrator has maintained to this point. These seventy are not simply sons of Gideon or other "men" who might rule; they are "his brothers."

Lest we miss the social relationship that now emerges in the recognition that these men, sons of Gideon, are really brothers, the narrator now in a few words goes back through the narrative for us by stating that Abimelech killed "his brothers, sons of Jerubbaal, seventy men." There we have it. They had been only sons of Jerubbaal (seventy) and men. Now in the space of five words in the Hebrew text we are reminded of all the social relationships that have woven these characters together, and kept them separate from another. The thread of the narrative comes together here "on one stone" (Judg 9:5).[41] The stone will be used to tie our narrative together, as we shall see, and here it perhaps functions to call our attention to "a common place of slaughter, an abattoir, or that the stone caught the blood so that it could not reach the ground and cry out for vengeance."[42] The narrative causes us to view Abimelech in unique ways. Hugh Page notes, "The story of Abimelek is also driven by both his social liminality, as the son of Gideon by a Shechemite concubine, and his transgression of social and political boundaries."[43]

One survives though, the youngest of the sons of Jerubbaal, for he hides himself. The youngest son had hidden himself but will soon emerge "atop" the people, standing.[44] The narrator lets us know that the "per-

---

41. The significance of this "one stone" in this narrative will be demonstrated as the study progresses through the narrative. In his commentary on Joshua, J. Alberto Soggin notes that the stone here might be connected with the stone of Joshua 8 and Joshua 24, where words are inscribed on the stone for the sake of remembering the covenant the Israelites made there with God. If Soggin is correct to find a connection between these three stones, then the covenantal words of Joshua quite literally have blood on them in this murderous act of Abimelech's desire to be the king (Soggin, *Joshua*, 240ff). Christopher Begg points out that in the version Josephus gives us, the seventy men help Abimelech murder the seventy brothers, but we note here that the Hebrew text has us read the narrative as if the one accomplishes the murder of the seventy. Granted that it would have been impossible to do it alone, still the one versus the many will be an important theme for us as we proceed with our Girardian reading (Begg, "Abimelech," 148). Boogart will use the emphasis on this stone to tie our narrative together, as we shall see, with its "retributive" end for Abimelech. Boogart's connection will tie this theme of retribution together (Boogart, "Stone for Stone," 51).

42. Boogart, "Stone for Stone," 51.

43. Page, "Boundaries," 47.

44. Jotham hides to save his life and then is later found standing above the people

fectly" seventy-shekeled rulership of Abimelech does not perfectly bring an end to the threat of rivalrous leadership of the seventy. Upon the one stone only sixty-nine were killed. One remains: his name is Jotham.

Having called attention to this one in hiding, the narrator hides him from our view as we move back to the lords of Shechem and the inhabitants of Beth-Millo, who join the convention. Beth-Millo is something like the house of fortification, stemming from the "filling" verbal construction in Hebrew. The archeological evidence of the Late Bronze Period suggests that the acropolis of the city might be the place referred to here as the Beth-Millo.[45] We shall see in the narrative if the house of fortification has the fortitude to inaugurate kingship in Israel.

Here they "king 'my father is king' king." The construction could not be more constricted. For the first time in Israel's history a "king" is "kinged" who is the son of the "king" who is never called a king and who, in fact, refuses the "rule" that this "king" seeks. Graham S. Ogden misses the point of this multiply explicit reference to kingship when he writes, "It is beside the point to then note that Abimelech was not actually offered the throne."[46] The fact that the term "throne" is not used seems to contribute to Ogden not seeing what is so obviously the point of this story.

And all of this takes place "at the oak of the pillar at Shechem."[47] The root of the word Shechem is from "shoulders" in Hebrew. Here it is Abimelech who is lifted on the shoulders, as it were, of the Shechemites. But we will see later in this chapter, at verse 48, where shoulders ironically play a part in destruction of this kingship event. This is the first appearance of king in the Deuteronomistic History for Israel's story to this point.

From this public event, the narrator sweeps our attention back to Jotham in hiding. And in hiding he must be, for he only hears of what

---

that he speaks to. Later in our analysis we will see Saul hiding for fear of losing his life but then emerging as one who stands a head taller than all the people.

45. Malamat, "The Period of the Judges," 150.

46. Ogden, "Jotham's Fable," 303.

47. The odd Hebrew construction here leaves us with a certain degree of uncertainty and ambiguity as to the location: what is the "pillar" that is located in this text as it is often translated? The LXX here suggests that it is here that the "discord" begins. Perhaps the Greek text recognized something that this study seeks to appropriate through a Girardian reading. With kingship there is ambivalence or discord, and especially if the kingship fails to redeem violence as we shall see that Abimelech fails to do.

has happened. Jotham himself, an insider in the story, is the orphaned child in the narrative; we may say the legitimate child in so far as the narrative has set him up for us: the last of the perfect seventy.[48] This is the second time in the Deuteronomistic History that we hear of the location Gerizim. What is interesting to us by means of this youngest son standing atop this location ("standing" and "highness" are important with Saul later) is what we know about Gerizim from Josh 8:33, particularly as that text embodies the Deuteronomic tradition of Deut 11:29 and 27:12. In the tradition of Deuteronomy and embodied in Joshua, it is from Gerizim that blessings are pronounced on the tribes of Israel, and from Ebal the curses are called down. But here, the one remaining perfect son, youngest, stands, atop the place of blessing, but calls down a curse on these baals of Shechem who "king 'my father is king' as king!" The bareness of the Hebrew is a pounding refrain of three verbal constructions laid side by side, which we might render as something like this: "He lifts up his voice and calls and says" (וישא קולו ויקרא ויאמר, Judg 9:7). The triplicate form calls our attention to the force of his speech—in the language of the idiom in the original language, he yells at them. He yells at them "Listen!" The youngest of the sons, the least experienced, calls on the seemingly eldest of the lords of the city, in a twist of irony not to be lost on the reader.[49] In any society it is the "elders" that are presumed the most wise, and particularly in Israel's later wisdom tradition! Here, the youngest has more wisdom to speak than the elders who establish and fund Abimelech's soon to be folly.

JOTHAM'S FABLE: THE IRONY OF KINGSHIP

The narrative breaks off here from following characters and the emerging violent rivalry that has already been displayed to the speech of Jotham. The "fable" of Jotham is an excursus from the primary narrative but remains an intrinsic part of this study as it details issues of kingship. It is in the fable that Jotham critiques Abimelech's kingship and the participation in it of the lords of Shechem. And, it is worth noting the argument of Barnabas Lindars that "kingship is the presupposition of the fable," and that therefore the fable marks the ambivalence about what kind of

---

48. Lillian Klein in *The Triumph of Irony* points out the play on words with Jotham's being an orphan here (Klein, *The Triumph of Irony*).

49. Maly, "The Jotham Fable," 300.

kingship should emerge, not that kingship is itself bad.⁵⁰ The fable will in many ways set the stage for the rest of the narrative here. At the same time, the critique of the kingship established by the lords of Shechem with Abimelech looks forward positively to the kingship of Saul when he will emerge as one "tall enough" to rule as king over Israel as we shall see in the narrative later.

The fable itself is simple enough. Trees prepare to "anoint a king" and when they ask the olive tree, the fig tree, and the vine, they all refuse the role. "All the trees" then ask the prickly thornbush to "be king" over them.⁵¹ The request is of trees that bear fruit or are productive. The thornbush tells the trees to "take shelter in my shade," which we know the thornbush cannot provide. In fact, the thornbush is not only diminutive in size compared to any tree, but it would literally have to take hold in the bark of the tree to attain any height up the tree at all. The thornbush would not be able to provide shade to any tree. The thornbush calls on the honor of the trees in requesting its kingship but warns that if there is no honor, then "let fire issue from the thornbush and consume the cedars of Lebanon." And as we shall see, fire does emerge with Abimelech—fire that literally burns trees to burn down towers to consume lives.

Eugene Maly's review of the fable suggests that the original fable was not against kingship itself, but "against those who refused, for insufficient reasons, the burden of leadership."⁵² He also notes that the fable is probably borrowed by Israel here from its non-Israelite origin. The fable's inclusion of the phrase "cedars of Lebanon" suggests how despite its non-Israelite origin, the fable had been incorporated both geographically and ideologically to suit Israel.⁵³ Maly does not note, however, that the reference to the cedars of Lebanon itself implies that the cedar was the tallest of these trees who were seeking someone to rule over them, which would have been impossible given the variety of trees in the land of Israel. This does lend credence to his seeming claim that the trees who look for someone to rule over them are not looking, in fact, for someone to provide them shade, but productivity or fruit, as already cited.

50. Lindars, "Jotham's Fable," 365.

51. The fable is littered with the terminology of kingship. Seven times in the fable the root word for *king* appears; these instances do not include other verbs of rule or leadership.

52. Maly, "The Jotham Fable," 303.

53. Ibid.

The function of the parable here does not seem to change any action in the narrative. The Shechemites do not retreat from having made Abimelech their king in this narrative. Rather, the parable exposes an ideology about kingship. As Meir Sternberg points out in the poetics of this biblical narrative, that may be precisely the point. The failure of Jotham's fable to move his audience to change their decision for kingship "serves to articulate the theme under cover of indignant repetition, and to propel the action toward the enactment of its moral: the mutual destruction of the townsmen and the usurper."[54] Here of course we would disagree with Sternberg's assertion that Abimelech is a usurper. The idea not only does not function in our narrative but quite the contrary; his having been empowered shows him as not stealing power, but rightfully gaining it.

The speech of this orphaned son of Gideon does not end with the fable, but with a continued critique of the actions of the Lords of Shechem in "kinging 'my father is king' king." Of note in his continued speech is the fact that he denounces the inhabitants of Shechem for having "turned on my father's household, killed his sons, seventy men on one stone." The repetition in the speech of Jotham attacks the multiple wrongs committed by the lords of Shechem. Not only did they do the first act in turning against Gideon, they also did the consequent acts Jotham details. Curiously he notes the destruction of "seventy men" "all on one" stone even when we know that he is the one who has escaped as the orphaned one. The use of seventy again here when the 'real' number is sixty-nine accentuates what was supposed to be the 'perfect murder.' The murder of the seventy is a means by which the Hebrew text suggests the 'complete' and 'ultimate heinous-ness' of the crime that took place, even if one did escape. Curiously here, Jotham refers to the "kinship" relationship that existed between Abimelech and the lords of Shechem, denouncing kinship relationship as the basis for proper kingship. And when Jotham speaks of Abimelech he is never named as his brother, as we already have seen. But Jotham does not call him the son of the concubine. He is instead the son of the "slave girl" (בן־אמתו Judges 9:18). The merit of the new term as distinct from the concubine we have met is not as crucial to us as is the fact that again in the narrative, Abimelech is marked as an outsider in a new way. It had been the narrator who had

---

54. Sternberg, *The Poetics of Biblical Narrative*, 429.

made Abimelech an outsider for us. Now Jotham identifies him as an outsider, but in a new way.

The geographic location of the speech of Jotham further seems to add irony to his speech as his location "on the mountain symbolizes [his] having the overall picture and moral superiority."[55] When he has finished speaking, Jotham goes to pit (וילך באׁרה) and there he stays (Judg 9:21). Oddly, this story that has so characteristically made Abimelech an outsider to Gideon and Gideon's sons finally says of Abimelech, literally the last words by the narrator of Jotham, that he was to Abimelech "his brother." While he is "brother" to Jotham, he has also been demonstrated as an outsider to his family particularly by his choice to murder them and do away with them as participants in his life and the life of rule in Shechem.

KINGSHIP, RIVALRY, VIOLENCE, AND GIRARD

Now, this Abimelech who was "kinged" to be "king" (את־אבימלך ותמליכו Judges 9:18) is said to have "ruled" (וישׂר, Judges 9:22). For all the attention to kingship in the naming, in the seeming inauguration at the tower of fortification, from the verbal emphasis so clear in Jotham's fable, this "king" who was "kinged" does not "king"—a verbal construction available in Hebrew—instead he "rules" שׂרר. This verbal construction is distinct from the verbal construction we shall see with the coronation of Saul later. And, the verbal construction here used for all the seeming gravity of Abimelech's rule is the same root used to describe "merely" Zebul's rule over a city, the city of Shechem itself in 9:30. This story seems ambivalent about what it means to be king and what it means to direct as king. The narrative is unable to choose מלך, משׁל, or שׂרר though we would expect מלך if this is a king. And we shall see different kinds of leadership emerge in our later narrative when, as we will argue, 'real' kingship emerges both in the narrative, and understood from categories of similar stories that share a Girardian perspective.[56]

---

55. Fokkelman, "Structural Remarks on Judges 9 and 19," 37.

56. The kingship of Saul will be characterized first by the category of being נגיד but also as one who "retains" (עצר; 1 Sam 9:17). Only late in our reading, at the very end, indeed, does Saul "reign over," (מלך) the people. Note here in our narrative that while different verbs for different kinds of rule have been used for Abimelech prior to and up to his pseudo-inauguration (contra the *real* one we'll see with Saul), once raised up Abimelech is never said to "reign over" (מלך) the people. Marc Brettler calls Abimelech here an "anti-judge" noting that in this unit "neither *wayyōša'* nor *wayyišpōṭ*,

While our focus is not theological in this study, that is, we are not trying to explore how God brings about kingship in Israel or how God was necessarily with or not with any character in our stories, our close reading of this narrative must recognize that God is a character in the narrative. In Judges 9, God is consistently "*Elohim*" and never "*YHWH.*" It is *Elohim* in the narrative who next acts, and the action of *Elohim* here regards an "evil spirit" sent "between"—and not "upon"— Abimelech and the Lords of Shechem (Judg 9:23). The nature of this "spirit" (רוח) seems to connote something of relationship between them, distinct from something that comes "upon a person" as it does for many of the judges and for Saul in our narrative (I Sam 10:6,10 and 11:6).[57] No matter the theological issues for us, what is important is that this one who is kinged, who hires worthless fellows, who murders his brothers, who "*sarrars*" Israel is now dealt a blow when the Lords of Shechem, who had hired him with their seventy shekels, now hire ambushes and "deal treacherously" (ויבגדו) with Abimelech. The narrator tells us it happened this way so that the violence of the blood of the seventy might be "put upon" Abimelech and the lords of Shechem (לבוא חמס שבעים בני־ירבעל ודמם לשום על־אבימלך).[58]

The Lords of Shechem with Abimelech killed the seventy. This same verbal construction for the killing will reappear in the speech of an unnamed Levite later in our review, cf. Judges 20:5. Ambushes are set to "contend" (מארבים) him and men carry out robbery (tearing, seizing, ויגזלו). One wonders if the lords of Shechem did not begin to reconsider whether or not it might have been better for them to have been ruled by seventy, for there is no טובטוב here—only מארבים and ויגזלו. Abimelech has to contend with the "terrorist" forces from the Shechemites themselves whereas all the other judges in the book of Judges encountered a foreign threat.[59]

---

typical of other judges, is used of him; instead we find *wayā šar* (9:22)" (Brettler, "The Book of Judges," 406). Tomoo Ishida says that in this verbal construction Abimelech's "*control* [italics mine] over 'Israel' was not regarded as the rule of" the other judges or *shopet* (Ishida, "The Leaders of the Tribal Leagues," 527).

57. The spirit that comes in these passages upon other judges is from YHWH.

58. The only other time the noun חמס is used in the Deuteronomistic History is in the poem of David in 2 Sam 22:3. This is indeed a unique kind of violence operating under the leadership of this "king."

59. Tanner, "The Gideon Narrative," 156.

ABIMELECH AND GAAL AS RIVALS FOR KINGSHIP

In the narrative then, the one who is such an outsider/insider, "my father is king" is kinged when he is sanctioned with authority and brokered with men and silver, he acts not with חסד or benevolence but with murderous magnanimity. He murders because of the perceived threat of his half-brothers' mutual desire to rule. Upon doing away with the threat, though, Abimelech does not bring peace, but only further division. He is inaugurated, but there is no peace, only more fracture. And as we shall see, rivalry escalates, and cannot be contained.

For all the narrative focus on Abimelech, the narrator turns our attention from him to a new character, Gaal son of Ebed (Judg 9:26). Gaal moves to Shechem and the lords of Shechem "put their trust in him" (ויבטחו־בו). The ones who "kinged" Abimelech only to "*bagad*" him, now enlist a rival. The triangle of rule over Shechem is again put in place, after all, he, too, is "kin" (Judg 9:26). And as the narrative continues we will discover the ambiguity associated with precisely who Abimelech lives in kinship and kingship with.

A. D. Crown says that the persons traveling with Gaal through Shechem are but vain and worthless fellows set off against Abimelech who is "simply hoist with his own petard."[60] The actual naming of Gaal in this narrative, itself, might be an intentional mockery of his status, as Burney and others have pointed out that the name derives from the Arabic Gu'al which might suggest that this person is a "dung beetle" of a character or perhaps a "black and ugly man."[61]

Volkmar Fritz used the character of Gaal to argue against the narrative unity of Judges 9. We side with T. A. Boogart who demonstrates the narrative consistency of Gaal with Abimelech in noting the commonalities in these two characters within this one story. In both stories:

> 1. a man comes to Shechem (9.1a; 9.26a): 2. the man is accompanied by his brothers/kinsmen (9.1b–3a; 9:26a): 3. the man conspires against the absent ruler of Shechem with a speech delivered at a gathering (9.2–3a; 9:28–29): 4. the speech emphasizes that the ties of the conspirator to Shechem are closer than those of the ruler (9.2b; 9.28): 5. the Shechemites put their trust in the

---

60. Crown, "A Reinterpretation," 95.
61. Burney, *The Book of Judges*, 278.

conspirator (9.3b; 9.26b): 6. the conspirator encounters the ruler (9.5; 9.30–42).[62]

Gaal's actions are spied upon by Zebul who is in league with Abimelech. Janzen notes that "Boling's alternative translation of the name 'Zebul' as 'Big Shot' nicely captures its narrative significance, standing in characterological [sic] contrast to 'Gaal' which, he notes, drives from the verb 'abhor, loathe. But the play with names and epithets is not over."[63]

Gaal does not lead the people in the murderous impulse to drive out Abimelech, as Abimelech had done so with his desire to kill the seventy. Gaal instead leads them to party. In their moments of imbibing they ridiculed Abimelech (וישתו ויקללו את־אבימלך, Judges 9:27). We might say they "revile" him with this new *rival* in town. The narrator tells us what it is that Gaal says as he questions "Who" Abimelech is at all.[64] It is a potent question in the narrative as Abimelech's characterization vacillates for the reader between insider and outsider from one verse to the next. Further, there is not one consistent verb used for his rule to nail down for us what it is precisely that Abimelech does for Shechem. And then Gaal tells us that another son of Gideon/Jerubbaal had ruled Shechem (Judg 9:28). This helps us believe better the threat that Abimelech had stated earlier in the narrative. At the same time, it confuses our belief since here Gaal makes reference to the prior rule of only one man, not "the seventy" that Abimelech had suggested in his speech to the Lords of Shechem.

Gaal seeks leadership of his own in a rivalrous speech challenging that of Abimelech. The rule Gaal seeks adds another verb to our narrative, as he claims if only this people were "under my hand" (ומי יתן את־העם הזה בידי; Judg 9:29). Then Abimelech could "increase his army and come out" to the challenge that Gaal represented. Zebul hears the words of Gaal. Here Zebul is referred to as the ruler (שר־העיר) of the city, though we might have expected a title like this, or something more specific to kingship, for Abimelech. Zebul gets angry.[65]

62. Boogart, "Stone for Stone," 50.
63. Janzen, "A Certain Woman," 34.
64. Robert Boling has noted the significance of Zebul in Gaal's question. Boling notes that Gaal's question is a critique of the rule of both Zebul and Abimelech. Of course our attention is on Abimelech in this narrative, whom Boling calls "a merely half-shechemite *mèlek*." (Boling, "And who is S-K-M?" 482).
65. We will see later that the same reaction happens to Saul, but not because of anger against his rival in Israel, but because of anger for the inhabitants of Jabesh Gilead, who

Abimelech travels by night, lies in ambush, and then rises to attack Gaal. Night is the cover for the violence to be inflicted and ambush is the modus operandi for the troops. Gaal sees people coming, Zebul calls them shadows, and soon the ambush is upon them. In direct discourse Zebul challenges Gaal to prove himself.

Gaal now leads the lords of Shechem, not Abimelech who we would expect to be leading those who crowned him king. Gaal and the lords of Shechem fall before the entrance of the gates. The text is specific that Zebul is responsible for driving them out (9:41). Interesting that for all the source of strength and leadership that Abimelech was supposed to provide for the inhabitants of Shechem, it is Zebul who operates to expel Gaal in this narrative. Alter says of this narrative, "When the trap is about to spring and Gaal realizes too late that he is caught in a pincer movement between two hostile forces, Zebul jeeringly reminds him of the language of his own speech."[66]

We expect that the problems with Gaal are over. We expect the narrative rising action to move towards a denouement. But we are surprised by what happens because the conflict that should have come to an end has not come to an end.

The next day, Abimelech meets the people of Shechem who have gone out to their fields. With three companies of men and the light of dawn, Abimelech attacks the inhabitants of Shechem and kills them. In the morning, the attack begins. We will see another corpse on another morning in Judges 19. The city, full of the persons who had kinged him king, is laid waste. And this city, unlike any other city in the biblical tradi-

---

themselves are very important in our next two narratives. Here the anger is about rivalry, but with Saul the anger will quell rivalry. To *arumah* ("the place of deceitfulness") the message is carried about Gaal to Abimelech. Stanley Gevirtz presents an interesting note on this *hapax legomena* in Hebrew: "*tormah*," that we have here read as *arumah* to tie it into the place name used for Abimelech again in 9:41. In Gevirtz's article he notes that it is indeed a *hapax* here in 9:31 and by analogy he "suggests for *tormah* a meaning 'separation, deviation, secret,' . . . one which suits the demands of context admirably, and which is furthermore in accord with the ancient versions" (Gevirtz, "The Hapax Legomenon," 59–60). The city is "besieged" (צרים); Zebul counsels Abimelech to take advantage of the night (night will play out poorly for us later) and then to come up from the field to attack. Later we will meet an unnamed old man in Judges 19 and then Saul in 1 Samuel 11 coming from the fields as well. In this narrative the ones who rise up from the fields bring violence. We will have to wait to see what it means in our other narratives.

66. Alter, *Language as Theme*, 13.

tion, unique to it and it alone, is sown with salt. We will later analyze how this odd series of events pertains to issues of kingship with Abimelech. For now we note that the sowing of salt on this city marks for the readers the fact of utter desolation. It is not just the case that all have been killed in Shechem, the kinds of growth/produce that Shechem produced will never occur again. A. M. Honeyman argues that the salting of Shechem demonstrates Abimelech's fear of "supernatural vengeance."[67] Believing this to be not simply a token gesture, Honeyman states that the "broadcast strewing of the salt was a last desperate attempt to neutralize the shades of the slaughtered Shechemites and to avert their vengeance."[68] While our focus is not on the "supernatural" or Honeyman's use of the term, it is important to note that Honeyman is aware of the issues of vengeance that might operate in the text as the extension of the rivalrous situation Abimelech and the Shechemites have fertilized.[69]

While this would have implications for the actual earthen fields of Shechem, of course, it seems to operate here in the context of the Deuteronomistic History for the kind of growth that Jotham's fable had articulated. No trees, whether olive, fig, grapevine or thornbush will take root here. The city and the archetypes of leadership that the city has produced, it seems, are coming to their end. And we shall see that not only is the city to be razed and no longer produce vegetation of any kind – but the kind of leadership of this king brings only humiliation following utter devastation.

The narrative, a second time, seems to have reached its climax, but the categories of this conflict have not ended until the one who brings the conflict—conflict perpetuated by the greed and rivalry of Abimelech—ceases to operate within the narrative.

It has not been enough to tell us the city of Shechem has been sown with salt. Abimelech must rise a third time. This time Abimelech rises against the tower of Shechem, the citadel, the stronghold. It too must fall for in this narrative we shall see that no stronghold can withstand the kind of conflict this kind of kingship brings. Marching to Mt. Zalmon this "thornbush" king takes up an axe and begins cutting down trees. If we recall here fully the fable of Jotham we see that not only will no produce grow from the salted city, but those trees which are standing

---

67. Honeyman, "The Salting of Shechem," 194.
68. Ibid, 195.
69. The pun is intentional.

must be brought down as well. And Abimelech picks up the fallen trees on his "*shechem*" (shoulders). Ironically the lords of Shechem had empowered Abimelech and now in a further twist the trees are lifted up on his shoulders—as it were, Abimelech is carrying upon his "*shechem*" the "trees" that empowered him, but what will now happen? His "*shechem*" (shoulders) will carry the fallen trees to the fortress and do that which Jotham's fable has anticipated for us—fire will break forth from the Abimelech and will burn down the Lords of Shechem (Judg 9:20). The men with Abimelech cut down their own branches and they lay down their wood at the citadel, the stronghold of Shechem and here they burn it down (Judg 9:49).

We expect that with no persons to empower this king any longer, the story should be over. Shechem is destroyed in our narrative. Day One; it was Gaal whose conflict led to siege. Day Two; it was the inhabitants of Shechem whose actions led to siege, then the tower of Shechem. We see how in this narrative the use of the third element sets the stage for what is most important. This third element theme will function in our other narratives as well.

Day Three; Abimelech does not cease but proceeds beyond Shechem. There is no logic in the storyline to explain or justify Abimelech's procession. He moves to the city of Thebez. As a city in the story, it exists only here in the Old Testament. And while there exists no explanation in the narrative by the narrator or in direct discourse for why Abimelech should move on to this city, we perceive one thing about this king and the kingship he has brought; it consistently involves conflict.[70] We expect nothing less as Abimelech gets to Thebez, and our expectations will be met. Perhaps with no one to "king," Abimelech needs persons "under him."

He camps around and occupies Thebez and here, as we had seen in Shechem, the inhabitants retreat to their fortified tower. They end up on the roof of the tower, taking refuge there. Perhaps it is roof-top experiences that confirm kingship.[71]

---

70. Wolfgang Richter notes of this story that here we have again or suddenly the start of a new narrative in which the characters are differentiated from each other (Richter, *Traditionsgeschichtliche*, 273).

71. Here we anticipate a rooftop conversation that will take place between Samuel and Saul in our narratives.

Abimelech had "shouldered" the "shoulder" city to their destruction. We watch to see what will come of the inhabitants of Thebez who are at this point in the narrative "over" Abimelech on the roof of their strong tower. But Abimelech wants to be over them, to rule them.[72]

Without belaboring our point, let me state again here, Shechem had kinged "my father is king" and they are now utterly destroyed with salt, fire, and with their trees consuming their fortified tower. Now, though, Thebez is a new fortified tower, not present in our story, not having empowered or called for this kind of kingship. Thebez has no claim to Abimelech that we know of. Nor do we know that Abimelech has any claim to Thebez.

ABIMELECH, ONE WOMAN, AND ONE STONE

Abimelech, whose first act of his kingship when empowered by the Shechemites was to kill seventy on one stone, sets fire to the tower doors. In a tightly constructed sentence in the Hebrew text we read about something new, a woman. At no point in *this* story apart from his unnamed mother has a woman appeared. There are plenty of women in the stories of the Deuteronomistic History, in narratives in Joshua and Judges that precede this story. And our only reference to women in this entire chapter has been to the total annihilation of Shechem. But here a woman, this "one" woman acts in the text. "One woman casts a millstone upon the head of Abimelech and crushed his skull." The difference-maker in the narrative is one woman and one stone. "One who would rule Shechem *single-handedly* as its *head stone*, in the end is killed by a *single* woman who drops a *mill-stone* upon ('al) his head."[73] And it is J. Gerald Janzen who also notes for us that this would be king of Israel, this one who should have lead armies and chariots into battle is killed by "a 'riding' stone, the adjective evoking overtones of chariots of war" which Abimelech clearly can no longer lead.[74]

Upon one stone Abimelech's conflictual violence brought his kingship, and with one stone's fall, his fall as king and as person is affected. The narrative construction tells us that both the "skull" of Abimelech is

---

72. While this narrative only uses the idea of Abimelech's being "over" the people in the Jotham fable, it does operate in the larger story. And we shall see that the idea of finding someone "over" the people will emerge in the height of Saul.

73. Janzen, "A Certain Woman," 35 (italics original).

74. Ibid.

crushed and the "head"—which can be used and is used in the Hebrew Bible for "chiefs" or "leaders" or "tops." The headship of this kind of kingship is crushed by one woman, one stone. Abimelech's death from the falling stone off the roof will be set in stark contrast from a latter scene where, upon a roof Saul's move towards the inauguration of kinship will commence.

The narrative should be over, but with the life of this king fading, the narrator adds further insult to injury. Mortally wounded, Abimelech speaks the words of his own destruction in the narrative. The one who brings kingship in the narrative and in his speech now brings the end of kingship in the narrative with his speech to his servant, the lad with him, to "Draw your dagger and finish me off so they may not say, 'A woman killed him.'"[75] The last words of this king reflect the tone of the narrative of kingship, "A woman killed him."

> Abimelech's last speech, like his first, contains an embedded quotation, in this case a prospective "text" he wants to forfend [sic] and, as we have already observed, fails to forfend [sic]. This is one of those rare moments when a biblical character sounds vaguely Homeric, actuated by the heroic code of a shame culture as against the Bible's more usual guilt culture. Abimelech, having achieved dominion through words leading to murder, is now faced with a legacy of mocking words alone, and his attempt to control them is futile.[76]

---

75. While a seemingly minor point in the story, the reference to the servant is important here and was brought to my attention in the work of Wolfgang Richter (Richter, *Traditionsgeschichtliche*, 274). The last "new" character introduced in this narrative is the נער. Our further study in Judges 17–21 and 1 Samuel 9 will demonstrate the significance of the נער since one appears as a central agent, unnamed, in each story.

76. Alter, *Language as Theme*, 14. While he goes beyond the scope of our narrative focus and intent in this study, Alter makes a connection between this final Abimelech episode and the final episode of the Saul narrative. Alter's link is instructive and connects with James G. Williams's article on Saul as the sacrificer and as the one who is sacrificed as king (Williams, "Sacrifice and the Beginning of Kingship," 73–92). In this narrative Alter notes that the last episode of Abimelech mocks his kingship in words, but that the last episode of Saul (the one who does mitigate and quell violence) is an episode of deeds. Alter writes: "The difference between his [Abimelech's] last command and the similar one that Saul issues to his armor-bearer is instructive. Saul, badly wounded, his forces defeated by the Philistines at Mount Gilboa, says to his attendant: 'Draw your sword and run me through with it, lest these uncircumcised come and run me through and abuse me' (1 Sam 31:4). Saul's horror is not of words but of deeds—the physical disgrace of being cut down, perhaps mutilated, by his pagan foes. Abimelech, who has ascended to the throne through words and has been countered by adversaries

CRUSHING ABIMELECH'S RULE

A woman kills kingship. And, "not merely 'a certain woman,' but a lone woman, whose singularity connects resonantly with an already established rhetorical pattern" to the one stone from the beginning of the narrative.[77] Abimelech's own speech, his dying words, utter his own deprecation.[78]

This one woman brings to the end the rule of this one man whose rule began on one stone. The narrative has worked us down from the four columns of Abimelech's march against Gaal (v. 34) to three columns (vv. 43–44), to two columns (v. 44) down to this one, one woman, one stone, one sword, one death of this one king.

As the narrative ends, we hear something we have not heard anywhere in this narrative until now. It was the "men of Israel" who had been following this king, this kind of kingship. We were told earlier in the narrative that Abimelech ruled in this local region, this city only—that

---

through words, has only a scrap of reputation to grasp at the end—and to lose" (Alter, *Language as Theme*, 14).

77. Janzen, "A Certain Woman," 36.

78. In the Hebrew Bible, the persons we know as the judges appear only in the book of Judges. Their character space is limited to this book. They affect stories here and here only in the whole of the Old Testament. The only place where they are mentioned outside this story is in one place, where the three of them are named side by side in a quick recollection of this entire period—the judges are Jerubbaal, Jepthah, and Samson. (Barak is included but he's never a judge in the story itself.) Judges are limited to their inclusion in the book of Judges. But I have intentionally left out one other verse in the Bible. In 2 Sam 12:11 when Joab, the commander of David's army seeks to deprecate the horrific act of David's murder of Uriah the Hittite, we hear of Abimelech. Joab says in 2 Sam 11:19–21: "When you have finished telling the king all the news about the fighting, then, if the king's anger rises, and if he says to you, 'Why did you go so near the city to fight? Did you not know that they would shoot from the wall? Who killed Abimelech son of Jerubbaal? Did not a woman throw an upper millstone on him from the wall, so that he died at Thebez? Why did you go so near the wall?' then you shall say, 'Your servant Uriah the Hittite is dead too.'" The only person "from the book of Judges mentioned in any other story outside the book itself is Abimelech. And when he is found in the Bible again, mention of him functions similarly to his function in his own story: mention of Abimelech functions to humiliate the kind of king that Abimelech had been, and the kind of king David was in the moment when he hears from Joab. For a slightly different read of Joab's use of Abimelech in 2 Samuel, see Sternberg, *The Poetics of Biblical Narrative*, 219–22. In their work on the traditions of David, Menahem Perry and Meir Sternberg say that in the David tradition Abimelech becomes explicitly what he did not want to become: a "keyword" (Perry and Sternberg, "The King through Ironic Eyes," 312ff.). See also Malamat, "The Period of the Judges," 133.

he had worthless fellows with him. But as the narrative ends, the narrator says that the "men of Israel" went to their "homes" (וילכו איש למקמו). The Hebrew word used to describe their homes here is not the more common expression of בית that we might expect used elsewhere in the narrative at Judges 9:5, 16, 18, 19. It is to their מקם that they head-off towards. In the larger book of Judges the earlier "judges" provided rest for one or two generations but for Abimelech and subsequent to him "no periods of rest are noted."[79] Things have changed in the Book of Judges itself as it characterizes its leaders.

What is more, the next time we have anyone return to a מקם in Israel is when an unnamed Levite carries the raped, murdered body of his concubine "home" (ויקם האיש וילך למקמו:, Judg 19:28). The conflict of Abimelech will appear as a pleasant story in contrast to the chaos that will break forth in Israel.

---

79. Mullen, "The 'Minor Judges,'" 194.

4

Micah, the Levite, and the Concubine

It has not been the purpose of this study to explore the variety of stories that appear in the narratives of the Book of Judges. Our selection to this point has been limited to Abimelech and to his narrative alone. That being the case, we call attention here to the basic framework of Judges as a narrative unit. The narrative we will read in Judges 17–21 seems so "out of place" with the larger narrative framework.

The book of Judges begins with a narrative framework that shapes the whole of the book. Explicitly stated in Judges 2 the framework is, "The Israelites did evil in the eyes of the Lord . . . they provoked the Lord to anger . . . the Lord handed them over . . . then the Lord raised up judges who saved them" (Judg 2:11–19). The basic framework orients the stories of the characters, the judges we read about in this book. There are numerous commentaries and books that give insight into the various characters in Judges and they follow the lives of the several judges within the book, usually following Ehud, Deborah, Gideon/Jerub-Baal, Abimelech, Jephthah, and Samson.[1] While the reviews of the scholars vary, it is generally noted that the length and effectiveness of the judges fades and wanes from the book's beginning to its end. In fact, as we have seen with Abimelech, the judges hardly deliver at all—and, of course, we have seen that he "ruled" Israel. By the time the reader of Judges gets through the lengthy Samson narrative, the formula of the book of Judges begins to break down. Samson has hardly even begun to deliver the Israelites from the Philistines. At the end of the narrative with Samson, we come to a new set of stories in Judges 17–21.

---

1. There are other judges in the book of Judges, but these are the judges given the most textual space. Technically the judges continue over into the stories of 1 Samuel, with Samuel and Eli being recognized as judges. But as we'll see, the narratives of Judges 17–21 break up the basic framework.

The issue that most specifically sets Judges 17–21 textually apart from the narratives that have preceded it is a new formula that operates for these final four chapters. The new formula is articulated slightly differently in its use four-times in these five chapters: Judges 17:6; 18:1; 19:1; and 21:25. It is not only the explicitly stated summary of this period of Judges, it also marks the final words of the book. In the first and final reference the formula reads in its fullness as follows: "In those days there was no king in Israel, all the people did what was right in their own eyes." These narratives in 17–21 are set apart with a new and unique formula marked by the specific introduction of kingship in Israel. In the middle references the formula is present only in the first part: "In those days there was no king in Israel." The narrator makes it explicit for us here at the end of the narratives of Judges, as the failure of the judges seems clear in the person of Samson and his death. A new reality is made textually present to the reader, kingship in Israel.[2] Building upon an Egyptian parallel, Frederick Greenspahn demonstrates the historical reality of this claim alongside a contemporaneous historical reality in Egypt.

"The force of this formula [to do good in one's own eyes] is illustrated by an almost identical assertion found in Egyptian literature dealing with a nearly contemporary period. Describing the chaos which preceded the accession of Setnakhte (ca. 1184–82), Harris Papyrus, No. 1 states that 'the land of Egypt had been overthrown with every man being his own standard of right (*s nb m 'k3.f*) since they had no leader (*r hry*) for many years in the times of the others.'"[3]

Greenspahn describes the historical realities in Egypt, which he assumes as narrating a real history, as being the "same claim as that made by the book of Judges for the coming of Israel's monarchy."[4] The idea that this reality of anarchy to monarchy has precedent in the "real history" of Egypt will be important for us in this study because we will argue that a

---

2. Gale Yee reads these narratives in a way (though distinct from the method of this study) that remains conversant with our aim here. Her reading "uses literary critical methods within a historical and social scientific frame in a comprehensive strategy for reading biblical texts" (Yee, *Judges and Method*, 146). She clarifies how the stories found in these five chapters serve to consolidate power for the rule of Josiah and at the same time marginalize the role of the Levites (and hence Levitical priests), who are depicted negatively here. Her assessment is meritorious and like ours seeks to appropriate the need for kingship that emerges out of our literary reading of these texts.

3. Greenspahn, "An Egyptian Parallel," 129–30.

4. Ibid.

real period of anarchy preceded the emergence of Israel's first monarch, Saul, as we move into his story in our next chapter.

At the same time, though, we want to remind the reader that the demarcations of these stories within the larger work of the Deuteronomistic History does not fracture them from being part of the larger story. To note their demarcation is not to separate them. We will demonstrate numerous literary connections bound up in these stories with the story we have read in Judges 9 and the stories we will read in 1 Samuel 9–11. We do not argue here that chapters 17–21 are an "interruption" to the story of Judges and 1 Samuel nor do we agree that these stories "disrupt the continuity of the Deuteronomistic history."[5] Mayes cannot suggest a solid reason for the inclusion of these stories at the end of the book of Judges.

"They have been brought very late into their present position, at a time after the composition of the Deuteronomistic history the continuity of which they disrupt. The intention of the editor who incorporated them is not clear. It need not have been identical with the original pro-monarchic concerns of the records; indeed, it may be that this late editor simply saw in them useful illustrations of the moral and spiritual state of Israel in this period, which he could use to mark off the book of Judges as a separate literary entity."[6]

We will argue here that the literary connections operating in this text mitigate against Mayes' claims in every respect. Other scholars have noted some of the connections between these stories with the content of the whole book, e.g., Yairah Amit.[7] Robert H. O'Connell argues for the coherence of these narratives with the whole in his chapter on the "double dénouement" in Judges and notes similarities in this story that move in a different direction than this study, the connection of these stories with the Samson narratives.[8] For us, then, they are not separate narratives. Neither are they just about the moral or spiritual state of Israel. Nor are they late separate entities.[9] These stories are fully in congruence

---

5. Mayes, *Judges*, 14–15.

6. Ibid., 16.

7. Amit, *The Book of Judges*, 314–16.

8. O'Connell, *The Rhetoric*. His discussion of the double denouement begins at page 229, and his references to the connections with Samson can be found at p. 169.

9. Here our work is in contrast to the argument of Uwe Becker, who dates Judges 17–21 from a late, post-exilic period. This study would suggest that while the entire

with the narrative and historical crisis about the problems and possibilities that kingship offers.

We will note connections and dislocations between what appears in Judges 17–21 with respect to the fact that Judges 17–18 are sometimes set-apart from chapter 19–21 by scholars who are working with this literature. While the intent of our focus will work towards what happens in the latter half of Judges 17–21, the stories are connected. As Philip Satterthwaite has written, "The two main blocks of narrative in Judges 17–21—chapters 17–18 and 19–21—seem to share a similar pattern. They both start by describing the doings of Israelite individuals (Micah in 17, the Levite and his concubine in 19) and then broaden their scope to Israel at the tribal or pan-tribal level (Dan in 18, all the Israelite tribes in 20 and 21)."[10]

At the outset of this chapter's close literary reading, however, we must again remind the reader of this study about what to expect in what follows. It needs to be remembered that the argument of this study is about kingship and the emergence of kingship in Israel's history. But it must also be pointed out that in these chapters there is no king and there will be little inclusion of kingship/monarchial language in my assessment of these texts for the following two reasons: first, as noted the narrative stories themselves apart from the framework device does not deal with a מלך or even נגיד or השפט, and; second, the emergence of violent, genocidal conflict is what lays the basis for kingship in our next story and this understanding will be explained using the Girardian hermeneutic that frames the work of this study.

It should also be stated at the outset of this chapter that the reader of this study may tire of the close, seemingly overly redundant use of introductions to characters within this narrative. We repeatedly use certain terms to refer to characters in this narrative in a way that I assume will seem exaggerated to the reader. This is intentional. In the books of Judges and 1 Samuel we meet many characters who are named for us. In this narrative, we meet several characters some of whom engage in significant events of discourse with several other parties, a few of whom never speak, but *all of them* are anonymous in the narrative. It is their an-

---

scope of the Deuteronomistic History may have been edited in a post-exilic context, these stories contain historical realities that predate the exile itself. See especially p. 297 of Becker's analysis (Becker, *Richterzeit*, 296–99).

10. Satterthwaite, "'No King in Israel,'" 77.

onymity that I heighten in my continued reference to them. Don Hudson notes that the narrative of Judges has digressed in its characterization of persons, leaving Judges 17–21 in "ironic mode" with anonymous characters.[11] "This use of anonymity brings the reader to the end of the narrator's descending characterization. As the plot [of Judges] unravels, so does the characterization."[12] This anonymity needs to be heightened for our ability to assess the implications of a Girardian framework for these texts in our review that will follow.

MICAH AND THE LEVITE AS PRIEST

In chapter 17:1 we meet a new character, who we might expect to be a new Judge in the narrative formula, Micah. Micah had stolen eleven hundred shekels from his mother, unnamed in the narrative.[13] Upon returning the shekels to his mother, she rejoices and hires a smith to create an idol of cast medal, a shrine, an ephod and ateraphim. Micah installs his son to be priest. This is the first time in all the stories of the narrative of Judges that we meet a priest, the first time we meet an idol (other than Baal who is named as Baal), and the first time we meet teraphim. Our only other reference to an ephod is, curiously, in the text that just precedes our narrative with Abimelech where Gideon, after refusing to become king, made an ephod, and set it up in Ophrah. We might remember this city as the city where Abimelech went to kill his seventy brothers. In creating a "shrine" we have a new event taking place in Israel's history in the Deuteronomistic History. The term occurs only in one other place in the Deuteronomistic History, in the narrative which introduces Saul to us and we shall explore its implications there.

This story which introduces sacerdotal implements and instruments breaks off and we read the formula that shapes our narratives

---

11. Hudson, "Living in a Land of Epithets," 51.

12. Ibid. We will demonstrate in the remainder of this chapter and the extended scope of this study that the unraveling of characters as named persons here sets the narrative connection to what happens in 1 Samuel. This story connects with episodes in Saul's life where Saul becomes a principally named and central character whose activities frame the start of kingship. Therefore the narrative unraveling here in Judges sets readers to interpret the actions of Saul as "binding" what has been unraveled, to borrow from Hudson's metaphor.

13. Of note here is this unnamed woman. We will explicate later in this chapter the issues of ambiguity and anonymity in this narrative as well as in the other narratives this study seeks to examine.

here: "In those days there was no king in Israel, every man did as he pleased." We move into a new story.

We are introduced to a new character who will be central to our narrative. Alongside his central role, though, he is an outsider to the story of Israel. In Judges 19:1 we are told of a young man who lives in Bethlehem of Judah, from the clan of Judah who resides there, but who is a "sojourner" (גֵּר):

ויהי איש לוי גר בירכתי הר־אפרים

This term for "sojourner" appears only here and in 19:1, 16 in the Deuteronomistic History. This Levite is an outsider, though he lives there. Curiously, it is only here in Judges 17–21 in the Deuteronomistic History that we read about Levites. In the 147 total chapters from Joshua 1 through and including II Kings 25, only in these five chapters do Levites appear. We who know the story of the Bible might know about the Levites from the book of Leviticus and the stories associated with them in the Torah. But here, in the history of the Deuteronomist, we do now know who or what this person is, this Levite. But a reader of the Deuteronomistic History would certainly know the connections between Levites and the Priesthood. Priests have important and clearly narrated responsibilities and functional duties with respect to the tabernacle or temple in many ways, not least of which is as the principle persons who officiate over sacrificial offerings.

Already set apart as גֵּר for us, the narrator reveals even more fully to us how "adrift" this unnamed Levite is, for he left Bethlehem to find a house "wherever he could" and he wanders to the house of Micah.

Micah queries him, "Where do you come from?" We shall hear this question again when the man from the fields in Gibeah greets the unnamed Levite there. The Levite's answer puts in his own words, for a third time, the extent of his wandering-outsider-stature. The Levite answers that he is traveling to take up residence wherever he can find a place (Judg 17:9). Micah stops the Levite and presumably takes his son out of the role of priest by placing this unnamed Levite in the role of priest. For the second time in the Deuteronomistic History we have met a priest (Judg 17:10). Micah installs the still unnamed man in his house, and for the third time we are told he becomes the priest (Judg 17:12).

The narrative has moved forward quickly, but so many pieces seem missing to hold the narrative in place for us. We have an unnamed woman/mother, a son who establishes a shrine with an ephod, idol and teraphim. Now we have an unnamed young man, a sojourner, a Levite, who has become a priest. We have a host of anonymous characters attending to priestly or sacred activities. And the narrator reminds us as we move into chapter 18: "this Levite has become my priest. In those days there was no king in Israel" (Judg 17:13—18:1).

We read how the tribe of Dan did not have a territory or allotment and therefore they go seeking another territory.[14] Upon coming to the vicinity of Micah's house, they hear the speech of the Levite and they recognize that he does not fit in.[15] We have already been told this in our narrative, but the Danites' speech to the Levite tells us yet again that the Levite does not fit in. They query the unnamed Levite, "Who brought you ... What are you doing ... What is your business?" The unnamed Levite replies, "Thus and thus, Micah hired me and I became his priest" (כזה וכזה לי מיכה וישכרני ואהי־לו לכהן, Judg 18:4). The men then ask this priest for a favor. "Inquire of God," they ask (Judg 18:5). And for the first time in the Deuteronomistic History we learn what might be the function or purpose of the priest. The priest is one who inquires of God.

The unnamed-young man-sojourner-Levite-priest gives a favorable word to the five spies, "peace" (לשלום, Judg 18:6). They move on. The Danites proceed to yet a further place of isolation and separation in the text as the narrator makes clear. They come to a place characterized by peace and they identify it as such. The come to Laish and we are told the people are "carefree," "peaceful," "unsuspecting" "with no one to molest them" (Judg 18:10). A. A. Macintosh has done an interesting assessment of the kind of rule operating here in Laish, connecting this narrative to our issues of rule/leadership/kingship in Judges 9, 17–21 and 1 Samuel 9–11. Macintosh notes that Judg 18:7 might best be translated as "There was no one speaking authority in the land, no one in possession of control."[16] Philip Satterthwaite points out that within the larger

---

14. We are reminded here of other stories in the biblical text where spies are sent to reconnoiter the land—by Moses or by Joshua perhaps, but our connections in this study will move us in a different direction.

15. We make the claim that he does not fit in based on the text. Van der Hart suggests that the reason the spies recognize him as different is that "he was presumably chanting hymns, hymns with which the Danites were familiar from other sanctuaries which they used to visit." (Van der Hart, "The Camp," 722).

16. Macintosh, "The Meaning," 77. Earlier in the article Macintosh writes, "It is now

corpus of the stories of conquest that we read in Joshua in particular, and in the Deuteronomistic History in general, the reference to Laish as peaceful is unique. Satterthwaite calls it "a rather unusual description for a non-Israelite city in the Old Testament, which is substantially repeated at verse 28."[17] What we will note here about this far-off city will be true about these stories in Judges 17–21; these stories are indeed all unusual for us as they characterize the leadership of Israel while there was no king.

KIDNAPPING A LEVITE, SACKING A CITY

We have met the separated, unnamed Levite. We have met a peaceful, tranquil separated people living in far-off, peaceful Laish. We expect to hear more about this peace and what this peace and place suggest, but our expectations will be shattered.

The spies return and in direct discourse repeat what the narrator has already stated, that the land is very good, sitting idle, an unsuspecting people, spacious land, with nothing lacking. And in their speech they state twice that they aim to "attack" and "invade" the land. They will leave Zorah and Eshtaol, the land where Manoah (the father of Samson) and Samson were buried. It seems the narrative is suggesting to us that the "peace" that Samson brought to Israel was not much peace at all when he ruled. The Danites, his people, have to look for another land. Clearly this type of ruler/leadership was not working for Israel and, here, not working for Dan.[18]

The Danites respond to the battle cry—the commission of the five spies—and we are told three times in the narrative that six hundred men

---

suggested that the particular use of *mklym* in Judg. xviii 7 is best explained by reference to the Arabic usage attested for the cognate noun. The meaning is not simply speech but authoritative speech, speech in the context of rule or government" (ibid., 73).

17. Satterthwaite, "'No King in Israel,'" 80. At this point in his article, Satterthwaite is characterizing the difference between narration and dialogue in biblical texts as part of his demonstration of narrative criticism at work in Judges 17–21. Satterthwaite in particular uses the work of Robert Alter and Shimon Bar-Efrat to demonstrate the narrative-critical work in these chapters.

18. The connection between the Samson narratives and the narratives here in the so-called appendixes to Judges has been statistically examined with the result that "the Samson cycle is more definitely to be connected with at least one or even both of the Appendixes to the book than is commonly assumed" (Radday, "The Book of Judges," 497).

are girt with their weapons of war. Three times we are told what to expect from these 600 men. Three times also the narrator tells us in the direct discourse of the spies that in the house with Micah is "an ephod, teraphim, a sculptured image and a molten image." The five spies lead the 600 men girt with their weapons to take/steal the ephod, teraphim, sculptured image and molten image, and when Micah protests, he is told, "Be quiet, put your hand on your mouth. Come with us and be our father and priest" (Judg 18:19). Then, reminiscent of Abimelech and the men of Shechem, the spies say to Micah, "Would you rather be a priest to one man's household or be a priest to a tribe and clan in Israel" (18:19). While the question is not a direct restatement of Abimelech's to the lords of Shechem, it functions in some ways as a directly inverted statement of Abimelech's place over Shechem. The intertextual links will continue to demonstrate their clarity as they are built in a compensatory way throughout the full narrative.

The narrator tells us that the priest chooses to go with the Danites, and, lest we forget, the narrator tells us a fourth time in Judges 18:20 that this is about the teraphim, ephod, household gods, and sculptured image.

The men leave the house of Micah with the still unnamed priest, placing their flocks and families in front of them. We might be reminded here of Jacob's return to see his brother Esau when he sent his flocks and families ahead of them for fear of Esau, his brother. If we call this to mind, we might expect that the story is setting up a theophany for us, akin to the one Jacob experiences at the place he called Peniel (Genesis 32). Coming up behind the Danites is Micah with his men. Micah wants to know why the Danites have taken "my priest" and "my gods." "In 18:23–26 the Danites are set over against Micah: Micah's words portray him as indignant, incoherent, and ineffectual; the Danites, by contrast, are cool, insolent, and in control. The narrator will go on to suggest that their assurance is less warranted than they think."[19]

In this moment, the Danites reply that some bitter or desperate person (מָרֵי נֶפֶשׁ) in their midst might attack Micah, and he would lose his life (Judg 18:25). Apparently fearing the reality of this, Micah simply turns and goes home. Violence is physically averted but textually present. The tension of the violence remains in the story as peace is not made

---

19. Satterthwaite, "'No King in Israel,'" 82.

manifest for the characters. In fact, Micah's arrival and departure only makes clear to us that the rivalry between the parties remains.

We are then told for a third time in this narrative, upon the Danites' arrival at Laish, that this people are "tranquil" and "unsuspecting" and "distant" from Sidon, and they had "no dealings with anyone." The Danites put these people to the sword and burn down their town. The story has framed several conversations for us between characters but in a single verse all the persons of Laish are wiped out and the narrative moves on.

The Danites rebuild a town there, and then, curiously, the unnamed Levite seems to disappear from the narrative. We are told that they set up "Micah's" sculptured images, maintaining them, but we are introduced to a new priest, Jonathan son of Gershom of the tribe of Manasseh (18:30).[20] In his own remark about the three fold pattern of narrative repetitions in this chapter, Satterthwaite writes, "Three times towards the end of chapter 18 we are reminded that the cult objects which the Danites place in their shrine at Dan are man-made, once by Micah's words of protest to the Danites ('You are taking my gods which I made', v. 24) and twice by the narrator's comments (vv. 27, 31)."[21]

In the larger scope of the narrative, we remain aware of the central role of the Levite and Micah's objects. But we are at a loss to understand the function of this unnamed "priest" or these objects. We use the term "objects" as intentionally ambiguous here because the narrative never tells us the function of the objects or the role of the priest; there is simply no language of worship, adoration, veneration, prayer, sacrifice, or anything in this narrative, even though the unnamed Levite priest is ostensibly present as are these objects! "Indeed, what we see in Judges is not that the Levites were markedly powerful but that they were unsettled (unlanded) and were forced to scrable [sic] for their priestly positions."[22]

When Micah comes with men against the 600 men, the crisis is averted when Micah turns back. Of course the crisis of war is not turned

---

20. Uwe Becker (*Richterzeit*, 242) details the "significant problems in the redaction history" associated with 18:30–31 ("Größte Probleme in redaktionsgeschichtlicher Hinsicht geben die beiden abschließenden Verse 18, 30–31 auf . . ." [my translation]). Since the concerns of our study are not on the redaction of the narrative, we will not detail the salient points that Becker offers except to note that 30–31 do represent difficulty for the narrative (ibid., 242–50).

21. Satterthwaite, "'No King in Israel,'" 78.

22. Simons, "An Immortality," 156.

back for the unsuspecting, peaceful persons in Laish. Violence tears their homes and towns down, another city built upon the rubble that had been their homes. Everyone doing as they saw fit in the days when there was no king brings the rumble of war and the tumble of homes.

And the narrator reminds us at the end of this story as we begin the next, "In those days there was no king in Israel." It seems, to a degree, the narrator does not want us to make sense of these days. The lack of explanation might be that there are simply too many items/objects/persons in the narrative that remain ambiguous, unexplained or unnamed. Perhaps the narrator does not want us to understand this time when there was no king in Israel except in so far as we understand that we cannot understand this time. It is full of its own chaos, its own anarchy.[23] Daniel Block suggests that in this narrative we begin to see a picture of what it means for people to do as they see fit, including

> (1) the loss of personal integrity in an Ephraimite household (17:1–3); (2) the establishment of private cults antithetical to YHWH (17:4–5); (3) the shiftlessness and opportunism of the priestly class (17:7–13; 18:20); (4) the glibness with which Levites performed their duties (18:5–6); (5) the unscrupulous disrespect of the Danites toward the rights and feelings of their countrymen (18:17–20); and (6) the centrifugal [sic] tendency of tribes to act independently in religious matters (18:27–31).[24]

Satterthwaite points out for us how these stories, set in the obvious context of Joshua and Judges emerging from the Exodus tradition, are almost antithetical to that tradition. "The account of the Danites' journey from south to north of the land in 18 seems to allude to the narratives of

---

23. We might also note in these narratives, though the focus is different than that of this study, that with respect to the "Commandments" of God (specifically the Ten Commandments), in these stories we have seen a nearly full abrogation of them. In the story with Micah we read about how he steals from his mother (in that sense he also dishonors her), how she utters an imprecation that she has to take back seemingly using the Lord's name in vain, how she casts in image, and how they seemingly disavow God in the narrative, worshiping other gods. (it is curious that the full name of Micah, Micayahu, also is absent at several points, literally taking out the divine name from the presence of this narrative). In the story with the Danites we have murder, theft, and coveting. The only commandments of the Ten that are not broken in the narrative regard the Sabbath and adultery. On this narrative, Nico ter Linden comments that the "accursed silver is laundered," and the "pseudo-sanctuary at Ephraim" flourishes when "Micah's relic shop has got official status" (Linden, *The Stories*, 74).

24. Block, "The Period of the Judges," 47.

the Exodus and Conquest in Exodus, Numbers, and Joshua. There are a number of elements common to the two accounts: the sending of spies; the mustering of fighting men; the named places where the Danites camped along the way; the capture and re-naming of a non-Israelite city at the end. But everything about this exodus and conquest is wrong: the Danites are unscrupulous plunderers, their cult is corrupt, and they destroy an innocent city."[25]

We have had only rivalry and violence, destruction and plundering. If this is the end of the narrative with the Levite, we are left with a defunct, a-sacrificial story. Perhaps this story then, apart from sacrifice, serves to introduce the story of a Levite and sacrifice we have yet to read.

THE LEVITE AND ANONYMITY

We turn our attention now to Chapters 19–21 of Judges. It is in these stories that we are told by the narrator of Judges again that there is no king. The statement is made explicit to us in 19:1 and then at 20:25. "In those days there was no king in Israel." So here we have it, a picture of life apart from the Judges that have dominated the book and apart from the institution/place/role of kings. That this narrative might reflect an actual pre-exilic event is disputed but "La grande majorité des exégètes est d'accord pour voir dans *Jud.*, XIX, un récit d'origine préexilique."[26]

We meet a Levite, but we do not know who this is. He will remain unnamed for us in the entire narrative, just like the unnamed Levite of Judges 17–18. Is this, in fact, the same Levite? On the one hand it seems that he must be the same Levite. After all, he lives in the hill country of Ephraim which could presumably be with the central character we met in 17–18, Micah. He took for himself a concubine from Bethlehem who, if this is the same Levite, would be from his home area and thus seems a likely possibility. But we do not know for sure. The narrator never tells us if this is the same Levite from chapters 17–18. If it is a different Levite, are we to read this narrative in total isolation from the narrative which has preceded it? If it is the same Levite, when did this story take place, given that by the end of 18 the Levite, we presume, was residing in Dan,

---

25. Satterthwaite, "'No King in Israel,'" 84. See also, Malamat, "The Danite Migration"; and Webb, *The Book of Judges*, 184–86.

26. Besters, "Le Sanctuarire," 26.

the former city of Laish where the Danites had carried him off. Or, is it possible that in some way not texted to us that when Jonathan son of Gershom was set up as priest they allowed this Levite to return south and he took up residence near the home of Micah where he had been? None of these questions can be answered by this narrative. The narrator, it seems, has no reason to let us know who this Levite is for sure. He and his concubine will remain unnamed through the narrative. For our purposes, then, we will call attention to the fact that this Levite, whoever he is and whatever his function is in the social code of the day, seems a total outsider to us. He does not seem to "fit" anywhere as he sojourns wherever he can find a place. We have no specific context, no family, no place of stature, or even specific role to place him in. He is simply the unnamed Levite living "at the other end" of the hill country of Ephraim as this narrative opens. That is all we can know. Perhaps he is left here by the narrator to reflect the separateness of persons, the non-unified persons. While it is the case that everyone does as they see fit when there is no king in Israel, it may also be the case that there is no unified sense of identity intended here.

This unnamed, outsider Levite though, is not alone. He has with him a concubine, also for us, unnamed in the entire narrative. The status and stature of this concubine in relationship to the unnamed Levite is problematic indeed.[27] And yet, we must admit that the nature or status or role of her is no more clear to us than that of the unnamed Levite. The text and the story told in the Deuteronomistic History thus far simply does not allow us room to understand who or what these characters are or what they are doing.

---

27. The concubine's identity is important for us. This unnamed character has been named by some scholars and left only as *pilegesh* by others. We will use "concubine" for this study, but the identity by naming is important, and other options might be better. Alice Bach chooses to leave the concubine as *pilegesh* in her work on Judges 21. She writes, "I have resisted supplying a name for the *pilegesh*, as Bal and Exum have done. Bal (1988b) calls her Beth; Exum (1993), Bath-sheber. Her anonymity creates a problem for the reader trying to identify her in a retelling of the narrative. This very difficulty underscores the gap or silence created by the biblical storyteller. By referring to her as *pilegesh*, I hope to maintain the narratorial vagueness and lack of subjectivity that anonymity of a character presents in a story" (Bach, "Rereading," 2). A detailed analysis of Bal and Exum will be undertaken as this chapter continues.

THE LEVITE'S CONCUBINE/*PILEGESH*

We have already met a concubine in our narrative in Judges 9 but have saved a full analysis of her status for this narrative. The word translated above "concubine" (*pilegesh*, פילגש) is problematic. The sentence translated reads "and he took to himself a woman, a concubine, from Bethlehem, Judah." The word translated women, אשה is the same word translated "wife" in the English. The meaning of פילגש is debated. That פילגש is not the same thing as אשה is obvious in that they are named and considered separately, as in the story of Gideon (8:31). A concubine is usually understood to be a woman purchased or acquired as a sexual object. But, this does not seem to be the position of this woman since she has the 'nerve' to leave her master. Nor does it make sense for him to desire to "speak to her heart" in order to get her back (Judg 19:3).

Gray has suggested that the word can also take on the meaning of a secondary wife, possibly contracted for a certain period of time.[28] The origin of the word #glyp is not Hebrew, but appears to be a loan word, possibly Philistine.[29]

To muddy the waters further, there appears to be some evolution of the word over a period of time. Mieke Bal, in perhaps the most interesting suggestion, harkens back to Koehler and Baumgartner's lexicon, published in 1958, which defines פילגש as "wife, in the older kind of marriage in which the wife stays in her father's house."[30] She argues that this explains the otherwise difficult verb ותזנה in Judges 19:2. Usually meaning "to play the whore", it can be translated "became angry." Bal suggests, again citing Koehler and Baumgartner, that this term originally meant marrying someone outside one's father's clan.[31] In the beginning, then, the sexual unfaithfulness was against the father, not the husband. Bal then argues that the פילגש was unfaithful to her father when she went to her husband's house. She is then attempting to go back where she belongs when she heads home.[32] Bal's suggestions do work nicely together and make sense of ותזנה otherwise difficult to render. However,

---

28. Gray, *Joshua, Judges, Ruth*, 347.

29. Rabin, "The Origin," 353–64. Interestingly, he attempts to prove that it is only found in reference to stories involving Judah and Benjamin, tribes that would have been in contact with the Philistines.

30. Bal, *Death and Dissymmetry*, 84.

31. Ibid., 87.

32. Ibid.

her translation rests on an entry in Koehler and Baumgartner that in subsequent editions is replaced. Furthermore, there is no reason to read this same definition into the earlier use of פִּילֶגֶשׁ, in the Gideon story.

Instead, this dissertation will follow Exum in acknowledging that the general breakdown in structure and coherence, accompanied with the gradual loss of names, mirrors the breakdown of a coherent world. As Exum states, "The political and moral instability in Judges is reflected in the textual instability."[33] The translation should, then, uphold the ambiguity of the text. "And he took to himself a wife, a concubine, from Bethlehem in Judah." Cleaning it up, far from distilling the proper meaning, clouds it further. The verse forces the question, "Who is she in relation to this man?" We will demonstrate in a full reading of the narrative that the text is ambiguous about the relationship because the words have lost their ability to differentiate between differing relationships, a fact driven home by the story of the securing of wives for the Benjamites in chapter 21.

This unnamed concubine and this unnamed Levite and their unclear roles 'for Israel,' 'to each other,' and 'in this story' remain ambivalent, ambiguous indeed for us. We are told in a series of verses that remain unclear that the concubine "played the harlot" from the Levite, and moved to her father's house, back in Bethlehem staying there a full four months.[34] The notion that she "played the harlot" or as the King James Version renders it, "the whore," is curious and problematic. Since the woman leaves the Levite "not in order to live with another man in either

---

33. Exum, "The Centre," 411ff.

34. Karla G. Bohmbach points out the remarkable accomplishment of this concubine to have traveled this distance successfully, particularly since we will see the Levite's inability to travel the same distance successfully with her later in our narrative. Her insightful comments can be read in Bohmbach, "Conventions/Contraventions." She also adds insight about the nature of what might have happened with the concubine's having "played the harlot." Separate from the insightful comments that Bohmbach highlights, we note Daniel's Blocks reading of this narrative and his view of the Levite as the agent of positive action. Block writes, "Even though the concubine had been unfaithful to him and left him, he goes to great lengths to maintain positive relationships with her family and to bring her back to his house" (Block, "Unspeakable Crimes," 51). Contra Block we should note that the words and actions of the Levite in the full narrative hardly demonstrate the great lengths he went to in order to maintain positive relationships—excepting perhaps the great lengths of cuts he made in the concubine's body when he dismembered her.

a marital or a sexual sense, as we might expect if sexual fidelity was the issue" but rather returns to her father's home in Bethlehem it is odd.[35]

For his part, after four months, the Levite, a servant, and a pair of donkeys heads to Bethlehem curiously to "woo" and "win" her back. Is it the "girl" (as she is now called and no longer פילגש or the father who admits the Levite to the house? And if there has been a "playing the harlot" role here how do we understand and interpret the warm welcome? (19:3) Victor Matthews asserts that the girl "has not offered him the hospitality of her father's home, simply directed him to it."[36]

The father of the girl becomes in the narrative the "father-in-law" to the Levite. For three days they eat, drink, and sleep. The man seems to be welcomed back easily enough by the father-in-law and his reception of the Levite has been characterized by several scholars as a model of hospitality, where "ambiance is created and emphasized by the author's skillful use of traditional repetition."[37] Eventually five days will pass in the narrative. The narrative itself is divided for us into three time periods as have become expected for us in these narratives. The fourth day's departure is imminent, but the father speaks to his "son-in-law," and now they feast.

We never hear the girl speak, not here or ever.[38] Marc Brettler notes that "at its beginning the story hints that strange things are ahead: the husband's father-in-law insists that his son-in-law stay for more than three days and does not allow him to leave on day four; instead the son-in-law departs on the fifth day. The typical three-four pattern which pervades the Bible is broken and is displaced by a (nonexistent) four-five 'pattern,' which suggests that the story depicts a world upside down."[39]

---

35. Stone, "Gender and Homosexuality," 90. "Whether the Levite was unable to keep his concubine from being sexually unfaithful, as the Masoretic Text seems to imply, or whether he was simply unable to prevent her from leaving him (and thereby securing a subject position seldom attributed to women in the Hebrew Bible) as the Greek alternative would have it, his prestige might be affected negatively in the eyes of a male audience, who could have been led to question whether this Levite is, in Herzfeld's terminology, 'good at being a man'" (ibid., 96).

36. Matthews, "Hospitality and Hostility," 7.

37. Niditch, "The 'Sodomite' Theme," 365–78.

38. Mieke Bal will call this woman, and others in this narrative who don't speak "A Body of Writing"— only her body/person is allowed to speak or write in the narrative (Bal, "A Body of Writing," 208–30).

39. Brettler, "The Book of Judges," 410. Brettler's reading of Judges 19–21 is intriguing. Its focus is different from that of this study. Brettler believes as we will argue that

Koala Jones-Warsaw points out that as the narrative flows, each time the father of the young woman offers for the husband to stay at the house under the "guise" of hospitality the "narrator uses *legal* terminology (father-in-law, son-in-law)" and "each time he concedes to his father-in-law's wishes, he is then referred to in a more *casual* terms (this is, simply husband in vv. 6b, 7a, 9a)."[40]

We might expect to see the girl particularly at meal time, since a cultural assumption seems to have included females preparing meals. But the wife-*pilegesh*-girl-daughter is not noticeable in this narrative of feasting![41] He implores to speak to the "inner joy" of this son-in-law in 19:5 and 19:6—using a construction that appears only here and in Samuel's speech to Saul at their shared meal in 1 Samuel 9.[42] In fact, seemingly against the father-in-law's counsel, the son-in-law starts to leave but is "turned back" to spend the night there.

Day Five and the servant (no asses) and the Levite's concubine (as she is now referred to again) are ready to leave and "his father-in-law, the girl's father" (both relational referents are made evident here) implores them yet again to stay, sleep, eat, and "enjoy yourself"(Judg 19:9). The imploring of the father here echoes the verbal construction of the Levite choosing to go with the Danites in 18:20. But here the imploring father is not listened to, not this fifth time, as "the man" (not the Levite, nor the son-in-law) refuses to stay the night and sets out to travel to Jebus.

Judges 19–21 and 1 Samuel 11 are connected, but his connection will argue that Judges 19–21 carries an "anti-Saul polemic," and we see the contrary to be true—namely, that Judges 19–21 points forward to the need for one like Saul to stop the anarchy. Brettler's work concludes, "Thus, Judges 17–18 is a polemic against the religio-political institutions of the north, and Judges 19–21 is a polemic against the kingship of the Saulide Dynasty" (ibid., 415). Contra Brettler we suggest that Judges 17–18 highlight the religio-political-priestly issues of sacrifice that can be redeemed in a pro-Saulide narrative that is not so much about the person Saul as it is about the inauguration of kingship that quells violence; this thesis will be defended in the full discourse of this study.

40. Jones-Warsaw, "Toward a Womanist Hermeneutic," 175 (italics original).

41. Bohmbach, "Conventions/Contraventions", 93ff. She writes, "The way in which the concubine manages to disappear from inside a house already near the beginning of Judges 19 is, in and of itself, rather disquieting. But it can also be read as a foreshadowing of the later effacement of both her and the virgin daughter of the old man of Gibeah while inside his house. Here the erasure prefigures particularly tragic ends—at least for the concubine" (ibid., 94).

42. In the books of Judges and 1 Samuel; elsewhere it appears only three more times in the Deuteronomistic History—one time in each of the books 2 Samuel, 1 and 2 Kings.

Phyllis Trible asserts that in this last day of dispute there is a "rivalry between males" that operates in the dialogical exchange.[43] Issues of rivalry will begin here and extend throughout this story.

NIGHT AND THE ANONYMOUS SERVANT

We do not know the names of characters in this narrative, nor do we know their roles in any definitive sense, either from scholarly perspective or from the perspective of the narrator. The father had said the day was declining as the Levite and concubine walk off into the night. The narrator has his readers walking into the darkness with these characters. Perhaps the author of this narrative wants us to understand something of the "ancient dread of malevolent darkness [that] can be most fully appreciated only by those who have spent time in places without artificial lighting . . . For the ancient reader the evening/night setting would almost certainly have imbued each narrative from the outset with an aura of foreboding and sinister premonition, of trepidation and anxiety, for night and violence, danger and darkness were inseparably joined."[44]

The servant speaks, imploring the man to head into the city (Judg 19:11).[45] The narrator reminds us, as if the discourse of the father was not enough, that the day was far spent (Judg 19:11). The direct speech of the servant says more directly, and for the third time in the narrative, that the night has come. Jones-Warsaw points out that the speech of the servant is "urgent, yet respectfully tempered by the enclitic particle *nā*."[46]

The Levite gets a new title here in the speech of the servant who calls him "master." This master will not listen to the words of his servant because the town of Jebus is a town of "aliens" (v. 12) who are "not from the sons of Israel." No statement is made by the narrator or in the direct discourse of the "master" about the kind of people the Jebusites are except that they are "not of us," "not of the sons" of us, not kin. The Levite's speech contrasts with that of the servant, with prohibition and imperative. He is acting here as "lord" in the conversation and perhaps has "overcompensated for his lack of power in the previous situation

---

43. Trible, *Texts of Terror*, 66.
44. Fields, "The Motif," 17–32.
45. In 1 Samuel 9 it is the servant who encourages Saul to go into the city to see Samuel, and he does it.
46. Jones-Warsaw, "Toward a Womanist Hermeneutic," 176.

[with his father-in-law], and now decisively and forcefully negates his attendant's suggestion."⁴⁷

They travel on, and as if we have not been told already the extent of night that is coming by father-in-law, narrator, or servant, the narrator tells us again upon coming to Gibeah of Benjamin the sun is setting (Judg 19:14). There they turn off and go to spend the night (Judg 19:15).

Sitting in the open square of the city, in the dark, no one takes them in.

THE ANONYMOUS OLD MAN

A man emerges. He is old, unnamed, coming from his field. He is from Ephraim, not Benjamite, living at Gibeah. He sees the "wayfarer" (19:17) literally, wandering man, (הֹאֹרֵחַ). This is another new title for this unnamed, Levite-sojourner-man-husband- son-in-law–master-wayfarer.

As the old man lifts up his eyes and sees the wandering man, he asks him, "Where are you going and where do you come from?" (Judg 19:17). Even as we, the readers, know the answers to the questions, we might find that we are asking the same questions as this story moves forward. Indeed who is this man standing before us in the dark, and where is he 'really' from, and where is he (or where is this narrative) 'really' going? We might also be reminded here of the question of the five spies to the Levite in the house of Micah in chapter 18, where they then carry him off and he goes with delight. Will the same be true here for this Levite and/or is this the same Levite?

In the reply of this unnamed Levite we have yet another curiosity. He replies that he is traveling from Bethlehem in Judah to the "other side of the hill country of Ephraim." "That is where I live." But he does not reveal what city he is from. What is more, the Levite continues to declare where he is going and introduces us to something completely new in the narrative, "I" (and it is first-person verbs used), "I went to Bethlehem of Judah and am going to the house of the Lord"

(וָאֵלֵךְ עַד־בֵּית לֶחֶם יְהוּדָה וְאֶת־בֵּית יְהוָה אֲנִי הֹלֵךְ).

The location of "house" is new to the narrative, at least in so far as the Levite having a house. Only the father in law has had a house to this point. And certainly, if this is "the house of the Lord" we have yet another sacerdotal highlight in this story.

47. Ibid.

We have emerged from a series of stories, narrative after narrative, involving characters and persons who are named for us in Judges 1–16. And obliquely we enter this new set of narratives framed with the referent that "in those days there was no king in Israel," and when there is no king, it seems that we have no 'real' persons either. We have been told the Levite has come from the "hill country" or "remote area." And, he seems to have no real history or home. We have the names of no one in this narrative, and, in fact, their roles and titles change as they intersect with new persons throughout the narrative as if they are building their history.

And whatever his role may be for sure, this Levite we now read is either on his way to his house or to the house of the Lord. But we do not know in truth where he is headed. The narrative opened telling us he went to fetch his wife/concubine and speak kindly to her, and to this point in the narrative he has yet to speak a word to her. We have to wonder and wait to see if this will ever happen.

The unnamed Levite assures the unnamed old man that they have want for no thing, only to be removed from the night and the open square. When the Levite mentions that he has brought supplies for his journey he mentions the animals first, placing the concubine, to whom he has gone to speak kind words, last. She was the cause of much journeying, but remains oblique in his discourse.[48] The unnamed man from the field speaks peace to the Levite, concubine, servant, and their ass(es)—but reminds us yet again in his direct discourse, "night" has arrived and one should not spend the night out in the open. Perhaps the Levite and his concubine will enter a house and move out of the darkness that has engulfed them now that the sun has set.

But something else happens as the Levite responds. Victor Matthews is correct when he points to yet another rivalry operating in this story in the statement of the Levite's possessions. Matthews characterizes the reply of the Levite as "disparaging" because "he claims to need nothing

---

48. Bohmbach has an insightful reading of the Levite and the concubine. She brought to my attention the placement of the concubine in the speech of the Levite. She writes about 19:10 that "in mentioning animals first and only then the concubine, [the narrative] seems to place the burden of significance on the matériel [sic] needed for the journey, rather than on the woman who is, as we will see, the point of all this journeying in the first place ... In Judges 19, then, a man has priority over beasts—even when the man is only a servant. The same cannot be said for the concubine" (Bohmbach, "Conventions/Contraventions," 87–88).

from Gibeah other than shelter, having all the provisions he requires, plac[ing] the guest above his host, setting the stage for a deadly rivalry to come."[49] No doubt we will (only later) see the irony that the Levite says he needs nothing, but it very nearly costs him his life.

The text narrates to us the details of hospitality extended by the old man, strengthening for the reader the clearly hospitable situation, at least to this point in the narrative. The narrator does not overwhelm us with detail, but highlights even the attention to foot-washing that is offered as the normal protocol of hospitality offered by the host (old man) to the guest(s).

The "sons of belial" show up and speak words, but before they arrive in the narrative, the story teller informs us that the "hearts" of the unnamed old man and the unnamed Levite are joyous or good. The last time we met a change of hearts in a narrative this study explores was when the lords of Shechem, with their changed hearts, welcomed Abimelech's kingship. And upon receiving it, violence broke forth with seventy being killed on one stone. In this narrative, hearts are merry, and as readers we ought to beware. The reference here to "merry hearts" may suggest something of the drunkenness of the crowd which is different from the more deliberate decision making of those who empower Abimelech in Judges 9. This focus on the specific rendering of the ideas may be important, but focused on too narrowly will cause us to miss the larger contextual interplay of the stories and the activities of its central agents. In each story a group of persons are acting, in Judges 9 to empower a man and here in Judges 19 to dispossess all the power of a woman.

We are prepared when the "sons of belial" arrive. They are the "men of the city, good-for-nothing-fellows" like the "hellions" described in Deuteronomy 13:13 says Susan Niditch.[50] As readers we wonder if we know what will come next in the story if these "sons of belial" are like Abimelech's hired men. The "sons of belial" who arrive do not merely show up, they surround the house. This is of "particular interest in the present instance [because of the] fact that there are only three places in

---

49. Matthews, "Hospitality and Hostility," 7. As this study already noted, the issue of rivalry is important here for the sense of rising action in the story, but it will become important to our Girardian reading as we continue in this study. The issue of the rivalry of this accepted but disparaged hospitality is detailed more fully in Pitt-Rivers, "The Stranger," 13–30.

50. Niditch, "The 'Sodomite' Theme," 372.

the Hebrew Bible in which the *Niphal* of bbs is used in the sense of 'surround, close round upon.'"⁵¹

The "sons of belial" (בני־בליעל) want the "old man," "the master of the house," to send out the man who has come to his house so they might "know him."

DESIRE, VIOLENCE, RIVALRY, RAPE: JUDGES AND GIRARD

The connections between this narrative, taking place in Gibeah and that which had taken place in Sodom in Genesis 18–19 are extensive.⁵² Convincing arguments for the intertextuality of this text with Genesis 12 and Genesis 24 have also been made.⁵³ Others have argued for literary connections from Judges 19 with 1 Samuel 13 and Genesis 34.⁵⁴ The "sons of belial" want to "know" the man and we might have the same question, as we too want to get to know this Levite—we know so little about him.⁵⁵ And, we might point out here that in the discourse of the "sons of belial", we have yet a new title for the unnamed old man; he is also a "master of a house." The text continues to "name" persons for us in ways that leave them un-named with personal names while it continues to characterize them in a multiplicity of ways. As a result we are left with an ability to understand that the persons who are unnamed but who bear several titles or appellations represent not just themselves, but all

51. Fields, "The Motif," 31 n. 34.

52. Block "Echo Narrative Technique." See also Matthews, "Hospitality and Hostility," 3–11; Lasine, "Guest and Host," 37–59.

53. Penchansky, "Staying the Night," 77–88. Penchansky works with Genesis 19 and 24, and with Judges 19. He notes that "all three stories concern hospitality, a festive reception provided for the guest. All three deal with women who are powerless to order and direct their own lives. All three, moreover, are marked by the repetitive use of the term *l-y-n* [sic], 'spend the night'" (ibid., 78). Penchansky's analysis also concerns the interplay of how "threatened guest" and "delayed guest" work in these intertextual stories.

54. Keefe, "Rapes of Women," 79–97. Keefe's attention is unique; she notes how the rape of women focuses attention away from that person-to-person event to the larger escalation of violence between men, with further victims made of women.

55. Obviously I am discounting or avoiding the sexual implications of the narrative in this sentence—and the sexual implications are very important, so I don't intend to trivialize those issues with this pun. But in fact I do want to point out the reality that we as readers really do not know who this Levite is! It seems the violent, vicious probing (rape) of his concubine will tell us little more about this character in the narrative. (Susan Niditch connects this story to the wife-sister tradition of Abraham and Sarah (Niditch, "The 'Sodomite' Theme," 370).

persons like them—all persons who bear similar roles or titles or appellations in the society of which they are members or participants.

The old man who is master of his house speaks to the "sons of belial" outside his door (we presume since he goes out to them) and he calls these men "brothers." Perhaps the narrator wants us to have yet another social relation by which we can identify with some person or groups of persons in this narrative.[56] The narrative is framed with the fact that there is no king in Israel and every person did as he saw fit and in this narrative we certainly have a host of "every person" operating in Gibeah. In her review of this story, Christiana de Groot van Houten notes that the men are characterized here in this story as "moral agents who by their actions bring about the crime of violence."[57] Further, "The narrative implies that the men are accountable for this gang rape. It did not have to be this way."[58] On the one hand we should note that the men in this narrative are characterized as "sons of belial" and not in some more honorific title. The narrative is not gracious to the men who arrive. At the same time, de Groot van Houten is correct about this narrative. The men in this narrative are nameless and perhaps representative of any group or any mob that comes to a lynching. As she continues to say in her analysis, "The text presents us with a picture of what human beings are capable of. It functions as a mirror that shows us a side of ourselves we do not want to see ... We need the sobering truth that, under certain circumstances, we are capable of such atrocities."[59] This reality will be important for us when we come back to analyzing this text in Girardian terms because when "the mob" acts there is a breakdown of any autonomous "selves" and the reality is true that in such moment, people act in different and often deplorable ways. The need, then, in Girardian terms, is for a difference maker to sway the violence of the mob away from using violence to make victims.

---

56. As Hudson notes, "The Levite, his concubine, his father-in-law, the servant, the old host, the men of Gibeah, the women and children of Benjamin, the daughters of Shiloh, and the men of leaderless Israel are nameless in this extensive story. What better way to portray that every Levite, every father-in-law, every host, every single man within that society committed such barbaric atrocities 'from Dan to Beersheba' (20.1) than by allowing every perpetrator in the narrative to exist nameless" (Hudson, "Living in a Land of Epithets," 60)?

57. De Groot, "The Rape," 14.

58. Ibid.

59. Ibid., 14.

NEBALAH: VILE, VIOLENCE, AND RIVALRY

The "sons of belial" want the guest in the old man's home to be sent out to them. There is much going on in this narrative about proper and improper host issues, honor and shame, and issues of sexuality. But here we note that while the men of the city want to "know" the guest as they pound on the door and ask specifically for the "man" who has come in, it is the old man who characterizes the action of the sons of belial. Issues of "homosexual rape" and the "vile thing" are important in this narrative. Geoffrey Miller suggests the door here is a sexual metaphor with the "battering of the closed door by the Gibeahites symboliz[ing] their intent to violate sexually an inappropriate object."[60] In her larger review of the issue of homosexual rape in this narrative, Susan Niditch notes that such behavior "de-orders modes of human interaction which make the Israelite's society ordered."[61] It not only characterizes (or caricaturizes) Israel here, it is also a "doubly potent symbol of acultural [*sic*], non-civilized behavior from the Israelite point of view [as] it is an active, aggressive form of inhospitality."[62]

The term the text uses to describe this "vile thing" they want to do is *nebalah*. The term is used to describe "serious disorderly and unruly conduct" and has "connections with outrageous sexual offences."[63] Keefe describes how this *nebalah* suggests that the stories are not simply personal, but about "disruptions of community life in Israel."[64] Anthony Phillips, in describing the use of *nebalah* in texts of the Old Testament notes that the noun form used here is connected to the verb form of *nabal* for "foolish" or "senseless" and is the opposite "to be wise." "Behind the Hebrew concept of wisdom lies the idea that life is ordered by basic rules which man can discern from his experience."[65] While it goes beyond what Phillips says, it is important in the rest of the monarchial

---

60. Miller, "Verbal Feud," 111. Miller perhaps overstates his case though when he writes that earlier in the story the "joyful opening of the doors when the Levite arrives at his father-in-law's house symbolizes the re-establishment of his sexual rights to his concubine as a result of appropriate behavior" (ibid.). There is no door in the texted story at the father-in-law's home, and the story narrated to us seems to suggest, at best, that the Levite is staying the night with the father-in-law and not with the concubine.

61. Niditch, "The 'Sodomite' Theme," 368.

62. Ibid., 369.

63. Phillips, "Nebalah," 237.

64. Alice Keefe, "Rapes of Women/Wars of Men," *Semeia* 61 (1993): 83.

65. Phillips, "*Nebalah*," 237.

tradition, particularly true of it with Solomon, that the monarchy is characterized by wisdom, not *nebalah*. That being the case, we note here that this period of time for Israel is markedly non-monarchial in its lack of ability to have the wisdom available in times of monarchy.

If we have not yet tired of unnamed characters, the unnamed old man will introduce us to another unnamed character, his "virgin daughter." To the sons of belial he entreaties with an offer of his virgin daughter and the unnamed Levite's unnamed concubine, "ravish them" as seems "good to you" but do not do anything bad to "this man."[66] While connections have been made with the inhospitality of this moment compared with the troubles of Sodom and Gomorrah in Genesis 18–19, Lasine notes the problems in this story surpass those of Genesis with "the old host [going] beyond Lot by explicitly telling the 'base fellows' to 'ravish' or 'rape' the women."[67] The sons of Belial refuse to hear, and a man from within—the text leaves ambiguous to us which unnamed man in the house acts—pushes only the concubine out into the night, into the open.

Anne Michele Tapp says that in this moment of casting the concubine out, though the narrative does not make explicitly clear to us who casts the concubine out, that the "Levite desperately asserts the only power available to him—that of master/owner of his concubine. As the object of the confrontation, the Levite's action is predicated on the hope that his opponents will accept his offering."[68]

Her insight is important here because it understands thrusting out of the concubine from the house as an offering, an attempt to scapegoat the violence of the sons of belial in the night. No matter who cast her out of the house, it seems self-evident she did not walk out on her own to the crowd who had gathered at the home. In harmony with our understanding of this event in ways congruent with her being an offering to the mob, Tapp notes that the issue here is one of sacrifice, but she reads the text as an issue of property as well. She writes, "In both Genesis 19 and Judges 19, the hosts acknowledge their limited power. Resigned to the

---

66. To "ravish" them as is "good" is an odd construction indeed! Shimon Bar-Efrat contrasts the use of the expression "for such a thing is not done in Israel" with a similar construction found in the story of the rape of Tamar by Amnon. He points out that in both instances the "expression is used in an attempt to avert a horrible crime" but does not keep the crime from being committed (Bar-Efrat, *Narrative Art*, 262).

67. Lasine, "Guest and Host," 39.

68. Tapp, "An Ideology," 164.

fact that their situations call for a sacrifice, they suggest a compromise. Both hosts invoke their rights as fathers and masters of a household to barter property."[69]

It will be important in our narrative with Saul that the barter of property is not used, but instead the invoking of violence to redeem violence is invoked as the means to cure violence.

The story reminds us two more times, as if we need to be reminded, that it is night, and the unnamed, unspeaking concubine who has not yet been spoken to kindly by her husband is "wantonly raped and abused" "all through the night." "The extraordinary effect of [the motif of night as danger] does not [merely] find its power in the mere number of references to approaching darkness and the night itself. It is the way in which the motif is combined with the other details of the story that gives it its signal prominence in the creation of an atmosphere of tension and gloom."[70]

Indeed in this narrative with no king and everyone doing as they see fit in their own eyes, it appears that is precisely what this old man/sojourner and unnamed Levite do; barter the life of their daughter/concubine in order to save their own lives. The Levite and his concubine both are in this situation with seemingly no power to retaliate, with no named kin or allies to avenge their crisis, offering no threat back to the lynch mob.[71] The Levite gives her to the mob.[72]

Having thus told us some six times that it is night, the narrator now tells us two times in one construction that morning has arrived (Judg 19:25). In the following verse we are told two more times that morning has arrived, and the woman, for that is all she is now—seemingly not a person in relation as a concubine, daughter-in-law, or wife—not in rela-

---

69. Ibid., 168.

70. Fields, "The Motif," 24. Fields looks at the narratives of Genesis 19, Joshua 2, and Judges 19–21 but finds the narrative of Judges 19–21 to utilize "the atmosphere-charging potential of the danger-at-night motif to the greatest extent."

71. Kerr, "'Rescuing Girard's Argument?'" 388–89. While Kerr's article is more central to analyzing John Milbank's critique of Girardian thought, his understanding of what happens in Girardian theory connects so closely to this narrative that we cite it here and will return to it again in chapter 6 of this study.

72. Alice Bach notes by comparison that another night scene (in the Samson narrative) has Samson emerging not as victim but as male hero on the night the Gazites lie in wait for him all night at the city gate but do not try to kill him until dawn arrives (Bach, "Rereading," 6).

tion to anyone it appears after her night of having been violated by so many she "comes" and "falls down" at the door of the unnamed man's house. And, and for the first time, he is now her "master." We have yet another inversion/change of relationships betwixt this 'couple.' There she lay "until it was light" (Judg 19:26). Light which so often could be used to mark the good of a situation is in this narrative used only to highlight the darkness of the night.[73] Light, which in other narratives brings liberation, in this narrative shines upon carnage and death.

If we have not been told enough that is had been night and now already four times that it is morning, we then meet "her master" who gets up "in the morning." Indeed, a new day has arrived in Israel for all these unnamed persons whose lives are played out when there is no king in Israel. Seemingly anxious to be on his way, after the "doors" are opened, there is "his concubine" "lying" at the door—somehow liminally between the place of safety and outside in the dark—with her hands on the threshold. She lies, as it were, in between so many worlds in this doorway. At this point in the story, when there is no king in Israel, Phyllis Trible writes of this woman: "Of all the characters in scripture, she is the least. Appearing at the beginning and close of a story that rapes her, she is alone in a world of men. Neither the other characters nor the narrator recognize her humanity. She is property, object, tool, and literary device. Without name, speech, or power, she has no friends to aid her in life or mourn her in death. Passing her back and forth among themselves, the men of Israel have obliterated her totally."[74]

Stone writes, "The men of Gibeah still manage to inflict dishonor upon the Levite, and to do so in a sexual manner: *by way of* the concubine . . . The men of the city convey the message to the Levite that was intended all along and which his own rape would have expressed as well, namely, that their power will prevail over his and at the expense of his honor as a man."[75]

Finally we hear the unnamed Levite speak to this concubine. He had sought her out to speak tenderly to her (Judg 19:3). Now we hear him speak these kind words to this woman ravished in the night, "Get up" (Judg 19:28)!

---

73. We might think of the opening hymn of creation in Genesis 1: "and there was light," and "it was good."

74. Trible, *Texts of Terror*, 80–81.

75. Stone, "Gender and Homosexuality," 100–101.

VIOLENCE UNDONE

We realize what has happened in the narrative. There is nothing to hear. Nothing is said. There is no reply. Perhaps we recognize the void of the narrative itself (19:28). The narrator does not say she did not answer. Instead, nothing is narrated at all in verbal reply. Perhaps in this way in a non-gendered body at the door the narrator is highlighting her personhood for us in this narrative—she now has no gender, no being at all.

The narrator leaves open for us all the gruesomeness of the scene, but in effect, we are left without a murder, without a sacrifice. Who killed the unnamed concubine and is she in-fact dead yet? Perhaps it is the case that we are not told of her death precisely because the narrator wants to leave us as readers with the idea that all are responsible for her demise. No one is free of the burden of this murder in a time when there is no king in Israel. Meir Sternberg notes the "permanent elision" in this text where we do not know if she is alive or dead and who actually murders her. About it he writes that the narrator uses permanent gapping to force on us

> two mutually exclusive readings, [and] he [sic] manages to blacken both parties to the crime at once. On the one hand, the woman died of pain and shock while still lying at the door, which exposes the townsmen to the odium of murder as well as gang rape. On the other hand, though speechless or unconscious, she was still alive till dismembered; and this gives the finishing touch to the portrait of her sanctimonious spouse, who pushed her out into the arms of the gang to save his own hide and then spent the night in bed while she was being subjected to horrors. His doings extend from 'seized his concubine and put her out' to 'seized his concubine and divided her, limb by limb'.[76]

We have finally heard the unnamed Levite's "kind words." But we hear no reply. "For him to talk to her as though she were not only alive but ready to continue their journey is totally absurd. He acts as though he were in a hurry to get on the road to beat the morning traffic."[77] The body/corpse is loaded on his donkey and they head to his home.[78]

---

76. Sternberg, *The Poetics of Biblical Narrative*, 239.

77. Lasine, "Guest and Host," 45.

78. The text seems to imply that it is to "his home" that they will travel, unless he is a priest heading to the "house of the Lord" as implied earlier with the priestly concern. The text is not clear, leaving even the home of the Levite anonymous in certain ways.

Perhaps this woman has no home of her own, no place of safety whether with the Levite, or her father, or in Gibeah.

Once he and the body/corpse are home, the final issues in the reality of this life and now death event can finally take place. Polzin argues regarding the death of the concubine that the narrator is being "deliberately vague" about whether or not the concubine was dead. Polzin believes though, that the narrative is "intent upon emphasizing . . . the inability of the reader to piece together crucial-aspects of the events in which these characters are enmeshed" and here we disagree with Polzin. The reader is fully able to hold all persons accountable to the crimes perpetuated against the concubine, as "one man" they all do right in their own eyes and all are enmeshed in the trouble.[79]

By setting off the "moment" of death in an ambiguous way such that the death itself becomes obscured in the text, the specific narration of the dismemberment becomes set apart in the story as a distinctly crucial element of the story. Or, said another way, the moment of dismemberment becomes the narrated scene left to create one of the strongest impressions on the reader of this story. And, as we will demonstrate, this narrated scene demonstrates a type of sacrificial act and will be understood in those ways even if the text does not appropriate specific Hebrew language for sacrifice.

The unnamed Levite pulls out a knife, the first and only time the knife appears in the entire Deuteronomistic History—and the last time in the Old Testament it appeared was in the *Akedah*, a narrative full of sacrificial influence. He "cuts" up this body, in twelve pieces, and sends pieces of the corpse to the "borders" of Israel. In rapid succession, four verbs report how the Levite '*took* a knife, *grasping* his concubine, he *cut* her into twelve pieces, limb by limb, and *sent* her."[80] Her body has been hacked into pieces.[81] The construction for the "borders" here appears only 6 times in Judges and 1 Samuel (twice in Judges 11 [vv. 8 and 22], once

---

79. Polzin, *Moses and the Deuteronomist*, 200. Polzin believes, though, that the narrative is "intent upon emphasizing . . . the inability of the reader to piece together crucial aspects of the events in which these characters are enmeshed" (ibid., 202).

80. Bohmbach, "Conventions/Contraventions," 95 (italics original).

81. I note the "hacking" here as a play on words back to Gideon, "the hacker" we met, who was the father of Abimelech. Gideon hacked away at Israel's enemies for the unity and near establishment of monarchy, but here the hacking will unite Israel in a war against self toward their own near destruction, or at least the near destruction of one of the tribes.

here Judg 19:29, one time in 1 Sam 6:12, then two times when Saul cuts up the yoke of oxen in 1 Sam 11:3, 7). "This gruesome episode illustrates well the metonymical meaning of the female body as the social body and the way in which violence committed against that body constitutes an act of 'decreation' (Scarry) in the dissolution of all forms of community coherence and sacral meaning."[82]

The Hebrew of text reads that he "cut her according to her bones." While it is the case that this is not a direct reference back to Abimelech being "bone of bone" with the Shechemites, we are still reminded here of the connection with the "bone" language of Abimelech in Judges 9. The cutting of these bones will muster the bones of the Israelites.

"Has such a thing ever happened since the day that the Israelites came up from the land of Egypt until this day? Consider it, take counsel, and speak out" (Judg 20:7). The reader is hard pressed to imagine any time in Israel's history when such an event as this had occurred since Egypt—and if the reader is reminded of Sodom, it certainly predates this question that is posed here from the time of Egypt and the Exodus. This new event that takes place when there is no king in Israel, is a *novum*, an event that beckons the unnamed Levite to implore his audience to do something that the desecrated concubine cannot do, "speak." Indeed, "the dead woman's divided body is a radical symbolization of Israel's 'body politics,' the divisions *in* Israel."[83]

Marc Brettler writes that "the action of butchering the woman is highly unusual and unnatural, and certainly not the typical way of mustering the army."[84] He cites this as part of his argument that the text here has borrowed and enlarged the claim of our next text, the story of Saul in 1 Samuel 11. We will demonstrate later that while Brettler is correct that it is not the "typical" way of mustering the army, the fact of Saul's not allowing this kind of muster to happen again allows for an atypical event to happen in Israel, the inauguration of a king.[85] In the larger frame of

---

82. Keefe, "Rapes of Women," 85.

83. Niditch, "The 'Sodomite' Theme," 371 (italics mine).

84. Brettler, *The Book of Judges*, 86.

85. Brettler's argument is weak. He writes, "In addition, the phrase about answering the call to arms in Judg 20:1 is longer than that in 1 Sam 11:7. Though I do not mean to claim that it is always the case that texts grow as they are transformed, it is more likely that 'and they came out as one man' would be transformed in 'thereupon all the Israelites—from Dan to Beer-Sheba and from the land of Gilead—marched forth,' than vice versa" (ibid., 86). As we will see later, the reference here to Gilead need not be

the narrative the Levite in Judges 17 and 18 had become the priest to an idolatrous sanctuary, and here the Levite seemingly presides over a horrific sacrifice.[86] We see in the stories cultic and social chaos that needs to be cured.[87] Karla G. Bohmbach notes that the dismembering takes place from within a house,

> a space not only normally associated with women, but also one with assumed connotations of safety and security for them. In this episode, however, such meanings are sharply reversed: the house becomes the setting for the most violent abuse inflicted upon her. Indeed, since the text is never forthcoming about the time of her death, her dying might well be coeval with her dismemberment. Thus, the place that is expected to serve as the secure center of a woman's life (and the locus of whatever authority she may have), becomes for this woman, the site where her husband finally and most horrifically, destroys her [sic].[88]

The dismembered body of the unspeaking and unspoken-to concubine elicits significant speech. As Milton recognizes, "in her death, the sacred significance of her narrative takes over, transcending the local myth of the scapegoated outcast, and the concubine becomes a powerful rallying point for morality and justice."[89] From Dan to Beersheba they gather—and the author notes for us that Gilead, too, appears. The convention is that "Dan to Beersheba means that all of Israel has gathered. The people of Israel gather. They gather as "one man" at Mizpah. We

---

mentioned again in 1 Samuel because we already know we are there in the narrative. An earlier or later use of the phrase is not within our focus here, however, as our concern is with the compatibility of the stories without positing any borrowing as functionally important for the coherence(s) toward which we are pointing.

86. Sweeney, "Davidic Polemics," 525.

87. Gale Yee points out the problems of cultic and social chaos in a way similar to but distinct from our approach. Her approach can be read in Yee, "Ideological Criticism."

88. Bohmbach, "Conventions/Contraventions," 96. And we note that while the observation goes beyond the scope and focus of our study, eventually the priests' sacrifices will take place in the "house" of the Lord—as this dismembered sacrifice takes place in the house of a priestly person, the Levite. But this profane sacrifice needs to be replaced with something acceptable; we will argue that Saul provides an acceptable alternative in his act of dismembering the oxen, an act that leads to the inauguration of his kingship and to new priestly roles that emerge in the Davidic and Solomonic periods.

89. Simons, "'An Immortality,'" 165.

might wonder why Mizpah has entered this story here. It has not been part of our narrative since we left off with Jepthah in Judges 11.[90]

The "congregation," "chiefs" "tribes" of all the people gather "as one man" (Judg 20:1). Perhaps we are meant to picture here all Israel. But ostentiously the Benjamites seem to have missed out on the news that has rallied all the other chiefs, tribes and congregation because they have "heard" that Israel gathered at Mizpah (20:3).

Once gathered, this group speaks in the form of a demand, "Proclaim to us this evil act!" (20:3). And "the Levite," who we are reminded again was "the husband" of the "woman," speaks from this position in Mizpah saying that in Gibeah of the Benjamites this "murder" took place. His speech reminds us that it was night, in case we had forgotten (20:4).

As the speech of the unnamed Levite continues, we here him refer to the 'sons of belial" from chapter 19 now as the "the Lords of Gibeah" (20:5). His speech implies that what happened in Gibeah was really about—and we might say exclusively about—him! He tells us it was the Lords of Gibeah who came against him. We have not encountered any "lords" in this narrative since the Abimelech narrative (where this same term appears in no less than 14 verses of Judges 9). The unnamed Levite asserts that these Lords of Gibeah rose up against him in precisely the same way that the Lords of Shechem are routed before Abimelech in Judges 9! The unnamed Levite reminds us again that he was in a house at night before telling us that the Lords "intended to kill me" and, only somewhat after the fact, notes that instead of him, his concubine was raped "until she died" (20:5). The unnamed Levite tells us in direct discourse what the narrator has already told us, that the body was hacked into pieces and sent to all Israel. And the unnamed Levite who had called the people to action through his messengers and the dismembered body now speaks to this congregation gathered as one man and encourages their advice and counsel "here," "now" (20:7). The Levite in this scene is acting like a judge rallying "all Israel." "The only other place in the book where 'all Israel' appears explicitly is in the sequel to the account of Gideon's suppression of the nomads (presented in 8:18 as a personal

---

90. While the use of Jephthah is not part of our discussion, noteworthy is that when Jephthah returns home to Mizpah, another daughter (his own) is made to be sacrificed.

vendetta), where he piously declines their offer of kingship but demands, instead, the making of an elaborate ephod" (8:22–26).[91]

Robert Boling suggests that the speech of the Levite "presents his case in the best possible light."[92] Susan Niditch suggests the Levite is "uncomfortable about describing the true nature of the event."[93] Stuart Lasine says the narrator wants the reader "to notice the blatant contradiction between the two accounts [what actually happened and how the Levite narrates it], in order to conclude that the Levite is an irresponsible liar."[94] The reader gets the impression that the Levite takes offense "not so much because actions have been taken against the woman, but rather because these actions are considered to impact in some manner upon himself" as Ken Stone states.[95] Lasine goes on to say, "The fact that the ensuing carnage is precipitated by the deceptive report of one irresponsible man is underlined by the self-centered tone of the Levite's speech. His speech stresses the emphatic pronouns 'I' and 'me.'"[96] What is interesting to note, though, is in the characterization of the events by the Levite all the acts were brought against "me" and "my," but the event was perpetuated by "they" [all the men of Jabesh-Gilead] and thus it beckons for a communal response as this is, at least in the eyes of the Levite, not just a personal matter but a community issue.

The people respond as "one man" stating they will not go home or to their tents[97] until they have cast "lots" and risen up against Benjamin for the "disgrace" they have caused (20:10). The event of carnage "becomes the spark in a powder keg; it serves as the exposition to, and opportunity for, the emotional chaos and civil war" that will ensue.[98] And we

91. Boling, "In Those Days," 42–43.
92. Boling, *Judges*.
93. Niditch, "The 'Sodomite' Theme," 371.
94. Lasine, "Guest and Host," 48.
95. Stone, "Gender and Homosexuality," 93.

96. Lasine, "Guest and Host," 49. We will see later how Saul reports to the tribes not in a self-centered way but for the benefit of others.

97. Is this reference a deliberate inclusion of pre-monarchial categories? We are reminded that after kingship begins to fail, Jeroboam will call the people of Israel back "to their tents" in an effort, one might argue, to de-establish what monarchy had become. That is, Jeroboam was not calling for himself to become king but was seeking to move back to a time before the dawn of kingship when (as in this time) Israel still lived in tents. This issue also occurs with Sheba, son of Bichri in 2 Samuel 20.

98. Fokkelman, "Structural Remarks on Judges 9 and 19," 43.

are told a third time in the narrative that this massive crowd, this mob of some 400,000 persons, gathers again, as "one man" with one intent, with one purpose in 20:11 to continue the cycle of violence perpetuated by the Benjamites by inflicting violence (Judg 20:10). And we only have to keep reading to see how the cycle of violence will indeed continue to perpetuate itself in this text. With no man to stop it, with the four hundred thousand united as it were as one man with nothing to differentiate or distinguish one from another—with no king—violence will run rampant.

The next time the reference to "lots" appears in the Deuteronomistic History is when Saul is chosen by lot in 1 Samuel 10. The next time disgrace appears is when Nahash threatens to disgrace the inhabitants of Jabesh-Gilead.

In direct discourse, the "one man" army calls to the Benjamites to hand over the "scoundrels." They will be killed for what they have done (20:13). They will be consumed by fire. The text tells us explicitly that the Benjamites, "kinfolk to the Israelites," would not give up the scoundrels in their midst. Lest we think the Benjamites are others to be scapegoated, the narrator reminds us that they are in fact part of Israel.

The Benjamites muster their 26,000 in Gibeah to face the 400,000 Israelites. All in Israel are warriors. The next time the term for warriors of this type is used is when Saul is anointed, but not yet inaugurated as king (1Sam 10:26). The last time the word was used was with Deborah summoning Barak to beckon his "warriors." The men of Gibeah have their left-handed slingshot aces to aid them and we read that "the men of Israel, other than Benjamin"—in case we have forgotten they are going to kill their brothers; inquire of God about who shall go up first to battle. The use here of left-handed sling-shot experts against the more normative right-handed option continues to point out to us the oddities of persons in these texts.[99] Sons of the right-hand, Benjamites, use their left hands to win the day.

We will see that the account of battle is complex but E. J. Revell's detailed analysis of the chapter demonstrates that "the complexity of the account is undoubtedly due, in part, to the need to present the activities

---

99. Hugh Page asks us to "compare the tenth century B.C.E. orthostat from Tell Halaf depicting the more normative right-handed sling bearing soldier" (Page, "Boundaries," 49 fn. 45). See also Miller, "Verbal Feud," 112ff., where he writes that "the left hand is associated with impurity or deviance."

of three different groups participating in the battle, a problem not often presented to the narrator, and difficult to solve within the linear convention of Hebrew narrative" but finally cohesively and "logically composed according to the conventions of Hebrew narrative standard in Judges and elsewhere."[100] Satterthwaite has extended the work of Revell to demonstrate how chapter 20, verses 29–48, we have a "deliberate and detailed account (three times as long as the accounts of the fighting on the first two days) with quasi-cinematic shifts ... forming a carefully-prepared climax."[101] We also note here that the question of God regarding who shall go up to fight first is used as an inclusio that holds together the narratives within the book of Judges.[102] Simcha Shalom Brooks has demonstrated the comparison of the attack at Gibeah with the attack of Ai in Joshua 7–8.[103] We will see that Joshua 7 has further Intertextual relations with the Saul story in 1 Samuel 9–11.

100. Revell, "The Battle with Benjamin," 432.
101. Satterthwaite, "Narrative Artistry," 82.
102. The inclusion is noted by many scholars in several places, but for a political reading of this inclusion, see Dumbrell, "'In Those Days.'" Marc Brettler offers an interesting read (Brettler, *The Book of Judges*, 5–418; see especially 399. Brettler's analysis is different from ours and should be read for its own intention. But it should be noted that one of the issues Brettler highlights is the role of the "ideal" judge pictured, he believes fictitiously, in Othniel in Judges 3. Building on the work of Wolfgang Richter, he notes that the first judge narrative centers on Othniel ben Kenaz, who defeats Cushan-rishathaim, king of Aram-naharaim. Evidence that the story is not based on historical events is presented when Brettler writes that the story "contains numerous clues that suggest this: the enemy king is named symbolically 'the dark double-wicked one'; the king's name and country of origin rhyme; the Israelite hero is 'borrowed' from a previous unit (1:13); and the unit presents a substantial historical improbability—it is Othniel, whose landholdings were in the south of Israel, who confronts the king who is Israel's northern neighbor" (Brettler, *The Book of Judges*, 404). What is important for us in reading this narrative is the ideas of light and darkness. In this first narrative, Othniel, the ideal judge, defeats the "dark double-wicked one" when the question is asked, "who shall go up first?" In the narrative we've read, darkness defeats the period of the Judges when each man does as he sees fit and when there is no king. In the first narrative of Judges, "dark double-wicked one" is defeated, but in this narrative, darkness of night triumphs with the rape and pillage of the concubine. Robert Boling also notes the inclusio function of this narrative and highlights some important issues with his comic reading of the narrative. Most specifically he notes how the questions were out of order insofar as "it was Yahweh's prerogative alone to declare war" (Boling, "In Those Days," 43). And "we may thus understand the narrative integrity of two severe drubbings in ch. 20; it was only after they got their questions in the right order and at the proper place of enquiry (before the ark of the covenant) that victory was to be expected (20:27ff.)" (ibid., 43).
103. Simcha Shalom Brooks writes, "In both stories, the Israelites are defeated in the first attempt, but then plan an ambush, with the cities eventually being burnt and the people there being exterminated. The military tactics used in both stories are identi-

The narrative here borrows from the opening chapters of the book of Judges where a similar inquiry is asked of God (Judg 1:1). Judah is commissioned to go up and, upon going to battle, they defeat the Canaanites. This narrative is not quite as simple. Here they advance or "go up" three times which participates in the threefold series of events we have come to expect in the stories we are exploring in our study.[104]

We expect, as we have read earlier in the Deuteronomistic History, that with this commission for war, Judah going first, the Benjamites at Gibeah will be defeated. But they are not. 22,000 Israelites are routed. Time and again the narrative in the time when there is no king in Israel confounds our expectations.

The Israelites inquire again of God. They remind God and the reader that they are going up against "our kinsmen, Benjamin" (20:23). Day Two fares no better for Israel and only slightly worse for Benjamin, 18,000 Israelites die.

In preparation for Day Three, all the Israelites, all the army, weep at Bethel, weeping before the Lord. Weeping will demarcate the story when Saul is sanctioned to prevent weeping in 1 Sam 11:5.[105] The next time the cries of people will elicit a response from God is the day of Samuel's anointing, 1 Samuel 9:16. A third time they ask, and we are reminded, "Shall we go again to battle *our kinsfolk* Benjamin." God's reply had been

---

cal, leading Malamat to suggest (1983:72–74) that the description of the battle against Ai (Jos. 7–8) was formulated on the basis of the model of the battle against Gibeah" (Brooks, "Was There a Concubine at Gibeah?" 32). Brooks posits that the story of the concubine in Gibeah reflects the story of Mephibosheth's nurse, who was trying to escape after the death of Saul narrated in 2 Samuel 2–3. That is, Brooks believes this story has been re-narrated here in Judges to explain a time when there was no king in Israel, because the story took place when there was no king in Israel—after Saul's death. Brooks writes, "The verses which describe a complete anarchy [in Judges 20–21 and 21:25] could very well be a description of the period extending between Saul's death and David's accession to the throne over the whole of Israel" (ibid., 35). Brooks's suggestion is interesting but not convincing.

104. The narrative also has connection to the conquest of Ai in Joshua chapter 8, though the construction does not follow in a linear pattern between the narratives (Becker, *Richterzeit*, 281–84).

105. In an article focused on an anti-Bethel polemic that operates in the book of Judges, Yairah Amit has demonstrated that the events of Judges 2:1–5 about the place of "bochim" or weeping are essentially about Bethel. In her conclusion, then, Amit writes, "The book of Judges thus opens and concludes with a concealed polemic whose aim is to criticize Bethel [as the place of weeping]" (Amit, "Bochim," 131). We shall see that Saul will respond in order to resolve a crisis that evokes weeping in 1 Sam 11:4.

"Judah First" and "Go up against them" and here it becomes "Go up, for tomorrow I will deliver them into your hands."

The ambush set for Day Three results in the Benjamites triumphing in battle. Numerically it is not tens of thousands, but only thirty men of Israel who die. But on this day, Israel's ambush triumphs and the battle becomes "furious" (20:34). 25,100 Benjamites die. The whole town is put to the sword. The reader might wonder about this city being put to the sword, as though this were an act of *herem* that has occurred elsewhere in the Deuteronomistic History and frequently in the book of Joshua that precedes this. But in several ways this is no *herem* and it had not been incited or "revealed" by God. It was incited by the violence of Israel's own doing against their own kinsfolk.[106]

The Benjamites look back on the ambush, having defeated only 30 men. They see their whole city up in smoke, even as Lot looked and saw Sodom as a tower of smoke (Gen 19:28). The language of 20:40 here is that it was not a *herem* but, in one option for translating the latter part of this verse, it was nothing less than a *holocaust* (כליל). Describing the narrative artistry of this passage, and verse 40 in particular, Satterthwaite writes, "The description of smoke rising from the burning city could logically have been placed before *v.* 38; but the detail is delayed until the moment when the Benjaminites [sic] turn to see it, so that we see it through their eyes (hence the use of *whnh*), as a menacing pillar of destruction. The impact is greatly increased. The vivid phrase *'lh klyl-h'yr hšmymh* suggests both the intensity of the destruction and the idea of retribution, the burning city being described as though it were a sacrifice to placate God's anger."[107]

Satterthwaite's ability to help us see the sacrificial issues at play alongside issues of destruction and violence again reveal to us how this narrative is conscious of its own sacrificial context. Here a city is burned for the sake of reconciliation, though we have yet to see if that reconciliation will be affective.

---

106. This study takes seriously the acts of violence in the narrative as part of some historical kernel of truth, some real event(s) that did take place in the history of violent fratricide in Israel's history. Not all agree, however. S. Schnitzer has argued that the narrative here in the story of the concubine is an example, perhaps the oldest example, of a literary parody used for political purposes, but a parody all the same.

107. Satterthwaite, "Narrative Artistry," 86. We note here that the use of sacrifice that Satterthwaite is referring to extends back to Deut 13:7, which describes punishment for cities caught in idolatry.

We are given a rendering of who among the 25,000 of Benjamin fell: 18,000 fleeing to the Rock of Rimmon, 5,000 on the road, and another 2000 on their way to Gidom. And 600 men made it to the rock of Rimmon, waiting there for four months, the same amount of time our unnamed concubine at the beginning of this story had fled from the dispute she had had with the unnamed Levite. It seems improbable that we would have missed it, but here it is made explicit, the men of Israel put the town, people, cattle, everything that remained of the Benjamites, "to the sword"—setting fire to all of their towns.

The violence, horror, and gore results from an unnamed Levite (whose role we cannot even ascertain) and his unnamed concubine and the "kind words" that the Levite anticipated speaking to this woman who never speaks!

Finally, the narration of this story and its unnamed characters and destroyed cities is at an end, we think. But it is only just begun. We have read here only the first (three-day) destructive event of three total events; we have yet to read of the siege on Mizpah or the kidnapping at Shiloh! Even when the text prepares us for moments of reconciliation to follow the horror we have witnessed, it brings reconciliation only through more violence; much more violence.

The narrator only now tells us that Israel had made an oath not to allow their daughters to marry Benjamites. We had not been told this earlier in the narrative, and we must wonder why an oath would have been necessary if it was the case that the Israelites planned to put the entire city to the sword. The Israelites, the narrative tells us, have now "relented" towards their "kinsmen" the Benjamites, and in verses 20:3 and 20:6 they declare in direct discourse that "one is missing" from Israel and "one tribe has been cut-off." Israel gathered as "one man" to cut off and sacrifice one of their own, one tribe now missing.

With one tribe now missing, those remaining inquire if any had not participated in routing the Benjamites. If any had not helped they should now be destroyed. And here the city of Jabesh-Gilead enters the narrative of the Deuteronomistic History, entering here only to drop off again until the day of Saul's inauguration to kinship. Here Jabesh-Gilead is besieged by the Israelites, and later in 1 Samuel 11 it will be to the defense of the inhabitants of Jabesh-Gilead that Saul leads the charge! Twelve-thousand warriors, the narrator tells us, are given instructions to put more persons to the sword—men, women and children (21:10)—but

Micah, the Levite, and the Concubine

to leave the virgin "maidens" and four hundred are found and brought to Shiloh.

Word is sent to the men at the Rock of Rimmon, words of peace. We last heard the term in the words of the old man who greeted the unnamed Levite. But in this narrative we do not know if we can trust peace to emerge. The men return, taking the "girls" who had been "spared" for them, but there is not enough.

Again the "elders of the community" (what they are called here), recognize the problem of finding wives for the men of Benjamin based on the oath they had sworn at Mizpah. They recall the annual feast at Shiloh. Curiously, we are told in the narrative where this location is. We are often not told where cities are, if we are told the name of the city at all. This city, Shiloh, runs on the same highway that passes through "Shechem" so it seems (Judg 21:19). We have heard of this city before, but not since the Abimelech narrative where it occurs 26 times there.

We might remember that Gaal had celebrated in Shechem and gotten drunk after celebrating in the vineyards (Judg 9:27). After their reveling in the vineyard, they reviled Abimelech. In this story, there is no Abimelech to be reviled, only daughters to be kidnapped. The men of Benjamin are given instructions to kidnap girls among the dancers, and the elders of Israel prepare in advance their answer for the fathers of the girls who complain to them: "Be generous to us." The dancing women will be met with violence as they are ambushed and then carried off.[108]

The Benjamites acted, taking wives from the dancers they "carried off" as many as they themselves numbered. This portion of the narrative, says Alice Bach, depicts not just the rape of the women from Shiloh but a double rape. As Alice Bach demonstrates, the fathers and brothers have been raped economically because "by ancient standards [the fathers and brothers are also] the offended parties. There is collective violation in both acts."[109] It is important for us to draw out the "economic" rape that

---

108. Alice Bach notes that the verb here translated as "ambush" "embodies both physical harm and action against an enemy" (Bach, "Rereading," 10). Indeed Israel has become enemy to herself in this narrative.

109. Ibid., 3. Bach goes on to note, "While an event of rape is not acknowledged openly in Judges 21, it is encoded within the ambiguity, the indirections of the text. The result is to naturalize the rape. By reading against the grain of the writer's intention to narrate the carrying off of women as wives for the men of Benjamin as necessary and natural, one sees how the biblical authors, men who possessed both benevolence and reason, could inscribe a rationale for oppression, violation, and exploitation within the

Bach notes in this narrative because it hints for us at the reality that the crime here, the violation that needs resolution, is not just one of sexual practice, but economic issues as well. It is economic issues that kingship will need to resolve if and when kingship can emerge in Israel. Not just this, Bach notes for us that the sexual exploitation and economic exploitation point to a further reality when she writes that the "national rape of the daughters of Shiloh, initiated by the tribes of Israel ... figured as a political necessity, not a sexual crime."[110] Indeed, the recurring phrase here in Judges 17–21 points us to the political necessity which Israel must come to reckon with in days when all men do as they see fit. Back in their towns following this episode of blood and gore, after all this violence, they settle as tribes and clans in their own territory (Judg 21:24). But as they settle, they are nameless.

ANONYMITY IN THE ABSENCE OF KINGSHIP

We have highlighted the anonymous character of actors and participants in our narrative. We repeat now that in Judges 19–21 every character is without a name, with the exception of Phinehas (20:28) "who is ironically more a name than an actant" in the story.[111] The anonymity of this final story in Judges contrasts with the opening stories we have in the book of Judges and at the start of kingship with Saul. And while in other stories, particularly in the judges, the names might have a double meaning as with Abimelech or Gaal in Judges 9, the frightfulness of the anonymous characters in Judges 19–21 seems to need no double-edged meaning.

Hudson suggests that there are five functions of anonymity in the Hebrew Bible, and that two of them function in this narrative. In our story, "anonymity 'universalizes' the characters and events of the narrative" and "anonymity as a socio-linguistic phenomenon deconstructs naming; anonymity parallels the loss of identity and personhood."[112] In this way, Hudson asks rhetorically about the nameless characters in Judges 19–21, "What better way to portray that every Levite, every father-in-law, every host, every single man within the society committed such barbaric

---

very discourse of the biblical text" (ibid., 3). Girard will help us understand these issues as part of the emergence of the culture from chaos.

110. Ibid., 7.

111. Hudson, "Living in a Land of Epithets," 58.

112. Ibid., 59.

atrocities 'from Dan to Beersheba' (20.1) than by allowing every perpetrator in the narrative to exist nameless?"[113]

> Ironically, the nation as "one man" assembled together to dismember and disunite itself. Every person represented by the anonymous "individual"—in the name of wholeness—sought the unity of the nation by punishing Benjamin (ch. 20), which in this case was the virtual destruction of the nation and the individual. Anonymity as a literary device reflects the universality of violence and dismemberment. The anonymous Levite, after leaving the anonymous host and the anonymous mob, dismembers the anonymous concubine. The dismemberment of the "one" leads to the dismemberment of the nation as a whole, which was nearly the loss of Benjamin's name.[114]

In the anonymity, says Hudson, the reader is forced to "endure the ambivalence and 'uncomfortability' [sic] of the namelessness."[115]

Satterthwaite states the obvious for us when he notes that when we compare chapter 19 with 20 and 21, all the killing, "carried out with the aim of avenging the concubine's death, has not made Israel any safer a place for women."[116] Robert Boling asks about these narratives, "how was this tragically inverted account . . . supposed to be relevant to anything at all?" and then submits "that the final chapters of Judges present a comic resolution to the chaos of the entire transitional period from Joshua to the monarchy."[117] Contra Boling we suggest that the narrative is not comic as literary convention, nor is it comedic. It is realistic about the chaos of violence among brothers apart from some form of mediation. The conflict between brothers is, indeed, a major story line of the biblical narratives from Cain and Abel, the first brothers. Conflict between elder and younger brothers will be a problem as well.[118]

The conclusion of the stories of Judges in effect disposes of the stories of Joshua that start the Deuteronomistic History.[119] We are left at the end of Judges with no leadership of Joshua or judges and with the seem-

---

113. Ibid., 59–60.
114. Ibid., 60. See also Girard, *Violence and the Sacred*, 39–67.
115. Hudson, "Living in a Land of Epithets," 64.
116. Satterthwaite, "'No King in Israel,'" 85.
117. Boling, "In Those Days," 42.
118. Greenspahn, *When Brothers*.
119. Crossan, *The Dark Interval*, 47–69.

ing disposal of every Deuteronomic code. We are left without individual, family or society. It seems there is no possibility for resolution or coming together.

And the narrator reminds us that the story of all this violence took place "In those days when there was no king in Israel, everyone did as he pleased" (Judg 21:25).

"The national level of violence and confusion ... the resulting problem of the right form of government are really the level on which the narrator wants to work, as the coda to his book ... the narrator himself [sic] indicates the framework within which we are supposed to interpret his material."[120]

This chaos is the result of no king, and no unity made available to the disparate persons acting out their own violence.

---

120. Fokkelman, "Structural Remarks on Judges 9 and 19," 43.

5

Saul and Kingship

WE BEGIN HERE OUR narrative review of Saul as a specific character, a person, in the narratives of 1 Samuel. We mention a few words regarding the nature of 1 Samuel as story, specifically as it relates to the story that has been shaped from Joshua and the introductory stories of the Deuteronomistic History. We want to pay attention to two things that have developed in and through the narratives of Joshua and Judges and that begin to receive focal attention here as Monarchy emerges in Israel's narrative history; dynasty and sacrifice. The two things to take note of deal with the reality/function of sacrifice(s) in these stories and the (im)possibilities of dynastic leadership in the form of any characters in the stories, but specifically with regard to Gideon and Samuel.

It is the intention of this study to attempt to understand how Girard might help us understand the stories we read in the emergence of monarchy. We will come to our more specific appeal to Girard later, but for the sake of clarity here we should be reminded that Girardian theory suggests that the practice of sacrifice harkens back to some primal experience in culture where mimetic rivalry is curbed by sacral victimage, scapegoating. Girard also hypothesizes that the formation of monarchy, choosing a king and accepting the dynastic rule of a monarchial family might derive from the primal experience of sacrifice that curbs rivalry and redirects violence in order to bring stability and peace. If this is true in the monarchy in Israel, with Saul as king, then stories of sacrifice and dynastic rule that play into our stories here will have import.

DYNASTY AND DYNASTIC SUCCESSION

It is interesting to note that as a general reference, the entire book of Joshua is about Joshua. Principally, the book of Judges is about the individual judges, approximately nine of them come to the fore. It is even fewer judges who receive significant textual space. The worst judge, Samson, intentionally and ironically receives the most space. As we enter the narrative cycle of 1 Samuel, the interplay of characters in the story quickly diminishes and Samuel and Saul become the two primary characters of the narrative. No doubt there are other characters (parents, contenders, and eventually David) woven into the story, but the narrowing of characters shapes and funnels our focus towards Saul as the first monarch.

The narrative that just precedes the introduction of Saul in 1 Samuel 9 is the dialogical exchange that Samuel has with the people before Saul is introduced. 1 Samuel 8 is a hugely important exchange in its own right and this study will pass over some of that importance in order to focus narrowly on our concerns here. It should also be noted that this speech-complex in 1 Samuel 8 is widely attributed to a much later period in the literary formation of the Deuteronomistic History, being one of several important speech-complexes that seem to pervade the entire Deuteronomistic History. The speech-complex clearly recognizes the import of monarchy, and, interestingly for us, point out to us the decisive problems of kingship, namely, that kings "take." The verb permeates the entire speech. Of greater interest to us than the speech, though, is the short narrative prelude to the speech of Samuel.

We are told in 1 Samuel 8 that Samuel has grown old (this narrative will sound like another we shall review shortly but from Judges). The aged Samuel has "placed" his sons as Judges over Israel (וישם את־בניו שפטים לישראל; 1 Sam 8:1). This is interesting because at this point in the story Samuel typifies the kind of rule of the judges associated with the book of Judges. But distinctly new, Samuel is the first one to appoint a sort of dynastic succession. The request of the people is for a king (מלך). This is a new title for our narrative for the tribes of Israel. Curiously, though, the verb used for this king's activity is the same verb used for the judges of Israel (Judg 8:6). They want a "king" who will "judge," thus suggesting in the story that the people recognize that something is different about the rule of kingship. To this point in the story, with the exception of our "anti-king" in Abimelech, the title of king has been used only for non-Israelite persons of non-Israelite nations.

While "all" the "elders" of "Israel" are asking for a king, they are also rejecting the kind of dynastically institutionalized rule that Samuel it seems with his sons was trying to establish. We note here that the "force" of those who "judged" was not able to carry over powerfully enough to allow for persons to recognize the judge as the "differentiator" who quelled rivalrous impulses in Israel. Kingship emerges within categories understood by Girard only when the King is seen as the one whom holds sway over the people by virtue of the sacral crisis that king resolves, or is reputed to resolve, in the mythic practices of sacrifice. Dynasties, at least to this point in Israel's history with Samuel, will not be accepted.[1]

And this is not the first place where a sort of dynastic rule is not accepted; we have already seen something similar to it in the narratives associated with Gideon. This study has already focused on Abimelech as the *pilegesh*-son of Gideon. We noted already that Gideon rejects dynastic rule, "I will not rule over you, and my son will not rule over you; the LORD will rule over you" (Judg 8:23).

Joshua, who of course precedes the entire period of Judges, does not even set up a ruler to follow him. Rather, the rule is spread for him to all the tribes of Israel.[2] The nature of non-dynastic rule here is important to us because we can see that whatever form of leadership preceded the monarchy of Saul in Israel's history, at least the narrative complex tell us that the "power" of rulers was not recognized in the same way that later dynasties of Israel would be recognized. The ability to lead Israel was limited in scope and time, until the Monarch, or the one who differentiates, emerges in Israel's history—and for us that person is Saul.

Sacrifice

The second important introduction we need to make to the narrative history moving from Joshua to 1 Samuel in the Deuteronomistic history has to do with the role of sacrifice(s) in the story. Simply stated, the central narrative significance of sacrificial acts only slowly emerges in the Deuteronomistic History and it is primarily within the stories associated here with the start of monarchy that sacrifice takes on a central role in the narrative. This is not to say that there are no sacrificial acts in the stories that precede 1 Samuel; it is to highlight the new functional

---

1. For a fuller explanation of dynastic rule or "hereditary leadership" in the first portion of Samuel, stories that are not the primary concern of this study, there is a good section in Garsiel, *The First Book of Samuel*, 63.

2. For an interesting perspective on how even Moses does not set up a dynastic rule but leaves on the text of Torah to rule in his place, read Olson, *Deuteronomy*.

role within the narrative of sacrifice in 1 Samuel. For example, in Joshua, there are only isolated narrative accounts of acts of sacrifice. In the two narrative complexes of sacrifices in Joshua, the stories are narrated in a way that suggests the sacrifice is something akin to a memorial event, a suzerain treaty perhaps. Those two sacrifice narrative unites include Josh 8:31 and the stories in Joshua 22.

Acts or issues of sacrifice are more central in Judges and no doubt we have already discussed the central role of a sacrificial-priestly-acts in Judges 17–21 that fails to quell the violence there. But in the larger stories of Judges, sacrifice does not play a central role. Sacrifice is only briefly mentioned in Judg 2:5. Interesting for our narrative, Gideon, the father of Abimelech, is the one who makes an offering in his rise to leadership in Judges 6. The only other reference to sacrificial language is that which has already been explored in this study in the Judges 17–21 complex.

When the narrative carries us forward to the start of monarchy and those associated with it—and even into narratives associated with the second monarch—we begin to read stories that are permeated with issues of sacrifice and offerings.[3] Saul's entrance into the narrative, and, as we will see, his inauguration wherein the people accept him as king is in the context of sacrifice. We will come to these important narratives in a more specific way within the context of this chapter.

SYMPATHETIC SAUL AND THE START OF KINGSHIP

So much has been written about Saul, the reputed first king of Israel, that one wonders what more can be said. It will be our intention to focus anew on Saul. Our attention will focus on how Saul was part of the struggle of culture that led to the creation of monarchy in Ancient Israel. It is with some gratitude that I begin this chapter in tribute to the continuing exemplary work of David M. Gunn whose work on the David and then Saul narratives was inspiration to my own desire to read more closely and study more diligently the many narrative units that permeate the entire narrative of the Deuteronomistic History.[4] It might also be of note to mention here that many of the books and articles about Saul are sympathetic towards him for his rejection or loss of kingship.[5] In fact,

---

3. James G. Williams has outlined other stories of sacrifice that lie within the Deuteronomistic stories (Williams, "Sacrifice and the Beginning of Kingship").

4. Gunn. *The Story of King David*.

5. Samuel Ridout's opening prefatory note to his study of Saul is simply, "The subject . . . is a depressing one" (Ridout, *King Saul*, i, prefatory note).

several titles of works themselves hint at their sympathetic reading of Saul.[6] That sympathetic reading will not be our focus! Instead, our aim will be to show how significant and important Saul is as a character in the narrative. We argue it is Saul who, through the scapegoat mechanism he enacts, quells violence. This suppression of violence leads to all the people inaugurating him as king, a *novum* event in the culture of Israel. Saul, who is normally viewed for how he loses kingship is still narrated as becoming the first king. Saul's start of kinship, not his loss of it, will be the central locus of our concern. Regardless of his later loss of kingship, it is with Saul that kingship begins![7]

1 SAMUEL 9–11 IN SCHOLARSHIP

Before we set ourselves to the task of following the narrative, it is important for us to note here that the framework of our reading, 1 Samuel 9–11 is not arbitrary or capricious, and several scholars note the same limits that we have noted here.[8] Sarah Nicholson writes about this narra-

---

6. Foresti, *The Rejection*.

7. We note here that there is significant and important scholarship available on the rise of David's monarchy, as well as on the succession to his throne eventually by Solomon. None of this is our concern here. The Girardian analysis has been applied to narratives in the History of David's Rise and within the Succession Narrative. While this is again not our concern here, such analysis might seek to validate the coherences found by other scholars with the work of Girard and the large corpus of narrative stories we find within the Deuteronomistic History. We also note here that the sympathetic reading of Saul might be read differently in the positive, powerful view of Samson that is present in the text of Judges 13–16. Again, this focus is not ours, but it has been argued that in the Samson cycle we have an account of Saul's greatness camouflaged in the work of Samson. See Brooks, "Saul and the Samson Narrative." See especially page 24, where she writes, "The pro-Saul author did not dare to write an openly true account of Saul, and therefore was obliged to conceal Saul's story behind the heroic image of Samson." The idea of Saul's story being hidden or concealed reflects something of our exposition, where these stories conceal a different reality than they bear on the surface, but that reading will be made more explicit as we apply our Girardian hermeneutic. For an excellent review of the "apologia" for Saul, see White, "The History of Saul's Rise." In her conclusion she writes, "We can conclude, therefore, that Saul's history was an *apologia* composed by his historian(s) to defend him from the charges of illegal arrogation of power and massive bloodshed perpetrated on a chartered priesthood" (White, "The History," 292).

8. No doubt there would be dispute over the textual limits; our point here is simply to note that our parameters cohere with other scholars' readings of these same texts. And readers are reminded that this textual section is framed by two speech complexes identified with anti-monarchial intent attributed to the Deuteronomic editor in 1 Samuel 8 and 1 Samuel 12.

tive section, "Although these ['two accounts of Saul's becoming king'] are often purported to be the result of discrete sources, the narrative flows so easily from 9.1 to 11.15 that it is difficult to tell at first glance where one source ends and another begins."[9] We have cited Nicholson specifically here because of her narrative purview of this same literary section, but also to highlight our incongruity with her sense of this story. As cited here, she reads in the narrative of Saul that there are "two accounts" of his "becoming king," and she goes on to outline these as the private and public anointings. We disagree that these are separate accounts of his becoming king. Our argument is that while these may be anointings that point towards a certain status for Saul—which we will explore in this chapter—he is not yet king until after he dismembers his oxen, quells the violence, and does not seek retributive conflict. David Gunn calls this event of Saul's oxen episode as being "the third phase in Saul's way to the throne."[10] Our argument here is that while these may be anointing scenes that prepare us for kingship, kingship itself does not emerge as an event until Saul has quelled conflict, chaos and brought reconciliation.

We also need to characterize here that our reading of these "three events" that lead to Saul's inauguration are narrative story, but narrative story that for us are about some kernel of real history. Volkmar Fritz says of these stories that "none of the three narratives goes back to actual historical events, so I Sam 9–11 cannot serve as a source for the history of the origin of the monarchy."[11] And yet, contra Fritz, A. D. H. Mayes cites along with Alt that "It has long been recognized that 1 Samuel 11, which recounts Saul's victory over the Ammonites, offers the most reliable source for our reconstruction of the event of Saul's elevation to the Kingship (see Alt, 1966, 183–86)."[12]

We note here, as well, that the characterization of these narratives by some, here by Garsiel, uses the same framework as this study, namely "ambivalence." Incorporating chapter 8 into his purview Garsiel writes, "Scholars have detected in chapters 8–12 an ambivalence both towards the instituting of the monarchy and towards the personality of the first

---

9. Nicholson, *Three Faces of Saul*, 55. See also Long, *The Reign and Rejection*, 174, on this same issue of textual parameters and narrative coherence found within it.

10. Gunn, *The Fate of King Saul*, 64.

11. Fritz, "Die Deutungen," 362. We disagree and will demonstrate our dissent in this study.

12. Mayes, "The Period of the Judges," 325.

king. Some passages in this narrative block reflect sympathy towards both, and others disapproval."[13]

It is also noteworthy for us to recognize that the narrative complex we find in 1 Samuel 9–11 is often seen to be early or "pre-Deuteronomistic." That is, while we recognize with the bulk of scholars that the Deuteronomistic History is finally shaped in and after the Exile, portions of it existed as literary history much earlier than the Exile. Those portions that are oldest, then, would have greater potential of narrating actual historical events. Nadav Na'aman argues convincingly, we believe, using the earlier work of J. van Seters, that 1 Sam 9:1—10:16; 11; 13–14 are regarded as pre-Deuteronomistic.[14] Our review will not include chapters 13–14 of the biblical text but it is important for us to recognize the possibilities that our stories here are more than "stories" and their early existence points to the possibility of "real" history narrated to us in the start of Saul's kingship. About these stories, J. van Seters writes that the individual stories about Saul "do not by themselves point to a stage of narrative development or historical consciousness that could be construed as a stage in the development of Israelite historiography."[15] Nadav Na'aman concludes that the stories of 1 Sam 9:1—10:16; 10:27b—11:15 are among those with the "safest point of departure for the reconstruction of [Saul's] place and role in the emergence of the Israelite monarchy. According to this story (whose date of composition cannot be established) . . . [Saul's] coronation by the people [is] closely connected with the campaign against the Ammonites."[16]

SAUL'S PIVOTAL ROLE

As the narratives of the Deuteronomistic History present the story, we have left the time of "there was no king in Israel" to proceed to the leadership of Samuel and then to Saul. We do not know how much time has passed for certain and any accurate reflection of dates is not important to our review. The actual dates aside, this study argues for some histori-

---

13. Garsiel, *The First Book of Samuel*, 76–77. Garsiel goes on to explain his own approach outlined in his introduction that "the author of Samuel [was] a conscious literary artist working upon older materials, and as being in consequence truly an author and not merely an editor" (ibid., 77).

14. Na'aman, "The Pre-Deuteronomistic Story."

15. Van Seters, *In Search of History*, 258.

16. Na'aman, "The Pre-Deuteronomistic Story," 655.

cal validity to the start of monarchy in Israel's history. David Washburn believes that "a fair amount of time would have been necessary [from the time of the civil war] for the tribe [of Benjamin] to rebuild itself to the point where it could produce a king such as Saul."[17] In fact, the liminal, marginal, almost totally obliterated sense of Benjamin's identity from the end of Judges might be important to highlight the marginalized status of Saul as we will meet him. Diane Edelman notes that the narrative unit has a "disproportionate amount of space" within the larger history suggesting the "importance of Saul's reign as a critical juncture within the Historian's purview of Israel's development. Saul's pivotal role is apparent from the use of his career to bridge two of the History's larger periodizations [sic] the era of the Judges and the era of the United Monarchy."[18]

1 SAMUEL 9:1—10:17

When we first meet Saul as a character in the narrative, the narrator draws our attention to him in 1 Sam 9:1-2. "According to the canons of Hebrew narrative, a new tradition clearly begins with 9:1. The full introduction with patronymics for Kish and the identification of his son, Saul, marks a new beginning in the narrative."[19] Saul's family status is important. A person's family and personal relationships—or lack thereof—frame the character for us. We have already seen this in Abimelech's relationship to Gideon and the unnamed Levite's relationship to no one. Samuel Ridout has offered an analysis of the characters named here that make up the genealogy of Saul. While his descriptions of their names are dated, the content of their names does play into our narrative in same way. After Kish, Saul's father whose name means "ensnaring," Ridout writes:

> The next in line was Abiel, "father of might," which seems to emphasize the thought of strength in which man does indeed glory, but which too often proves to be utter weakness. Zeor, the next, "compressed" or "contracted," suggest the reverse; we can readily understand how one, himself hedges in and oppressed, would seek a reaction and give expression to his desire in his son. Bechorath, his father, "primogeniture," is that which nature makes much of and Scripture has frequently set aside. Aphiah, "I will utter," would suggest that pride of heart which tells out its

---

17. Washburn, "The Chronology," 425.
18. Edelman, "The Deuteronomist's Story," 208.
19. Campbell, *1 Samuel*, 89.

imagined greatness. The last person in the list is not named, but described as a Benjamite, a member of the tribe whose territory had been one of such glorying self will and rebellion.[20]

Ridout notes that even in this genealogy "desire" operates as he writes, "Thus, the genealogy of the man of the people's desire would suggest the pride, the self will, the experience of nature, together with its feebleness, too, and its deceit."[21] Indeed, Saul comes to us from an interesting genealogical lineage. He will be marked for us in these texts as the man of the people's desire. "The seven-generation genealogy in 9,1 indicates that he is a man destined for greatness from birth, and his status as the son of a *gibbor ḥayil*, a man of wealth or importance, also dispels any possible rise from lowly origins."[22] The "intent of the genealogy is surely to emphasize the high status of Kish and therefore of Saul."[23]

It is not enough to know that Saul is the son of someone, in our case, Kish. More than just the son of Kish, the narrator wants to demarcate Saul for us. We are introduced to the manner in which Saul literally stands. He is a "young man" both handsome and tall. As a "young man" (בחור) not a "man" (איש) neither a "lad" (נער). As a בחור, he is a young man about to enter adult life, "who had not yet married, i.e. about seventeen-to-twenty years old."[24] Saul is, by most interpretative standards, "handsome" (בחור וטוב). This בחור we are told a second time in the narrative, stands apart from the "sons of Israel" by virtue of his being "handsome." In Israel's family stories narrated in the Bible, certain sons are favored or chosen from the other sons. Often it is this story line of a favored son that drives entire narrative complexes throughout the Hebrew Bible.[25]

But this introduction to Saul is not yet complete, his standing among the people is not by virtue of being "good/handsome" alone, he quite literally stands over or above (ומעלה גבה מכל־העם) them. His appearance among the "sons of Israel" is as one who is "tov" but here he stands "over" or "above" the very "shoulders" the people of Israel. And perhaps, as it is stated here, Saul is "head and shoulders" above "all the

20. Ridout, *King Saul*, 82–83.
21. Ibid, 83.
22. Edelman, "The Deuteronomist's Story," 212.
23. Klein, *1 Samuel*, 86.
24. Brooks, "Was There a Concubine at Gibeah?" 36.
25. Greenspahn, *When Brothers*.

people." Saul, we can safely say, is narratively set apart from those among whom he lives, both sons of Israel and all the people. Shimon Bar Efrat writes that with this height, Saul had "won [the people's] affection and loyalty." [26] We will demonstrate in our study that this narrative is much more complex than issues of Saul simply being tall. Height alone will not win affection and loyalty necessary for kingship to be inaugurated.

At the same time, though, with attention to 1 Sam 9:1 we need to note that Saul, while clearly, textually unique and perhaps we could say textually alone, his family status within the home of his father Kish makes us aware that this new character Saul is not removed from the larger social/political/family fabric of Israel's story emerging within the Deuteronomistic History. "The Bible presents Saul as the son of a landed aristocrat."[27]

We have been told as we met him that his father Kish is none other than a Benjamite (1 Sam 9:1). The tribe that was obliterated in tribal genocide. It is not enough to tell us only one time in the introduction that Kish, the father of Saul, is a Benjamite. We are told a second time in 1 Sam 9:1 that he is himself a "man" (again, distinct from the בחור that is Saul that we will meet in the next verse) of the מבן־ימין. The textual construction in Hebrew is different in the second complex. Interestingly here, this second mention of being from the clan of Benjamin points us to the root of the word itself. To be "*ben*" (son of the "*yamin*") is to be of the sons of those "on the right hand." [28]

Such is the nature of our introduction to Saul in this narrative. The man who will become in the scope of a few biblical chapters the first monarch is here both entrenched in the familial traditions and heritage of Israel and at the same time distinct from any other family member

---

26. Bar-Efrat, *Narrative Art*, 49.

27. Van der Toorn, "Saul and the Rise," 520.

28. Although it is nowhere in the purview of this study, it is striking that in the post-monarchial period a new descendent of Kish is raised up to face the same threat of Saul in a later narrative of 1 Samuel. That new descendant faced with the threat of a new Aggagite is none other than Mordecai of the narrative we read in Esther. Readers of the larger narrative complex that is the Hebrew Bible might remember here that when the patriarch of this tribe was born (Benjamin) his mother died in bearing him. The narrative of Genesis tells us that his mother, the favored wife of Jacob/Israel, whose name was Rachel, cried out that his name should be "Ben-Oni," meaning something like "Son of my Sorrow," but for Jacob this son is as his "right hand."

or any other person. He is at one and the same time as it were like and unlike the persons with whom he dwells and over whom he will rule.

We have been introduced to Saul in the narrative. Saul's status as a Benjamite is important as this narrative connects with the narrative of Judges. As the narrative continues to introduce us to Saul in 1 Samuel 9 we meet characters and persons who serve to move the story forward, but who remain unnamed for us. We shall first examine the significance of these characters within this narrative here. Later we will explore the connections between these characters and the stories we have already detailed in our study.

Saul seeks his father's asses with the company of a servant.[29] They arrive at a location near Samuel's home. Unnamed girls join the story and give instructions regarding where Samuel is and what it is that Samuel is doing.[30] It is curious in the story here how the unnamed characters and the narrator speak of Samuel. In the previous narratives he was one who judged Israel and who set up his sons in an attempt to continue in his role as judge. Chiefly in this capacity, we had been told that Samuel would "make the rounds," to serve as judge. His travel circuit through Israel is narrated to include: Bethel, Gilgal, and Mizpah, and Ramah, his home (1 Sam 7:15–16). In this story where Saul is first introduced to us and where we again encounter Samuel, we learn something new about *Samuel* and his role.

Marsha White points out that this otherwise "mundane search," which would have been common for farmers of the period with unpenned livestock, carries a nuance of meaning that we might miss.[31] She points us to the nuanced use of "to find" (מצא) in the narrative where the verb is used twelve times and has a double meaning, not only "to find" but also "to discover." "Saul could not 'find' (i.e., discover) the missing donkeys

---

29. Ludwig Schmidt suggests that 9:1–13 of this story about Saul are the beginnings of an old story that have been adapted (Schmidt, *Menschlicher Erfolg*, 63–80).

30. Moshe Garsiel compares the intimate literary connections and thematic issues here with Moses's "call" when he was in the wilderness with Jethro's sheep, and with the "call" of Gideon in Judges 6. The textual connections are revealing but are not our focus here. With Garsiel, however, we would note that by picking up on these interconnections and themes, the narrator frames for us the rise of a new kind of leader in Israel's history. The thematic and textual connections, says Garsiel, "are not so clear and sharp that they would certainly be noticed, were [they] not reinforced by the dialogues between Samuel and the Lord and between Samuel and Saul" (Garsiel, *The First Book of Samuel*, 78ff.).

31. White, "'The History of Saul's Rise,'"284.

(1 Sam 9:4), but instead he 'finds' (i.e., encounters) first the girls who direct him to Samuel (1 Sam 9:11–13) ... Finally Samuel tells Saul that Yahweh will bless whatever his new power 'finds' (i.e., discovers) to do (1 Sam 10:7) ... The twelvefold iteration of המצא unites the ordinary search with its extraordinary outcome."[32] In sync with the anonymity operating in the narrative is the fact that the location itself, while assumed to be Ramah, is technically unnamed for us in the narrative. The assumption, for example, of Ralph Klein marks the normative response for 9:10–14, "Within the present book that unnamed city should be understood as Ramah."[33] What is more, alongside the unnamed characters, even the "unnamed" asses shape the narrative in a small way towards kingship.[34] The extensive accumulation of unnamed persons after having so clearly named Saul for us points to the central concern for the narrative operating around the introduction of this person in this story.

SAUL'S PRIESTLY PORTION

The servant and Saul have crossed "the district of Shalisha" (1 Sam 9:4). They crossed "Shaalim." They traveled the entire territory of Benjamin, finally reaching the district of Zuph—territorially a place not yet encountered in all the stories of the Deuteronomistic History. Even though the district of Zuph is mentioned in the narrative, we know from the end of 1 Samuel 7 what city this is where Samuel resides, Ramah. The story is infused with references to persons of Benjamite origin and the Benjamite territory. We are also geographically in the place where chaos might have been avoided in the end of Judges. Saul has arrived here in this story in the city of Ramah. Saul arrives then at the city the Levite

---

32. Ibid, 285. White notes in a footnote that the turning point of the iteration happens at the seventh iteration, I Sam 9:20.

33. Klein, *1 Samuel*, 70.

34. Krondorfer, "Response," 103. "The ass, we know, is a royal and messianic symbol. Howard Eilberg-Schwartz further argues that the ass is also a metaphor for the resident alien, 'for it stands in the same relation to the herds and flocks as the resident alien stands in relation to Israelite society. Like the resident alien, the ass is a loner ... [Both] are neither complete insiders nor total outsiders." "The task of finding the asses ties Saul symbolically to the animal that is neither insider nor outside. Like the ass, Saul is a marginal figure (a resident alien?), whose status is ambivalent" (ibid.). Ralph Klein writes "Stoebe points out that asses were the riding animals of nobility (cf. Judg 5:10; 10:4; 12:14 and Zech 9:9 where the Messiah rides on an ass) and that their loss would mean both poverty and an inability to fulfill a leadership role" (Klein, *1 Samuel*, 86).

was not able to reach in his journey (Judg 19:13). The Levite had walked with a pair of donkeys (Judg 19:3), and here Saul looks for his father's donkeys.

When the unnamed servant first speaks in this narrative it is in reply to the speech of Saul. Saul, ready to go home lest his father Kish should worry about him, appeals to those traveling with him that they should go home. The servant encourages Saul to consider heading to "that town"[35] where they will encounter "a man of God" (איש־אלהים) who has some 'merit' (והאיש נכבד). This unnamed servant says that all that this "man of God" says it "comes true" (1 Sam 9:6). In direct speech, the Hebrew of the "comes true" is something like this "it comes to become," or colloquially, "It happens" (כל אשר־ידבר בוא). Saul discusses with his servant the need to pay this "man of God" and the servant has silver. "The narrator insists on this 'farm boy—reluctant king' aspect of Saul. When Saul finally asks Samuel how to find his father's asses, it is significant that Saul has no money on him and has to borrow from his servant to pay Samuel."[36] In the midst of this dialogue, the narrator pauses to tell us something about the person who has been introduced to us as "man of God." The narrator says, "Formerly in Israel, when a man went to inquire of God, he would say, 'Come, let us go to the seer,' for the prophet of today was formerly called a seer" (1 Sam 9:9). In this story, focused on this insider/outsider Saul, there is not yet a single mention of Samuel by name, but he has been newly introduced to us as "man of God" and "prophet" and "seer."[37] We shall see that Saul's servant boy gives him good advice. In connection with the story in Judges 19 we note that in this story Saul heeds the advice of the servant, unlike the Levite of Judges 19. It is when the Levite fails to heed the servant's advice that the atrocities of Judges 19 begin when there was no king.

---

35. The name of the town is not identified in the narrative.

36 . Preston, "The Heroism of Saul," 31–32.

37. These appellations are used nowhere prior to this narrative to describe Samuel. The term "man of God" in the Deuteronomistic History has only appeared in Judges 13 with the man of God appearing to Manoah's unnamed wife and with an unnamed person approaching Eli in 1 Sam 2:27. This man of God conversing with Eli confirms for him the end of his priesthood and anticipates the inauguration of a new "faithful" priest. The term for prophet is used in the Deuteronomistic History to this point only in the Gideon narrative, then in 1 Sam 3:20 to describe Samuel in his role as he who sees God at Shiloh. "1 Samuel 9 is often thought to be the story of an anonymous seer that has been assimilated to the Samuel Tradition" (Grabbe, "Prophets, Priests, Diviners and Sages," 53).

The narrative proceeds to tell us that unnamed daughters come out to draw water. They are not full characters in the story, but they suggest a curious anonymity alongside the detailed genealogy of Saul from the start of our story. The nameless nature of the daughters alongside the fact of their coming out to draw water might cause the reader to think that this story is about the unwitting acquisition of a wife for Saul. As a sort of type-scene, the narrative idea of unnamed girls drawing water has before led to marriage for Isaac, Jacob, and Moses. The reader might be prone to think this story will "twist" for us towards some marital. But instead of marital, the issues become monarchial.

The nameless girls are questioned, "Is the seer in town?" Their reply adds new elements to our story. "Hurry," is the response to Saul and his servant; not only is the seer in town, but he is about to "sacrifice" at the "shrine." There is only one other appearance of a shrine apart from this story in the entire Deuteronomistic History, in Judges 17. While there have been limited references to sacrifice throughout the Deuteronomistic History this particular kind of sacrifice is heralded by a unique term at a unique location in the Deuteronomistic History, the "shrine." As we have already seen and will explore more fully later, the shrine is central to the issues of rivalry operating in this story. At this event, I suggest there is no sacrifice. Later in 1 Samuel, Samuel uses the ruse of a sacrifice to anoint David. I suggest here and will further explicate in this study that the sacrifice in this story is also used as a ruse for initiating but not yet inaugurating Saul's kingship. In fact, in the stories introducing us to Saul, the first true sacrifice of this narrative is with Saul's dismembering the oxen and being heralded by all Israel as king.[38]

In this story we have been told by unnamed girls who will not become the wife or wives for Saul that a "sacrifice" (זבח) is to take place. Curiously, though, at this "shrine" there is no altar, no fire, no covenant, no priest; (only, remember, a man of god/prophet/seer). The function and purpose of this thrice-called person, Samuel, is interesting in our

---

38. The David narrative is not a concern of our exposition, but it is interesting that when David is anointed, the use and plan of the sacrifice is intentionally a means of providing "a cover story for the visit to Jesse in order to deceive Saul!" (Gunn, *The Fate of King Saul*, 62; emphasis original). As we will argue in our narrative here, there is also no sacrifice, only a meal. Perhaps the idea of the way sacrifice serves "to cover" and "to deceive" will arise for us in our Girardian reading though. Despite Gunn's very different approach to this story, it is of merit that he uses, unbeknownst to himself, Girardian terminology to describe the act of sacrifice.

narrative not the least of which is because when he is first introduced, it is not by name, making him initially another anonymous person.[39] It might be the case that we would associate power or public office of significance with this person, but the ambiguity of titles associated with this person in the narrative seems to draw our attention away from his office and to the office being created in kingship. Meir Sternberg whose work with this narrative does not focus on the issues of kingship as we do here ponders:

> [why does the narrator] suddenly multiply and switch referring expressions to prophecy, arrest the dialogue to interpolate a philological comment, revive a term that the speakers could manage without (as they have done so far) and his own audience would find archaic? All these incongruities make sense in terms of image shattering—a thrust against the inflated figure cut by the prophet in the popular imagination ... To cut the prophet down to size, the narrator brings to bear on him a series of three referring terms, each pointing to a different side or view of the office ...[40]

The effective dramatic performance for us in this narrative, then, is to draw us away from the office of prophet effective in Samuel towards the newly formed office emerging in the person coming to be anointed, Saul. "Three designations, three denigrations" writes Sternberg, "variously undermining cultural through verbal clichés and culminating in a full-scale exposure of presumption. On the threshold of the monarchy, the outgoing prophet-judge hardly appears in an attractive light."[41] Indeed, a new office was needed to stabilize the archaic complexity of this older tradition. The previous biblical chapter, 1 Samuel 7, explored Samuel expounding on the anti-monarchial tone that operates within the larger Deuteronomistic History. Here, though, we read the pro-monarchial tone cast over against the vagaries of the office and tradition maintained by Samuel.

What actually takes place in the story, that which is narrated to the reader as taking place and that which is anticipated by the unnamed

---

39. Hertzberg writes, "At the beginning, the man of God is given no name. He is as little known to Saul as Saul is known to him ... Moreover, the way in which the man of God is first described as a professional diviner does not at all fit the picture of Samuel which we have been given hitherto" (Hertzberg, *1 Samuel*, 79).

40. Sternberg, *The Poetics of Biblical Narrative*, 95.

41. Ibid., 96.

girl's story, is a meal. This is perhaps an uncommon meal, a 'banquet' but any impending sacrifice that Saul might have rushed to preempt is not narrated.

It is important to the argument of this study that some mention is made with regard to the kind or type of sacrifice that is made here in 1 Samuel 9. While it is the case that the language of the text uses זבח and thus, has the idea of sacrifice clearly within its purview, we will argue that the sacrifice itself is not narrated, and, instead, the focus on the meal and eating shifts the focus away from the non-narrated sacrifice to other actions and activities going on that are central to the story. These other elements are, we will argue, so central to the story with respect to the movement towards Saul that while the idea of sacrifice is present, its lack of narrated reality in the text leaves the sacrifice proper as being not present in the narrative and only present, as we shall argue, in the later activity of Saul in 1 Samuel 11. Our argument is not without merit in the scholarship pertinent to these chapters in 1 Samuel, though our read of it will take on a uniquely Girardian perspective.

The lack of sacrificial highlight or significance in this text is noted by Ralph Klein when he writes: "After inviting Saul to a banquet, Samuel promises to tell him in the morning everything in his heart, but discloses immediately that the asses have been found and that everything desirable in Israel will be his. Saul professes his insignificance (vv. 15–21). At a subsequent banquet, Saul and his servant are given honored positions and special food which Samuel had reserved for them (vv. 22–24)."[42] No mention is made of anything specific with regard to the animal or place of sacrifice, there is only the hint that this banquet has "sacrificial" connotations given the characteristic use in Hebrew. The *New International Dictionary of Old Testament Theology and Exegesis* notes that in connections with Aramaic usage in the Ancient Near East the root "was certainly conceived of as a meal, at least for the gods" and that the basic meaning of the qal verb and the "overwhelming pattern of usage" for the verb is "undoubtedly sacred slaughter."[43]

This being true for the definition of זבח in its Hebrew use, the text itself is absent of any direct reference to sacrifice itself taking place or happening as an event in the narrative—other than being anticipated. It is anticipated, but not narrated. And, instead, the focus on what is nar-

42. Klein, *1 Samuel*, 83.
43. Averbeck, "זבח (2284)," 1068–69.

rated in the text is on what is eaten and who eats. The narrative construction of sacrifice is present, but not detailed and instead the narrative focuses on the actors and their "roles" or "status" at the meal. The verb for eating (אכל) is used no less than seven times in this short story, it is the unnamed girls who anticipate eating, it is guests sitting for a meal with a "cook" in a "room" (1 Sam 9:23). When the special portion has been given to Saul, the one who is specifically narrowed out by the narrator and by Samuel at this meal, the people are instructed to "eat." The suggestion of the Hebrew word and the language of the unnamed girls suggests sacrifice, but that is not what is formally and explicitly narrated to us. So that the language of sacrifice is operative, without a sacrifice being narratively present.

About this meal, Ralph Klein writes: "The purpose of this meal is never explicitly described, but Mettinger and Schmidt may well be correct in understanding it as the anticipation of a coronation banquet (cf. 1 Sam 11:15; 16:1–33, where Samuel visits a city, performs a sacrifice, and anoints David; 2 Sam 15:7–12; and 1 Kgs 1:9). Note that the guests had been *invited*, an apparent technical term in the coronation ritual of Adonijah (1 Kgs 1:41, 49; cf. Ezek 39:17 and Zeph 1:7)."[44] At this meal we are told that the meeting hall was large enough to accommodate at least thirty people at 9:22. The last time thirty persons had been narrated to us in the Deuteronomistic History was when, in Judg 20:31, 39 the Benjaminites of that story inflicted casualties on thirty men.

Our focus is on Saul and how he is characterized in this narrative. We are detailing how he will become the monarch who brings reconciliation to Israel by means of sanctioned sacrificial violence. The narrator reveals to us Samuel's thoughts about monarchy. After the girls had told Saul and his servant to head for the shrine, the narrator pauses the story to tell us about what had been revealed to Samuel (in Hebrew it is literally that YHWH uncovered his ear) "the day before" by YHWH. YHWH, so the narrator tells us in 1 Sam 9:16, had revealed to Samuel that he would see someone who he should anoint as "ruler" (נגיד) over Israel. Curiously, this person is not to be made "king" (מלך), which we might suspect from the dialogue that took place in the preceding chapter, 1 Samuel 8.[45] In this narrative, apart from the speech complex that is so

---

44. Klein, *1 Samuel*, 87 (italics original).

45. Wolfgang Richter studied the use of this formula in 1 Samuel 9:16 and 10:1 and noted the relationship of the *nāgîd* connected in early traditions of kingship. See Richter, "*Die nāgîd Formel.*"

clearly late in the biblical tradition, Saul is to be anointed not as king, nor even as "judge" like those who had preceded in leadership. He is to be "prince" or "ruler" (נגיד). Regarding the curiosity of this reference even Ralph Klein writes after advancing some options for attempting to understand it that the "precise denotation of *nāgīd* seems difficult to demonstrate."[46] This same appellation appears at the time of Saul's "anointing" just a few verses away from this, but precedes what I am arguing is his real "coronation" as king after curbing violence in the narrative. The argument of Hertzberg coincides with that of this study, but for different reasons. Hertzberg notes with our reading that "the word 'king' (*melek*) is not, in fact, used here; twice we have *nāgīd*, prince, properly the 'one who has been announced.'"[47] Distinct from this study, though, Hertzberg understands a theological reason for this title where we will explore its function in sacrificial and sacral categories. Hertzberg writes, "Thus, the king is entitled 'the one designated of Yahweh' until political honor is added to the theological recognition by the 'acclamation of the people (11:15).'"[48]

With this reference to Saul as "prince" or "ruler" over the people we should note a few things. First, with respect to this study and the arguments made about Abimelech's "rule" over the people in Judges 9 and chapter three of this study, this is a new title. The term used for Abimelech's rule is different than the נגיד used here for Saul. Second, the association of נגיד here is tied with a formula already used in the biblical story of Exodus. Here it reads; "He will deliver My people from the hands of the Philistines; for I have taken note of My people, their outcry has come to Me" (1 Sam 9:16). This is the speech of YHWH to Samuel but here it sounds almost verbatim like the speech of God to Moses in Exodus 3. Here, then, in this narrative, we have been introduced to Saul as a Benjamite deeply embedded in the family history, but he is unique from among them. He is seemingly at a sacrifice, so the girls would lead us to believe but it is eating that takes precedence. He is anticipated by a man of God/prophet/seer as one who is like Moses, perhaps he will be their first נגיד but before our narrative introduction to Saul is over we will discover that he becomes their king.

46. Klein, *1Samuel*, 88.
47. Hertzberg, *1 Samuel*, 82.
48. Ibid.

Yet more curious in this narrative, when YHWH continues his speech in declaring to Samuel who Saul is, God does not use the term "govern" or "judge"—which was the request in the speech-complex of 1 Samuel 8. Rather, in 1 Sam 9:17 God says that this נָגִיד who is here recognized will "restrain" or "retain" (יַעְצֹר) the people. The use of עצר is significant, especially since other terms associated with political power are more common in Hebrew. Hertzberg writes that the word used only here and in 10:1 "has the meaning of 'keep in check.'"[49] Our study will highlight the idea that there is something operating with desire leading to rivalry and mob violence that Saul must restrain the people from enacting through scapegoating. I submit that in this narrative exchange, in the speech of Samuel, we have here revealed the yearning of Israel for the Benjamite who can retain the violence that was horrendously meted out in Judge 17–21.

We do not need to look far in the text for a reminder of Saul's status. Saul replies to Israel's yearning and Samuel's speech, "I am only a Benjamite, from the smallest of the tribes of Israel and my clan is the least of all the clans of the tribe of Benjamin. Why do you say such things to me?" (9:21). Ostensibly, Saul is from within the clan, but recognizes himself as being unique from the clan/tribal allotments. David Gunn says the story here is of "the unlikely hero."[50] Ridout suggests that the reason for Saul's affirmation of his smallness is in direct correlation to the narratives we have studied that demarcate the near destruction of the Benjamites. He writes, "He was doubtless familiar with the history of the tribe, and how it came to be reduced to such small proportions, because of . . . Gibeah."[51] As this narrative began he was "tallest" and here he is "smallest." As a character, Saul's presentation is mixed and unique. In some ways he is just like others in the narrative, where in other ways the contrasts to his unique status and stature are drastic.

The meal is consumed. Saul's meal is unique. A special portion had been set aside for him—yet again marking textually for us the difference of this character in this story. "Bring the portion," which had been "set aside" (1 Sam 9:24). The "reserved" thigh portion was set before Saul. The allotment "kept" for "this occasion" which normally needs a priest to partake, is consumed by Saul. As we move through these narratives

49. Ibid., 83
50. Gunn, *The Fate of King Saul*, 61.
51. Ridout, *King Saul*, 92.

and come later to our Girardian understanding we will note more fully how the one who brings kingship does so through means of sacrifice, a sacrifice that we will note moves to enable the scapegoating mechanism in the story. In Israel's history it is the priests who offer sacrifice, and we have seen the complexities of the horrible "sacrifice" offered by our unnamed Levite in Judges. In our narrative at this festive meal, the portion set aside that Saul consumes, given to him by this man of god/prophet/seer, is the "shoulder." In the priestly traditions narrated in the book of Leviticus, the priests are described as the only persons who consumed the "shoulder" (cf. Leviticus 7:32 and 10:14 as two examples). With reference to this special portion set aside for Saul, Ralph Klein notes: "Both the thigh (Exod 29:22, 27; Lev 7:32, 34; 8:25–29; etc) and the fat tail (Exod 29:22; Lev 3:9; 7:3–4; 8:25; 9:19) are mentioned in ritual texts as items to be burned on the altar though the thigh could also be given as a prerequisite to the sons of Aaron."[52] More deliberately in line with the assessment central to the argument of this study is the statement of McCarter when he writes that here "Saul is being treated as if her were a priest!"[53]

In our narrative, this tall/small נגיד consumes the priestly portion. In some ways this tall/small נגיד is sacral, in addition to being set-apart in other ways already in our story. Samuel, the man of god/prophet/seer and this tall/small נגיד who will retain Israel, departs from this shrine to the town and then ends up on the roof for conversation.[54]

The next day Saul is asked by Samuel to send the servant ahead, which he does. Saul is only then privately anointed with oil (1 Sam 10:1). Samuel kisses him and proclaims him—not as king—but the נגיד. Saul is then told to head out so that he can become recognized as one who is among the prophets (1 Sam 10:2). The story seems so odd here, given the speech-complex of 1 Samuel 8. We find here not a king, but a נגיד and he will not be recognized as a king. He will first be recognized as one who is "also among the prophets," or so the people wonder (1 Sam 10:12). 1 Samuel 8 led us to believe a king would be found. And while some

---

52. Klein, *1 Samuel*, 90.

53. McCarter, *1 Samuel*, 180.

54. Roofs appear in the narrative about Rahab in Joshua 2, about Ehud and Eglon in Judges 3, about the woman who throws the rock that shatters Abimelech's skull in Judges 9, and about the Philistines partying on the roof as they gloat over the blinded Samson in Judges 16.

veiled hints at kingship are implied, perhaps in asses, it is only there that kingship operates. Saul, in fact, privately eats like a priest. Publicly, he will be recognized as a prophet but even that will cause for some suspicion. We expected kingship, but find ourselves in priestly and prophetic roles. Antony Campbell notes how the story opens with a search for asses but ends with the need for a king but a king not yet having been named. He says that this causes disequilibrium for the reader.

> Taken at face value, the opening disequilibrium in the story is the loss of the asses. From the end of the story, it is clear that the real imbalance that drives the story is the need for a king in Israel. The term "king" is not used in the story, and one might think a deliverer would do, but deliverers were not anointed. Even at its earliest level, the story appears to be moving in the direction of kingship. [The] ultimate equilibrium [in the text] is to be found in Saul's emergence as king. As a way station in this direction, it offers balance enough. At the level of the present text, the story moves from the lost asses to a specific commission of Saul as "ruler" (*nāgîd*). This too is only a way station toward kingship."[55]

Campbell is correct that the text presents levels of ambiguity that cause the reader to be in a state of "disequilibrium" with regard to what is going on. With Campbell the focus of this study is to demonstrate that kingship has not yet arrived here in chapter 9 and 10. At the same time, in this study we will not agree that this is a "way station" toward kingship. Rather, this story sets up the one decisive act heralding kingship narrated in the full text of chapter 11.

In the series of persons and events that Saul is told to expect that day, it is noted that Saul will pass by Rachel's tomb and end up in Gibeah. Gibeah has been significant in our exposition already. We saw in Judges 17–21 that in the later part of the narrative in chapter 19–21, Gibeah appears over 20 times in 20 verses.

Once in Gibeah, Samuel tells Saul, "you will become another man" (10:6). We might hope that he would become another man in terms of becoming מלך instead of just the נגיד that he is after his anointing, but he is not yet מלך and he cannot yet be מלך in the narrative. We will learn in this narrative that Gibeah becomes Saul's hometown base (10:26). Not too much farther it becomes bound up with Saul by title: "Gibeah of Saul" in 11:4. This is certainly a call for us to remember the

---

55. Campbell, *1 Samuel*, 109.

events of Gibeah in Judges 19–21, where the references to Gibeah occur 22 times.[56]

With reference to the signs Samuel tells Saul to expect, the second sign has to do with bread. On the one hand this might be a reference back to the fact that, on the previous day Saul and his servant had consumed all their bread on the search for the lost asses. Klein notes that at a later point in the story with the next king, David will accept bread from the priests of Nob and that "it may be understood as the first installment of royal tribute promised earlier by Samuel (cf. 9:20)."[57] In addition to its royal status with kings, though, it may connote something of significance towards the priesthood, even as the portion of the meal consumed by Saul brought in the import of priestly issues. Here, McCarter suggests that the gift of wave offerings in the form of bread connotes priestly dignity of Saul. "As in the incident of the consecratory thigh (v. 24), therefore, Saul is again being given the priestly share . . ."[58] In another reference to how this passage connects with the activity of the next king, David, Hans Joachim Stoebe notes the connections in this passage with the anointing of David and the spirit coming over him in power as a later reflection on how Saul is empowered here in 1 Samuel 9 and 10.[59]

The Spirit of the Lord carries Saul off and he is encouraged to "do whatever your hand finds to do, for God is with you" (1 Sam 10:7). We hear again the importance of the "hand" of the would-be king as a sign of power, and this from the one of Benjamin. Peter D. Miscall interprets the charge "whatever your hand finds to do" as a call for Saul as the would-be

---

56. Amit, "Literature in the Service of Politics," 31: "The name that keeps recurring throughout the incident is that of Saul's city Gibeah, which is referred to 22 times [in Judges 19–21]. In the entire Bible this name is mentioned eight more times: six times in Samuel (1 Sam. 10.1, 26; 14.2; 22.6; 23.19; 26.1) and twice in Hosea (9.9; 10.9); as 'Gibeah of Saul four more times (1 Sam. 11.4; 15.34; 2 Sam. 21.6; Isa. 10.29)."

57. Klein, *1 Samuel*, 91.

58. McCarter, *1 Samuel*, 181.

59. Stoebe writes with reference to 1 Samuel 16:13 and David: "Dieser Zug hat eine stärkere innere Verwandtschaft mit Kap. xi als mit der in ihrem Zusammenhang enthaltenen Salbungsgeschichte. In beiden Fällen ist die Mitteilung der rûaḥ nicht durch Samuel vermittelt, sondern erfolgt zur gegebenen Zeit aus einem sich gerade ergebenden Anlass; in beiden Fällen handelt es sich um die Ausrüstung zu einer unmittelbar folgenden kriegerischen Rettungstat. Auf eine solche Konkretisierung zielen die Worte ʿaśeh lekā ašär timṣāʾjādäkā x 7 unmittelbar hin; wenn schon die Sache selbst, die einmal folgte, um der Gesamtkonzeption willen jetzt weggebrochun und durch xi ersetz ist" (Stoebe, "Noch Einmal," 368).

king to go to battle and act in violent ways.⁶⁰ In the narrative, though, it is not violent battle that Saul seeks.

Indeed, Saul becomes not just another man (1 Sam 11:6), he seems to have a whole new inner disposition, a new heart (1 Sam 11: 9). We have already seen in Judges 9 and Judges 19 what happens in social and political situations when hearts are changed. The reader of this narrative should be prepared for the violence to break out if this narrative reads like those already encountered in our study.

A proverb is spoken concerning Saul here, "Is Saul also among the prophets?" David Gunn characterizes the proverb as neither positive nor negative in its view of Saul. The raving seems to be "an ambiguous gift."⁶¹ We have read the three-fold incongruity of 'man of god/seer/prophet' that starts the narrative introduction to Saul via Samuel. This proverb that Saul, too, is considered among the prophets continues to suggest the multivalent and liminal character that Saul is as we meet him. Like other characters in our study, he may be among many persons and with many titles, but these relationships only highlight the lack of specificity Saul has in any one role. Picking up on David Gunn's characterization and the literal roots of "ambiguity" we will wait to see where this raving, prophesying anointed one will "drive us around" in the narrative.

SAUL'S TEXTUAL INTRODUCTION AS KING

Saul arrives back home and is questioned by his uncle. We should not be surprised that the uncle is unnamed. In this narrative, only Samuel and Saul are named. We only know the family status of the uncle with reference to Saul.⁶² Saul is asked specifically what it was that Samuel said to Saul. Saul reveals only that Samuel had told him that the asses were found. In fact, the narrator tells us explicitly in verse 16, "[Saul] did not tell him anything of what Samuel had said about the kingship." Importantly, it is the *narrator* who introduces "kingship" to the narrative

---

60. Quinn-Miscall, *1 Samuel*. Alan Culpepper also reviews the use of 1 Sam 9:16 and 10:7 in his larger review of 1 Samuel 13, where he is trying to understand Saul's failure in his "vacillating, and failing to seize the opportunity to lead out in battle against the Philistines" (Culpepper, "Narrative Criticism," 37).

61. Gunn, *The Fate of King Saul*, 63

62. Steven L. McKenzie says of this encounter with the uncle that it is "odd because it is he [the uncle] rather than Saul's father who questions him and because the uncle appears unexpectedly, is nameless (not identified as Ner, 14.50), plays no other role in the stories about Saul, and is never mentioned again" (McKenzie, "The Trouble," 292).

complex even when the narrative has not yet used the term. The text did not narrate that Saul's anointing was about kingship and Samuel never calls Saul king. Saul attended a meal. Saul had become a different hearted man among the prophets. But only the narrator calls him king. The narrator seems to read back into this story from what he knows happens later when, in Gibeah, Saul restrains the people in the midst of their outcry from violence. As Hertzberg notes, "From the passing mention of the 'kingdom', we see that we [the readers] are being led on ... the hearer waits in burning expectation."[63]

SAUL'S LOT CASTING INTRODUCTION AS KING

Having thus explored this narrative up to a transition that takes place in 10:17 we will move back through this narrative again with a different "lens" attentive to our reading. We have been introduced, as it were, to the unnamed girls in this narrative. We heard their speech regarding the need for Saul and his servant to "hurry" but we do not know their names, nor will we ever know their names. They have assisted this journey for the lost donkeys. There seem to be several ways in which Saul, the Benjamite, is connected to similar persons and events we have already heard about in Judges 19–21.

In Judges 19 we also met an unnamed girl, the פִּילֶגֶשׁ of the Levite. In that narrative she never speaks as the unnamed girls in this unnamed location do with Saul, but her presence implies a sense of "hurry" when the Levite seeks her out. In Judges 19 when the Levite goes to the house of his father-in-law to seek the girl, he remains there for five days, feasting with the father-in-law before he heads out. It is an opportunity for eating, a verb that operates in both, Judges 19 and 1 Samuel 9–10. In the narrative of Judges 19, it is the servant who speaks to the Levite, exhorting him to go into the city of Jebus for the night saying in the text, "Let us turn aside to this town of the Jebusites and spend the night in it" (19:11), much as the servant of Saul exhort him to head into the city to look for the man of God/prophet/seer. Upon arrival not in Jebus, they are eventually treated to eat with the man who himself hailed from the country of Ephraim but who resided in Gibeah. The story of Judges 19 moves on with the men of the town showing up, moving us away from our connection to Saul and towards connection with the cities of the

---

63. Hertzberg, *1 Samuel*, 86.

plain at Sodom and Gomorrah, but they return to narrative connections with our text before the story is over.⁶⁴

In this narrative about Saul, we are told that he shall go from the presence of Samuel where he has eaten with thirty persons and his appointment there to be the one who restrains/retains for Israel will be marked by a curious pattern of meeting persons with three items: three men carrying three loaves of bread, three kids (goats) and a jar of wine. After this, in the words of Samuel, Saul is to go to Gibeah. In Judges 19–21 we have been in Gibeah. In Judges 19–21 after a series of failed attempts to come out as "one man" to destroy the Benjamites, we are told that an ambush has been laid for the men of Gibeah. Three items stand out here. First, the general nature of the ambush itself harkens us back to the violence of Judges 9 with Abimelech where he lays in ambush in order to destroy all the inhabitants of Shechem, leading only to his own demise. Second, the connections to Israel that have here come together as "one man" points us forward to Israel coming together as "one man" under Saul's rule. We shall read more on this in a moment. And third, when the Israelites do lay siege successfully to the Benjamites in Judges 20, we meet an odd pattern of numbering. We had been told on the first few days of battle that the tribes of Israel, whose numbers were 400,000, were routed before the Benjamites (who themselves had 26,000 fighting men, not including the inhabitants of Gibeah or the 700 chosen left-handers!) with 22,000 persons being killed on day one and 18,000 persons being killed on day two. On day three, however, the day that the Israelites ambush the Benjamites, we are told not once but twice in the narrative that the Benjamites killed "about thirty men" in battle (Judg 20:31 and 20:39). Whether or not we assume the numbers garnered for battle are exaggerations, it remains curious that the numbers are so high for days one and two, and so meager for day three! And, what is more, this reference to thirty is yet another curious way in which this narrative in Judges 19–21 connects with our narrative here with Saul On the night Samuel and Saul ate together, thirty nameless persons joined them (1 Sam 9:22). In both narratives we have the location of Benjamin and this unique character of the Benjamites acting and the Benjamite Saul who makes the difference in our narrative in 1 Samuel 9–10.

We left off the narrative with Saul having been recognized not as a king, not as a נגיד, but as one who was also among the prophets. Our

---

64. Fields, "The Motif."

argument remains that Saul is not yet the king nor has he been anointed as one[65], nor recognized by the people as one! Not yet.

1 SAMUEL 10:17—11:1

At 1 Sam 10:17 then we enter another location, another place where Samuel and Saul meet. This time it is at Mizpah. Samuel summoned the people for a public meeting. We have been to Mizpah before in our narratives. It was from this location that the "one man" assembly of Israel agreed to inflict violence upon Benjamin for their "evil thing" (Judg 20:3). Mizpah has been the site of declarations in the past. We will see that new declarations can herald from here again.

Samuel reminds the people of what YHWH had done for them, hearkening back to their important traditions of delivery from Egypt. Samuel reminds the people that they have asked for a king. For the first time since we met Saul, a character in the story names kingship for us.[66]

We move towards a scene where lots will be cast to recognize publicly this new office yet to be inaugurated in Israel. Casting of lots reflects the ambivalent nature of kingship. First Samuel 10:17–19 is viewed as negative towards kingship and verses 20–25 being favorable towards Saul. This narrative has literary connections to the choosing of Gideon as would-be-king, but who rejects it in his narrative.[67]

As kingship arrives, lots are cast.[68] We last encountered the casting of lots in Gibeah in Judg 20:9 where Gibeah was also being narrowed out. But here we have Saul, the person being singled out.[69] Benjamin is

---

65. We should be reminded that he has been anointed, and we might assume kingship; but the narrative does not use the language of king but of prince. We need to listen to the narrative for what the narrative says here and not assume "king" where it has not yet been used.

66. There are 57 total verses in 1 Samuel 9–11. We are 44 verses into the story, 80 percent into our narrative pericope, and two chapters removed from the request for a king before any character names kingship again.

67. Bruce Birch summarizes the earlier work of Wolfgang Richter in Birch, "The Choosing of Saul," 451.

68. Lindblom, "Lot-Casting in the Old Testament." Lindblom demonstrates that evidence suggests that lot casting could only give a yes or no answer to the question asked, thus making it unlikely that someone not present could have been chosen by lot.

69. Garsiel connects the choosing of lots here with the story of Aachan in Joshua 7. His connection, while intriguing, is dependent upon connections found with lots cast when Jonathan is singled out in 1 Samuel 14 for "troubling" the land (Garsiel, *The First Book of Samuel*, 82ff.).

selected, then the Matrites, then Saul son of Kish.[70] But this one who has already been singled out for us in 1 Samuel 9 where we met him, this tall man (we are reminded of his stature here in 10:23) is doing nothing less than hiding! Hiding among the baggage! Samuel proclaims his *difference*, "There is none like him among all the people" (1 Sam 10:24). Note carefully, Samuel does not call him or proclaim him king. Samuel had said he would cast lots and have the people assemble but he never proclaims Saul king. He notes he is the "chosen" man (1 Sam 10:24).

The people acclaim and shout (but do not yet serve or are ruled by) the one they say about, "Long live the king!" Finally, it appears, Saul has the title of king, the naming of king, but for our argument he has not yet functioned in a role that marks his kingship as effective.

At this time, we suggest, Saul is no more significant a king in his role than Abimelech was in Judges 9. In fact, we have a literary connection between Abimelech in that narrative and Saul in this narrative. In the Abimelech narrative, as we have seen, "outlaws" maraud in the land. Here, after being publicly proclaimed, the narrative comes to conclusion in fact with the words, "But some scoundrels said, 'How can this fellow save us?' So they scorned him and brought him no gift." We might be reminded here that when Gideon ruled, "everyone" gave him a gift. But here, not all bring gifts to Saul. Perhaps not all shout or recognize as one man that Saul is king. He is not yet king. He has had a private and public anointing, but his kingship has yet to be inaugurated. Inauguration of him, done to him, can only become effective about him once he has mechanized the scapegoat that allows for him to be both proclaimed and *inaugurated* as king.

Moshe Garsiel points out that Saul is not acting like a king here after he "starts his rule."[71] Of course, we have already stated that we do not believe he has yet been made king in the full and final sense of his inauguration and thereby we disagree that he is yet "ruling." Garsiel's analysis we believe to be faulted in that his rule has not started, as Garsiel states, but Garsiel's further analysis of the narrative here is correct with how and why Saul is not yet acting as king. Garsiel notes that Saul "does not behave in accordance with the 'custom of the king'; he does not

---

70. Birch, "The Choosing of Saul," 449: "The mention of Saul's family as that of Matri is a piece of information not given to us elsewhere and adds weight to the conclusion that this is a fragment of genuinely old tradition."

71. Garsiel, *The First Book of Samuel*, 70.

conscript men by force into the army (10:26–27), and (in the Masoretic texts) makes no claim for gifts from those who oppose him and is silent in the face of their contempt for his ability."[72] On this point Garsiel is correct. We argue that he is not acting like a king because he has not yet been *inaugurated* as one.

SAUL: THE DIFFERENT ONE

We return to that which we have just explored to draw out yet another insight. In our narrative we have seen how Saul is selected out by virtue of his stature—both in 1 Sam 9:1–2 and here in 10:23. He is the different one, even though he is in their midst. Oddly, though, Saul is hidden among the baggage. The only other time someone is said to be "hidden" (חבא) in the entire Deuteronomistic History is in the Abimelech narrative. It is Jotham who hid from the upstart pseudo-king. Jotham, of course, delivered his fable about the bramble. In our narrative here with Saul, unlike Abimelech—Saul is perhaps a "tree greater than all the other trees" that can provide shade by virtue of his stature. He is indeed a person who stands "over" the others.

The term used here for Saul among the "baggage" (1 Sam 10:22) is nowhere used before this in the Deuteronomistic History, but it is used after it, כלים. Of the 58 verses that use this noun in the rest of the Deuteronomistic History, nine verses are about items/utensils housed for their functional use in the Solomonic Temple or the House of the Lord. The most common meaning in the books of Samuel is with reference to military equipment so that the use here might "indicate that Saul was part of some kind of military entourage."[73] But it is also possible that Saul hides among the priestly utensils, pointing forward to the priestly role he will serve as the one who brings the scapegoating mechanism to Israel's history.

More central to the issue than the place of his hiding, however, is the means by which Saul is found as he hides. We should not be surprised that Saul is hiding when the lots are cast. There is another story in the Deuteronomistic History that precedes this one where, when lots are cast, the one upon whom the lots fall becomes the bearer of the ills and burdens of the community. In that narrative, of Aachan at Ai, he and

---

72. Ibid.
73. Klein, *1 Samuel*, 99.

his family are stoned then burned! Perhaps Saul knew to hide lest *he* be scapegoated as Aachan had been before him!

1 SAMUEL 11:1-15: SAUL'S INAUGURATION

Our review of 1 Samuel 9-10 is come to its conclusion at this point. From the outset, Saul is set apart as different. Numerous literary connections permeate this narrative with the narratives of pseudo-kingship and chaos that we have seen in Judges 9 and Judges 19-21. Saul has had a private and public anointing for the one who restrains/retains, but we have neither peace nor violence operative yet. Saul has the title "King" by some, but by others he is brought no gift.

We move now to the final biblical chapter we will study. We will argue that in this chapter, through the scapegoating mechanism, Saul differentiates in order to bring reconciliation for Israel and thus becomes king in their history. Chapter 11 becomes the crucial story for us about how Saul finally becomes king. Citing Wellhausen, Birch, Mayes, and others Nadav Na'aman writes, "It is accepted by many scholars that the old story in chap. 11 is in vv. 1-11, 15 and that this is the oldest story of how Saul was crowned by the people."[74] As the oldest story we have at least the greatest possibility of some historical reality underlying the emergence of monarchy in Ancient Israel.

Nahash of the Ammonites threatens a city of Israel. It is not just any city of Israel that Nahash threatens; it is none other than the city of Jabesh-Gilead, the city that failed to rise up against the Benjamites at Mizpah in Judges 19-21. In the narrative of Judges, because of their failure to participate in the violence being inflicted upon Benjamin, they became the subject of violence by their brothers. The cause of the violence was ostensibly to save the tribe of Benjamin by proscribing the virgins of Jabesh-Gilead as wives for the remaining 600 men of Benjamin who had returned from the Rock of Rimmon. Gibeah's crime led to their near destruction by their brother Israelites. That near destruction led to further total destruction of Jabesh-Gilead. It was brothers who threatened to exterminate their own brothers at Gibeah and at Jabesh-Gilead. In our narrative here with Nahash, this "serpent"[75] comes against Jabesh-Gilead

---

74. Na'aman, "The Pre-Deuteronomistic Story," 642.
75. Etymologically his name sounds like "serpent" in Hebrew.

and we must wonder if any one of Jabesh-Gilead's brother-Israelites will care to redeem this city they are already said to have destroyed.

Upon hearing the report in "Gibeah of Saul" (11:4) "all the people break out and weep." The news caused for public weeping, but no one was dispatched to tell Saul so that, had he already been king, he could now lead as king. This story, which we assert as being historically early and authentic, does not know about the private or public anointing or acclamation of Saul. Saul has not yet become king in the perspective of this story—and he was not named king in his encounter with Samuel at the banquet-sacrifice where he ate the priestly portion and with the bread offering received another priestly allotment.

Apart from the individual person, Hannah, in 1 Samuel 1, we have not heard this kind of weeping since the last time we heard mention of Gilead in Judg 20:1. What makes the introduction of Gilead significant in Judg 20:1 is the way it is singled out, as we noted already. In both these texts, Gilead and Benjamin are singled out in the stories. In Judg 20:1 we read how the men of Israel muster "as one man" to respond to the violence that has taken place in the rape, murder, and dismemberment of this concubine. And, the narrator of the text uses a conventional expression within the Hebrew Bible at first to explain how all Israel musters. We are told that "from Dan to Beersheba" the people assemble. This phrase is used numerous times in the bible as a means of describing "all the land"—the northernmost location of Dan to the southernmost location of Beersheba. What marks Gilead as noted in Judg 20:1 is that the narrator has told us, as we recall, that not only did all turn out, "but even Gilead." And here we have Gilead yet again in our narrative at the time of Saul's possibility of kingship.

If Saul had been made king, as we have been led to believe in chapter 10, we might expect him to be in some situation of pomp or circumstance, in his palace perhaps. But here, with the people weeping over the possibility of a city being cut off from Israel—much like what had taken place or potentially taken place in Judges 20–21, Saul is instead coming from the field where he had been driving his cattle! Saul is not in a palace. Saul is not leading armies. Saul is not taking or taxing. Rather, like the old man of Judg 19:16 he comes from his field. In that narrative the man had come up from his fields and on finding the Levite and his concubine offered them protection saying he would provide for their needs, which he was unable to do for the later ravaged concubine. In our narrative, Saul returns to the city much like the unnamed man in Gibeah, but now the narrator has caused our attention to fall on Saul, this new man from Gibeah, to see what protection he will offer, to see what victimage will result at his behest. The Levite's concubine met rape and murder. An outbreak of violence tore the people apart, brother-killing-brother in Israel when there was no king in Israel. But that was before Saul had been recognized for his difference, chosen by lot, and now emerges from his field.

The Levite dismembered his concubine and violence ravaged Israel. Violence escalated beyond its original call, leading to more violence, more rape, more kidnapping, more victimage. The reader of the story, we suggest would wonder in advance what melee will break forth.

Here, in Gibeah again the people weep. When the situation took place in a similar way in Judges 19–21, the people channeled their violence together "as one man" against their own kin. Here, though, we shall see that Saul effects a different though similar social outcome through the sacrificial scapegoat he offers and the threat of violence it carries.

Hearing the cry, Saul takes a yoke of oxen, and like the Levite, cuts them up into pieces and sends them throughout the territory of Israel. Like the Levite, Saul scatters a dismembered body to the inhabitants of the territory. In both stories messengers carry the dismembered pieces. Unlike the Levite who dismembers a human corpse, Saul takes live oxen and sacrifices them here. With the messengers carrying the dismembered, sacrificed body of the oxen Saul sends the message, "Such shall be done to the cattle of anyone who does not follow Saul and Samuel into battle!"[76]

The people respond by "coming out as one man" just as in Judges 20. Baruch Halpern cites with seeming cynicism that misses the point, "The notion that any bucolic butcher could assemble the league army of Israel, then lead it into battle, should raise an eyebrow at least? The savior-judges, by contrast, hold their positions through Yhwh's or the league's pleasure."[77] What we are suggesting is that Halpern misses the point entirely. Not only was it *not* by some means of "pleasure" that the former judges had held their positions, but more importantly as we have

---

76. Birch, *The Rise*, 55. Bruce Birch demonstrates that the inclusion of Samuel here is probably supplementary and might be built upon the introduction of Samuel to the entire narrative complex of 1 Samuel 1–7. See also McCarter, *1 Samuel*, 203.

77. Halpern, *The Constitution of the Monarchy*, 155.

demonstrated through the preceding exposition, Saul is not just "any bucolic butcher." On the other hand, in this story the "butchering" brings peace. So, in that sense, Halpern is correct, this is not just "any bucolic butcher" but the one whose sacrifice inaugurates kingship. Contrasting the "bucolic-ness" of this story, Martin A. Cohen writes that "there is no reason to doubt the essential historicity . . . with all the other facts at our disposal regarding the inception of the monarchy."[78] The readers of the story might wonder how their coming out here as one man will affect violence and fratricide, rape and pillage.

SAUL'S USE OF VIOLENCE, AND GIRARD

The narrator has deftly added a line of dialogue into our story that we dare not miss. After Saul has dismembered the oxen and called for the "mutual protection clauses of her treaty to be honored by Israel," and after mustering the troops, but before proceeding into battle, the narrator shifts our vision back to the crisis which has precipitated all this action.[79] In 11:10 our attention is drawn to the direct discourse the men of Jabesh-Gilead have with the Ammonites as they say, "Tomorrow we will give ourselves up to you and you may do to us whatever seems good to you." We are to be reminded in this statement of the days when there was no king in Israel, when everyone did what "was good" in their own eyes. And, as we have read through this narrative we have seen what that amounted to in Israel—it amounted to rape and anarchy, whole tribes being cut off in genocidal conflict. Not only that, but the earlier threat of the Ammonites had been to "gouge out" (11:2) the eye of the people in Jabesh-Gilead. In effect, then, here in 1 Samuel 11 the intent is to blind or mar the vision of the inhabitants of Jabesh-Gilead.[80] In Judges 19–21 we

---

78. Cohen, "The Role of the Shilonite Priesthood," 68. Cohen believes the emergence of monarchy fits well the Philistine threat of the tenth century BCE. He also believes the evidence in the Bible demonstrates that the monarchy "was subordinated ideologically to the Shilonite priesthood" (ibid., 69). While our concern is not explicitly with the issues that Cohen outlines, it is important to this study to note that we are not alone in seeing a real history that lies behind this text. Further, like Cohen, we believe the bond between priesthood and monarchy is intimate indeed.

79. Polzin, "HWQY' and Covenantal Institutions," 240.

80. Omanson and Ellington, *A Handbook on the First and Second Books of Samuel*. We suggest the issue of vision in the narrative as pertaining to social vision that plays into our narrative here. And this we do believe is within the scope of the narrative. Omanson and Ellington note that "no reason is given for wanting to gouge out the right

had seen already the way that night functioned to effectively cloud their sight, without gouging out their eyes, "as was good" in that day when there was no king.[81]

Further, we suggest that the narrator is intentionally playing with the speech of the old man from Jabesh-Gilead. In Judg 19:24 the old man said he would "bring out" (יצא) the women to the "sons of belial" gathered at his door. Here, the inhabitants of Jabesh Gilead promise to "come out" (יצא) to the Ammonites who symbolically wait outside their door. "The crucial difference is that in 1 Samuel 11.10 the citizens are not really offering themselves up to the enemy for their right eyes to be gouged out. They have already been told that they will be delivered by Saul and his forces the next day, because Saul has rallied the league."[82] And, I note, Saul's rally of the league is not by divine sign. Saul does not amass troops who come to him by the appeal of YHWH. Saul's army amasses as a result of his scapegoat threat.

Saul proceeds to divide the men into three columns and we see echoed here the actions of another almost king. In this study we only quickly met Gideon in chapter three, where he served as the person who would not become king. The reason the people of Israel beckoned him to be king was as a result of a battle he fought against Midian. It is of merit that the battle that Saul begins to fight here is likened to the battle Gideon fought in Judg 6:34–35 and 7:16–19. Narrative coherence between these stories and 1 Sam 11:6, 11 operate around the ideas of sending messengers, dividing in three columns, watching, and laying at

---

eyes" in the narrative. At the same time, they suggest that since "most soldiers held their shield in their left hand, blocking the view of the left eye, they would not be able to see the enemy well in a fight if their right eye was blinded" (ibid., 225).

81. Stuart Lasine highlights similar themes in "Guest and Host." Specifically in footnote 17, on page 54, he draws attention in his review of Genesis 19 and Judges 19—that both of these stories are preceded with someone's doing right in their own eyes, followed by a scene of rape or abuse. In this story of Samson, though, that which is good or right in one's eyes is categorically not followed by rape or abuse, but by victory! "In Gen. 16.6 Abram tells Sarai to do what is good in her eyes to Hagar, whereupon Sarai 'abuses her' or 'treats her so violently' that she has to flee from her mistress. The verb used here ('*innâ*) is also used to describe the rape of the concubine in Judge. 9.24. In Judges 16.3, Samson chooses a wife from the Philistines, because she is 'the right one in his eyes'. Although Yahweh is actually behind Samson's choice (16.4), Samson's choosing on the basis of what is right in his eyes soon leads to violence, and eventually to his eyes being poked out" (Lasine, "Guest and Host," 54).

82. Ibid., 43.

the edge of camp, as Garsiel points out in fuller detail.[83] Gideon was not king and our analysis has demonstrated only a pseudo-kingship for Abimelech and its failure, but Saul will become king.[84]

Having divided the troops into columns of three, Saul and the men he has mustered defeat the Ammonite threat. Survivors scatter, though— it is not genocide nor is this an event of *ḥerem*/the ban in Israel. Saul and the men he has mustered as "one man" have aptly defeated the threat from Nahash. Where the dismembering of the concubine in Judges 19 had led to the near annihilation of Jabesh-Gilead, here the dismembering of the oxen and the mustering of troops leads to its salvation. And the act will inaugurate one more thing for Israel.

It is not truly an army that Saul has mustered, the forces are strong, some 330,000 strong if we take the text at full value. But to be an army, one needs to first be a King, and that is not yet what Saul is.

Saul mustered the people of Israel as "one man." In 11:7 Saul has all the persons come out as one man, but at the end of the narrative describes survivors scattering, each running off by himself. The reference here is to the surviving Ammonites, and must be noted, but it highlights the lack of cohesiveness that holds them together in the narrative at this point. Each person escapes alone. It was a mob that descended upon the Levite in Judges 19 and the mob violence prevailed in the remaining violence that took place in Judges 19–21. But here, after the king acts the threat of the mob is turned around completely with the mob being dis-assembled, each man now alone.

Saul sacrificially victimized not a person but the yoke of oxen. This scapegoating effect warns of the threat of further violence that could be spread. But, having now defeated the external threat of violence, the Ammonites, the Israelites respond now with an act described only here in all of the Hebrew Bible (and of course only here in the Deuteronomistic

---

83. Garsiel, *The First Book of Samuel*, 80ff.

84. With reference to the coherence of Gideon and Saul here Garsiel writes: "Even though some of the motifs and shared phrasing mentioned in the discussion and appearing in the paired texts above can be matched elsewhere in the Bible, or can be accounted for in some other way, the sheer accumulation of parallels creates an association for the reader, and it is hard not to conclude that a comprehensive comparison between Saul's personality and actions and those of his predecessors (especially Gideon) formed part of the author's intention from the outset" (ibid., 81). And of course while we've chose to focus on the specific issues of Abimelech in our narrative, we agree here with Garsiel that the accumulation of parallels ties us with the predecessors of Saul, particularly for us with Abimelech.

History), they inaugurate their first king and confirm kingship a reality in Israel.[85]

The reader of these stories might expect that the "violent" rampage of the Ammonites will lead to further violence within Israel. We might be reminded here of how the violence of Abimelech did not end with Shechem being destroyed but had to continue to Thebez as well, leading to his own destruction. We might be reminded here of how when the Benjamites were routed in Judges 19–21, the violence did not end there but was carried out in other ways, through destruction of those who did not muster at Mizpah and the kidnap and rape of the dancers at Shiloh. So we expect the continuation of violence here.

We had been told in 10:27 that some persons who did not accept the new role and anointing of Saul had said, "How can this fellow save us?" In this text, 11:12 it is reported by the crowd that some have said, "Shall Saul be king over us?" And the violent men who have followed Saul "as one man" cry out "Hand the men over and we will put them to death!" The reader, remembering Abimelech and the Levite, would expect the violence to continue. In fact, we are textually assumed to believe the violence will continue for these same phrase starts all the violence we saw in Judges 19. It was in attempt to avenge the death of the concubine that the tribes of Israel cry out "Give up the men (the repugnant characters who raped the concubine) that we may put them to death" (Judg 20:13). And here in 1 Sam 11:15 the same words are cause for what we would expect as more violence, "Give up the men, that we may put them to death." Violence, we expect, will break forth.

But it does not.

Saul, the one whose sacrifice of oxen mustered the people as one man, replies "No man shall be put to death this day!" (11:13). And no person of Israel dies in this narrative, not 70 sons, not 30 men, no Gaal, no inhabitants of Shechem, no persons in Thebez, no pseudo-king, no Benjamites, no virgins of Mizpah, no dancers at Shiloh—only a yoke of

---

85. With respect to the verb used here that we will translate "inaugurate" David Gunn says that the kingship is "'renewed' (confirmed?)" in this event (Gunn, *The Fate of King Saul*, 64). Gunn passes over as a blip that issue most central to our thesis: in this moment monarchy arrives in Israel. Andre LeMaire too misses the point that this study argues for—that it is only in this moment that Saul becomes king at this event of his inauguration. He writes, "In each of these accounts, Saul is installed and anointed as king by Samuel" (LeMaire, "The United Monarchy," 87).

oxen has been slain. The violence within Israel has ended with this Saul who retains/restrains.[86]

David Gunn calls Saul in this moment, "magnanimous."[87] Ralph Klein says that here "Saul himself emerges as a savior."[88] Peter Miscall notes this is "Saul's finest hour."[89] "This is the true climax of the narrative."[90] "By granting amnesty he also exercised responsibilities . . . in the sacral, legal realm."[91] Saul is on the cusp of kingship, acting in sacral realms. And the magnanimity of Saul in this moment is not lost to the larger witness of the Deuteronomistic Historian. Not only does Saul save from destruction on this day, but in tribute to Saul, the people of Jabesh-Gilead redeem the corpse of Saul from certain vandalizing corruption at his death (1 Sam 31:11–13).

We read: לכו ונלכה הגלגל ונחדש שם המלוכה׃

For the first and only time in the narrative of the Hebrew Bible we hear these words coming from the one who has anointed privately and publicly this נגיד, "Come, let us go to Gilgal and there inaugurate the

---

86. Sholom J. Kahn cites a rabbinic reading of this text that does not cohere with any of the textual tradition or with the argument of this study. Kahn writes, "After the victory, his seeming magnanimity to his former opponents (11:13) is interpreted as follows by Rabbi Levi ben Gershon: 'There shall not a man be put to death this day: Perhaps they killed them after this day, or perhaps Saul said: "There shall not a man be put to death this day in a cunning fashion to cause those people to escape from Israel by showing them that it was his intention to kill them the next day"'" (Kahn "The Samuel-Saul Story as Drama," 10). I quote this text here not to comment on its accuracy—it is conjecture by Rabbi Levi ben Gershon. Instead, I quote it to note the tendency of human persons to read the as sanctioning violence in its spiraling rivalrous-mimetic-contagion. Rabbi Levi ben Gershon's reading then is so typical of, and correctly typical of, mimesis. It is also, however, categorically wrong for understanding how Girard will help us see the rise of monarchy and the rise of Saul as monarch as a break from violence through scapegoating.

87. Gunn, "A Man Given Over to Trouble," 91.

88. Klein, *1 Samuel*, 98.

89. Quinn-Miscall, *1 Samuel*, 66.

90. McCarthy, "The Inauguration," 404.

91. Klein, *1 Samuel*, 108. The full content in the Klein commentary is worthy of full reference: "By granting amnesty he also exercised responsibilities (as future king?) in the sacral, legal realm. According to 2 Sam 19:23 David refused to execute Shimei, who had insulted him and hurled stones at him in connection with Absalom's revolt, since it was the day on which he had again become king, but in 1 Sam 11 there is no *explicit* reference to Saul's coronation day as providing the reason for amnesty. The positive evaluation of Saul's performance in the sacral, legal realm is reverse by Samuel in chaps. 13 and 15" (ibid.; italics original).

monarchy." And all the people go to Gilgal and there they all—no outlaws, or scoundrels—not at the threat of violence against them—they all declare Saul king "to the face of"/before the Lord. The "fact that the verse describes the elevation of Saul's election as something carried out quite spontaneously by the people, and not by Samuel, gives it an indisputable aura of authenticity."[92] This was not, we argue, a renewal of kingship in Israel but its genesis. As with Hertzberg, "originally it will have been no 'renewal', but an institution of kingship."[93] Klein notes that this "one of the oldest and most authentic [events] about Saul."[94]

As in other narratives in the Deuteronomistic History, Gilgal becomes the place of assembly after the crisis, the place for solemn activities (Josh 5:10; 10:43).[95] Now it is the place to meet after a new kind of crisis, to formulate a new kind of sacred activity, the inauguration of a king. In these actions, "Saul demonstrates the difference between the way a disaster is prevented by a newly chosen king and the way a disaster is avenged by an irresponsible, callous, and self-absorbed man who lives at a time in which there is no king in Israel."[96] Lasine is correct, there is difference in these stories because Saul is the difference maker and the one who ceases the "avenging" rivalries that take place with a group of people. At this time in the story we agree with Edelman who writes that "it is only after the official act of coronation that kingship exists as fact."[97]

The argument of this study is that what happens in and with this inauguration of Saul is not an extension of the rule of the judges that preceded him. His is not simply a charismatic rule based on some form of new political control. The emergence and unique inauguration of Saul here is a new event for Israel based out of violence that is used to unite the brothers of Israel around sacrifice.[98]

92. Mayes, "The Period of the Judges," 325.
93. Hertzberg, *1 Samuel*, 94.
94. Klein, *1 Samuel*, 104.
95. The textual specificity to Gilgal is unique in that in this verse (11:15) "there" is repeated three times. It is "there" "before the Lord" that they proclaim Saul king and proclaim other sacrifices. The Ammonites had been sent off "each alone," but here a united people "celebrate" the unity of the kingdom brought about by a king they inaugurate.
96. Lasine, "Guest and Host," 37.
97. Edelman, "The Deuteronomist's Story," 208.
98. Here we stand in contrast to W. J. Dumbrell, who states, "As for the figure of Saul, the continuance of the office of Judge in his truncated kingship is clear from the

The violent sacrifice of oxen and the presence and person of Saul that curbed violence leads to the full and formal inauguration of kingship in Israel. From the chaos of these stories emerges a unique reconciliation in Israel, through the violent sacrificial scapegoating of this King. And "Saul and all the men of Israel held a great celebration there" (1 Sam 11:15).

1 SAMUEL 12—AFTER SACRIFICE AND THE END OF VIOLENCE

What follows this narrative that we have tracked so closely in 1 Samuel 9–11 is another speech complex in the Deuteronomistic History. Like the speech complex we encountered in 1 Samuel 8 we read in chapter 12 how Samuel gave yet another speech. Passing over this speech-complex and assuming its editorial insertion by a late hand in the Deuteronomistic History, we read in 1 Sam 13:1 that "Saul was ___ years old when he became king, and he reigned over Israel two years."[99] This, it seems, is the likely extension of the story we have just ended. Saul was inaugurated as king, they celebrate and we have record of his kingship. Interestingly, the record of his age and the length of his reign has left us with a corrupted text. The fact is that we do not know when Saul began to reign or the length of his reign. All we have is the inauguration of his reign, at least to this point in the story.[100]

---

narrative of 1 Samuel 11. Such a narrative well illustrates a belief in the tenacity of charismatic rule and the reluctance of Israel to depart from it. The replacement of the office of Judge by kinship and the struggle which ensued for political control . . . displays the view that judgeship and kingship were incompatible, and that, at least in Samuel's view, kingship was a political degeneration from earlier ideals" (Dumbrell, "'In Those Days,'"26). It is interesting to note that in Dumbrell's estimation "Judge" is capitalized in English and "kingship" is not. This seems to tip toward his own hand about his view of kingship in Israel. And, contra our view, he sees kingship in nominal significance, and that this narrative is not really about kingship, which we argue emphatically against. The inauguration of Saul is a new event in Israel's history, the wording and context used only here in all of the Old Testament story.

99. The verse is problematic in its structure in the MT and LXX.

100. My suggestion is that the actual reign/extent of Saul's leadership has been lost or confused in this narrative, but the history of his relieving the violent crisis by sacrificial scapegoating has remained. As noted previously in this study, Simcha Shalom Brooks believes the text has been lost or confused here with reference to the story of Saul's end of kingship and his leaving behind Mephibosheth. Brooks suggests that the reason for the dating of Saul's reign here was intentional: "The confusion between the two chronologies is probably the deliberate work of a later redaction. Its purpose was

Saul and Kingship

What we have seen in this narrative introducing us to Saul is the voluminous literary connections that compel us to consider again the literary issues operating in the Deuteronomistic History. We explored in chapter 2 the compositional perspectives on and the history of arguments related to the Deuteronomistic History since Martin Noth. In these stories we have read together, Abimelech, the Levite and violence in Israel, and Saul as monarch there is a history of chaos that is restrained and brought to Reconciliation through the Sacrificial Office of Kingship.

The Deuteronomistic History is ambivalent about kingship—not because the Deuteronomistic History is anti-monarchial or pro-monarchial as some would hope or want us to believe, but because kingship itself reflects the chaos of an earlier period that is reconciled through violent sacrifice.[101] The peace that kingship brings comes with a cost,

---

not only to give a false chronology for Saul and Ishbosheth, but also to ridicule both of them, to belittle Saul, on the one hand by making him a one-year-old baby, and, on the other, to make Ishbosheth look ridiculous by making him a forty-year-old who was still under the guardianship of his uncle" (Brooks, "Was There a Concubine in Gibeah?" 37.

101. Before we end our analysis of these chapters, we pause to make specific reference to a section of Mark Brettler's work on Judges, specifically Judges 19, where he deals with the issue of "Polemic and Allusion in Judges 19," *The Book of Judges*, 88. Brettler demonstrates in his narrative a similar set of correspondences that we have pointed out here in Judges with the narrative of Saul in 1 Samuel 11. He writes about these correspondences in a way that is demonstrably unique from our analysis here. We make reference to it here at the end of this chapter, not to weaken our argument presented here, but to show the inadequacies of Brettler's position. The allusions between these stories, argues Brettler, function to "make Saul look bad." "[Saul] comes from a tribe, indeed from a city of rapists and murderers, who are unwilling to own up to their wrongdoings. Through these allusions, chapter 19 [of Judges] in particular serves to de-legitimate Saul even before he becomes king." But we believe Brettler reads the text in the wrong way. Quite the contrary, rather than bringing violence as had happened in Judges 19, Saul redirects the violence. Saul is not seen in our narrative here as some sort of lowlife character from a city of rapists. Instead, his outsider role allows him to be the one who acts to redirect the violence of the narrative not towards a woman, not against a brother, but to a yoke of oxen so that violence can be quelled. Contra Brettler, then, we have attempted to show that the Judges 19 narrative set us up to see Saul as the hero of the narrative not necessarily because the narratives are pro- or anti-Saul, though, but because the narratives are "pro–sanctioned-violence" in sacrificial form to redirect violence from butchering another person or tribe within Israel. Brettler also points out the connections to the Sodom themes that appear in Judges 19, as we've already demonstrated in this study. About the connections with Genesis 19, Judges 19 and 1 Samuel 11 Brettler writes that these aspects are "being alluded to here; the sins of the people of Gibeah, namely Saul, are heinous and the house of Saul deserves the fate of Sodom; no future descendent of Saul possibly deserves to reign." That Brettler has this all figured out in such simplistic form is undermined by the next statement of his argument states,

a victim. So while there is peace to rejoice in, to celebrate, and that we might call pro-monarchial, there is violence, too—that reminds us of the death and destruction, the victimage, the scapegoating and about this, the author of the Deuteronomistic History wants us to not forget, to remember, that which is not to be celebrated about kingship and monarchy, hence the necessary incorporation of the so called anti-monarchial aspects of kingship.

"It is not clear when such a polemic would originate." And before the paragraph is over Brettler will state that a positive Saulide ideology remained alive in the post-Exilic period. The fact that "much later rabbinic texts also seem to preserve traditions that laud Saul" is for Brettler "quite surprising given the ultimate victory of David in the canon, and might suggest a continuing Saulide royal ideology." In short order then, Brettler notes the positive ideology associated with Saul that remained alive, but discounts it entirely by his reading of the texts' coherence that we believe to be a misreading. That is, this study argues that these texts do not serve the purpose of delegitimating Saul but in fact set the stage for his reconciliation of conflict and chaos in Israel that sets the appropriate stage for him to be inaugurated as the first king over Israel. Contra Brettler's, our reading has aimed to convince us that Saul is the appropriate one to be inaugurated as king because, though he is from the city of rapists and murderers who are unwilling to undo their wrongdoing, Saul turns the community from wrongdoing and saves his brothers from their annihilation.

6

Assessing a Girardian Hermeneutic within this Study

SUMMARY ASSESSMENT AND LITERARY REVIEW

THE FOCUS OF THIS study has two aspects. First, to assess the literary character, coherence, and connections that operate in the narrative of the Deuteronomistic History with the texts we have examined thus far. In and through the context of the preceding chapters we have accomplished this task. Alongside the literary analysis that is now complete, we have hinted at the second aspect of this study, to assess the extent to which the hypothesis of René Girard helps us to read these texts.

We have argued across the previous three chapters for narrative connections and patterns of locations, places, and persons that demonstrate how the passages connect. Our analysis wove together connections in the stories while only hinting at how we might understand the import of these stories in Girardian ways. By analogy, what we did in the previous three chapters was the "needlework" task of examining the threads that have connected these stories. As if we might turn over a tapestry and look at the back of it to see the weave of the fabric, the individual threads that connect it together. In this chapter I aim by analogy, to turn the tapestry over and step back from the narrative and show broader patterns that have emerged from the threads that have made up our narrative. By nature then, this chapter will include the threads of the narratives we have examined to this point. More importantly, the threadwork of the preceding chapters will now allow us to see what picture the tapestry contains and not simply the threads that hold it together.

That which has been examined to this point in the study is itself already a new and unique contribution to the study of the books of Judges and 1 Samuel. We are now able to understand and discern new issues of emerging kingship with a closer examination of these texts as literary units.

Again by analogy, as we step back to look at the pattern the narrative has woven for us, we will aim to show that, in addition to the literary coherence of these stories, there is a second way to review and examine these narratives using the formulation of René Girard. The import of this study, then, will be both its contribution to our literary reading of Judges and 1 Samuel and for how it suggests another application of Girardian Theory in another literary text.

We will argue in this summary chapter that the literary connections that have been outlined in the preceding chapters point towards a common desire for people to live in peace with one another. In the midst of this desire to live in peaceful ways, though, violence continually breaks out. In our texts, Abimelech attempted to start a kingship, but it enacted violence that did not bring peace and only killed brothers and then others. In the midst of Levitical issues, the Danites seek peace, but steal and murder. Then the Levite himself along with his concubine becomes the victim of violence escalating to anarchy. It is only in Saul who connects the priestly roles with the ambivalence they inherently possess in sacrifice that kingship emerges. The rivalry that had preceded his inauguration is quelled, at least for a time.

GIRARDIAN PERSPECTIVES FOR JUDGES AND 1 SAMUEL

In the literary analysis of our Biblical texts I have at times pointed forward to themes and issues that will find their explanation in this chapter. Throughout this study I have pointed toward the Girardian issues that I will now seek to explicate. In the former chapters I have connected literary issues in the stories, I have attempted to (both) point toward this chapter and not make the preceding an exclusively Girardian schema for reading the narratives. I have waited to present a full reading of Girard until this section of the study in order to allow the literary reading to have its full hearing. The reader should be aware that this chapter will proceed on the foundation of the full reading that has already been established.

DELIMITATIONS OF A GIRARDIAN METHODOLOGY

Arriving now at this review and analysis of Girard we want to offer two points of clarification by means of delimitation. One, it is not our intent here, after having read the narratives, to lay over them a sort of "Girardian Grid" that says, "This text is Girardian because we can connect these dots." It may appear that is what we are doing in this chapter and while we will be attempting to draw distinct connections between Girardian theory and the stories we have examined, we want to articulate again that which has been demonstrated in the heart of this study; these stories share coherence and literary tradition regardless whether Girard helps us read them. Second, while we do apply a Girardian hermeneutic here that we do believe helps us read the cultural issues of kingship emerging in Israel's history, we do not mean to suggest naively that this then "proves" how kingship emerged in Israel's history. Nor do we mean to suggest that after having applied a Girardian hermeneutic to these texts we can now say there is no other way to understand the emergence of kingship and sacrifice in Israel's history. Rather, we hope to demonstrate that the insights of Girard find important confluence with our stories, even as the insight of Girard has found important confluence with many other stories. Our texts help support the theory of Girard as much as Girardian theory helps us understand our texts.

In this way, then, the argument of this study does not "prove Girard is correct" nor does it "prove this is what happened in Israel's history." It does, however, add another text to the many studied with a Girardian Hermeneutic, that suggests the import of Girardian hypothesis is perhaps as large, as inclusive as some might argue.[1] Our argument here will not be for or against the largeness of Girardian theory and applicability, but rather, with regard to this text we will say, Girard helps us read these texts in new and important ways.[2]

---

1. One of the chief critiques, if not the chief critique, of Girard is the all-inclusiveness of his method. That is, Girard suggests that all issues about all cultures can be understood through his hermeneutic. Certainly John Milbank critiques Girard for this (Milbank, "Stories of Sacrifice," 46).

2. It has been already noted, but to reaffirm, this study is not the first to apply a Girardian hermeneutic to stories found within the Deuteronomistic History. Nor is it the only to read the stories of Judges 19–21 and 1 Samuel 11. It is, however, the first attempt to connect these stories to Judges 9 and to connect them specifically and most deliberately to the ambivalent crisis that Saul resolves in sacrifice, commencing in his inauguration as king. The other works are distinguished in their own right, and the

As a starting point, "In *Reading in Communion* Stephen E. Fowl and L. Gregory Jones address the variety of approaches toward biblical interpretation in terms of *communities of interpretation* and of *interpretive interests* [italics original]. Such an approach acknowledges the existence of multiple approaches, but avoids the error of having to claim that one, and only one of those approaches is 'correct.'"[3]

Our Girardian reading will be unique from McGinnis' reading of 1 Samuel, but like it, will suggest another approach to reading this text correctly. We intend that our reading of these texts will offer "correct" ways to discern the importance of these stories.

SUMMARY OF GIRARDIAN METHOD

The broad scope of Girard's theory and its extensive use can be discerned in a growing corpus of texts within a divergent field of disciplines. We will proceed with the assumption that a full-reading of Girard's work consistently points us to certain fundamental concepts within his theory that are pointed out by numerous scholars in their review of Girard's work.[4] Most common among the issues outlined by reviewing Girard's work and summaries of it is the attention to certain categories: desire and mimesis, rivalry and conflict, and violent resolution through scapegoating. Each of these will be reviewed here in brief. These serve as the basis of understanding a Girardian literary reading and a Girardian social theory or anthropology of culture. What is important in Girardian scholarship is the nature by which scapegoating not only leads to peace, but leads to ritualized peace. What is less often seen in the work of Girard or in reviews of Girard, is the means by which scapegoating leads to ritualized peace *in the form of sacral kingship*, which is at the heart of the presentation of this study.

---

work whose argument is most proximate to our own but distinct from it are cited here: Schwager, *Must There Be Scapegoats?*; Williams, *The Bible, Violence, and the Sacred*.

3. McGinnis, "Swimming with the Divine Tide," 241.

4. Numerous scholars, books, and articles could be cited here. In fact, several pages could be devoted to a bibliography of Girard's work and summaries or reactions to it. The bibliography of this study will serve as the basis for the articles reviewed that could be cited here but for the sake of space will remain in the bibliography.

GIRARDIAN ANTHROPOLOGY[5]

Throughout this study we have used key terms to point to our understanding of René Girard's hypothesis for emerging culture through scapegoating. In the process we have assumed much of the reader regarding the essential framework for understanding Girard. There are numerous accessible resources that lay out models, ideas and frameworks for understanding Girard's perspectives many that are cited within this study and within the bibliographic resources. Additionally, a full reading of Girard's perspective would certainly require more than just summary statements about what he believes as presented in a multitude of secondary sources. Here we will present the summary position of Girard in outline alongside primary source reading from Girard himself. This will not suffice to summarize all that Girard has to say, but should demonstrate the import of his work in categories significant for the purposes of this study.

We will review Girard's understanding of human persons and formation of culture through an assessment of desire, rivalry, conflict and violence, and conflict resolution in scapegoating.

DESIRE AND MIMESIS[6]

Girard understands that fundamentally all human desires are imitated. Girard understands that humans learn language, for example, by means of imitating others who speak in their hearing. Human persons learn how to act and react based on imitating those around them. Indeed, all human learning is acquired as persons imitate or copy those around

---

5. Our review of Girard within the scope of this study will highlight the means by which Girardian insight lines up with the essential story we have read from Judges to 1 Samuel. It is obvious that Girard's work is not accepted by all scholars as the answer for understanding myth, hominization, culture, ritual, or sacrifice. As a point of fact, the scope of Girardian hypothesis that addresses all these issues is one of the chief critiques of his work. That is, those who disagree with Girard tend to do so for the meta-quality of his hypothesis of answering so many questions.

6. "Desire" is the term we will use here, and it is the common term used by Girard and others who use or critique Girard's work. It should be noted though that Girard is specific in his later work that the term "desire" is not the best term to be used because it is too often associated with a sexual or erotic need as a result of the popularity of Freudian work. In an interview with James G. Williams, Girard suggests other terms to replace it without naming one as uniquely better (Williams and Girard, "Epilogue: The Anthropology of the Cross," 268).

them. It is not the case that human persons learn physiological desires through imitation, as if one needs to see someone else hungry to know that they themselves are hungry. Instead, the means of fulfillment for the physiological need is learned through imitation. The body is hungry as a function of physiological need but a person learns how to satisfy the hunger by copying those around them, eating what they eat or drinking what they drink. Imitation is a necessary condition for living life. The lion cub imitates its mother or father as an infant human child copies her mother or father.

What marks a Girardian understanding of desire occurs not so much in the root physiological aspects of life, but in the objects of desire. That is, Girard understands that human persons can acquire a desire for not only the same *kinds* of things to satisfy their desire, they can acquire a desire for *the* same thing. Girard suggests that persons attain their desires for things by imitating others. But, the objects of desire can be sought after in such a way that what is at stake is not a mere "copying" or "imitating," but "mimetic desire." For understanding the nature of imitation that takes place, we will henceforth use the term mimesis and mimetic desire since it better serves the nuance of meaning that Girard suggests for his work.

Girard developed his understanding of mimetic desire from his study of the novels of Cervantes, Dostoyevsky, Flaubert, Proust, and Stendhal as detailed more fully in his early published work, *Deceit, Desire and the Novel*.[7] The character of Don Quixote in the novel with the same name is a primary example of how Girard understands desire to be mediated. Don Quixote's quest stems from his mimetic desire to become like his model, Amadis the Gaul. Girard distinguishes "appropriative" or "acquisitive" mimesis for this kind of mimetic desire, seeking the objects of desire by imitation. This is to be distinguished from another understanding of mimesis which is "metaphysical" in nature. That is, metaphysical desire is the imitation of some person not for the sake of the object they possess (or seek to possess) but for some more transcendent state of becoming the person that has the object. In order to do this, though, they must in effect become the person who has the desire—the subject who seeks the object they seek to possess. About Don Quixote's quest Girard writes, "Chivalric passion defines a desire *according to the Other* [sic], opposed to this desire *according to*

7. Girard, *Deceit, Desire and the Novel*.

Assessing a Girardian Hermeneutic within this Study

Oneself [sic] that most of us pride ourselves on enjoying. Don Quixote and Sancho borrow their desires from the Other in a movement which is so fundamental and primitive that they completely confuse it with the will to be Oneself [sic]."[8]

Girard describes the idea of children playing on together with a room full of toys, where more than one child desires not just any toy, but the same singular toy another child possess in *Violence and the Sacred*.[9] Gil Bailie extends the picture that Girard suggests in more detail. In so doing, he illustrates mimetic desire for us in the following way:

> Imagine a scene. A small child is sitting alone in a nursery that has a couple of dozen toys scattered about it. He sits there rather dreamily, exhibiting only a casual interest in the toy that just happens to be nearby. Another child comes into the nursery and surveys the room. He sees the first child and a great number of toys. There will come a moment when the second child will choose a toy. Which of the toys will he most likely find interesting? The first parent you meet will be able to tell you. It will likely be the toy with which the first child seems to be interested, although the first child's interest is as yet only a casual one . . . (this scene continues in footnote)[10]

---

8. Ibid., 4 (italics original).

9. Girard, *Violence and the Sacred*, 146.

10. Bailie, *Violence Unveiled*, 116–18: "All parents have seen this sort of thing happen hundreds of times. Dealing with the resulting squabbles is an almost constant aspect of child-rearing. We joke about it. We shrug our shoulders. We even try to exploit it in order to elicit the behavior we want. But we almost never ask what this familiar phenomenon tells us about desire, and about the little bundle of [desires] that we like to call the self. Imagine, now, what most parents would predict. The second child becomes interested in the toy for which the first child has shown an interest. The second child reaches for the toy. What happens? The first child's nonchalance vanishes in an instant. Suddenly, he clings to the toy for dear life. Extremely vexed, the first child says, 'I had that!' His intense reaction arouses in the second child a desire for the toy vastly more powerful than the rather mild one with which he had first reached for it. The two children simply feed each other's desire for the toy by demonstrating to each other how desirable it is. Each further intensifies the desire of his rival by threatening to foreclose the possibility of possession. As the emotions rise, the opportunity for parental compromise declines rapidly. Each child treats the suggestion that he take turns playing with the toy as a betrayal by the adult who makes it. If a perfect facsimile of the toy is produced so that both children can have identical toys, the dispute may well sputter out, but each child's interest in the no longer disputed toy will in all likelihood begin to cool at the same time. As long as the conflict remains unresolved, the suggestion that both children bear some responsibility for the squabble will be resolutely rejected. Each child will be certain that the other is the sole cause of the conflict . . . In children old enough

Girard distinguishes his work from others when he rejects what he considers to be the Romantic idea (the Romantic lie) that humans possess a desire for being that is independent and autonomous. About this Girard writes in *Violence and the Sacred*: "Once his basic needs are satisfied (indeed, sometimes even before), man is subject to intense desires, though he may not know precisely for what. The reason is that he desires being, something he himself lacks and which some other person seems to possess. The subject thus looks to that other person to inform him of what he should desire in order to acquire that being. If the model, who is apparently already endowed with superior being, desires some object, that object must surely be capable of conferring an even greater plenitude of being."[11]

The force or power of mimesis is distinguished in Girardian thought from what he characterizes as "external mediation" and "internal mediation."[12] When the subject who desires to be like the model

---

to be verbal, something of the following dialogue can be safely predicted:

FIRST CHILD: I had it first!

SECOND CHILD: You weren't playing with it. I wanted it first!

FIRST CHILD: No you didn't. I wanted it first!

SECOND CHILD: No, I wanted it first!

Now, let us ask: who's right? Who wanted it first? The astonishing thing is, we cannot completely answer that question. Should either of the children be told that his desire for the toy was aroused by the desire of the child who is now his rival for it, he would vehemently deny it. In a way, he would be right, inasmuch as there has probably been no conscious attempt to copy. That is why the term 'imitation' is not entirely satisfactory. It implies a degree of conscious intention that the term 'mimesis' does not necessarily imply. The most glaringly obvious fact about the squabble in the children's nursery, the one that is so familiar we hardly notice it, is the very one that the two children will most vehemently deny and whose implications we adults seem predisposed to ignore, namely, mimetic desire. Clearly, each child's desire for the toy evoked and reinforced the desire of his rival ... Should it be pointed out to either child that he wants the toy just because the other child wants it, he would passionately insist that his desire was original and that the desire of his rival was secondary and derivative ... Desire, that most cherished essence of both the romantic and the Freudian self, is not the infallible gyroscope the modern age has acclaimed it to be. It is the most fickle and capricious compass imaginable, whose needle always quivers in the presence of someone else's desire."

11. Girard, *Violence and the Sacred*, 146.

12. Girard writes, "We shall speak of *external mediation* when the distance is sufficient to eliminate any contact between the two spheres of *possibilities* of which the mediator and the subject occupy the respective centers. We shall speak of *internal mediation* when this same distance is sufficiently reduced to allow these two spheres to

is removed by social or cultural distance from the model of the desire, external mediation prevents the likelihood of the relationship becoming rivalrous. When, however, the distance between the subject of the desire and the model is close or proximate in internal mediation, the model / mediator becomes the source of rivalry. Girard characterizes this with Don Quixote, Sancho Panza (his servant) and Amadis the Gaul (the model).

MODEL/MEDIATOR, THE *VANITEAUX*, RIVALRY, AND CONFLICT

When the subject and the model/mediator mimetically desire the same object, and that object is limited, conflict will result. The model/mediator may act in ways so as to impede the subject's ability to acquire the object. It is possible that by obfuscating or hiding access to the object, the subject only has an increased sense of desire to act like or become the model/mediator. This may increase the value of the object for the model/mediator resulting in what Girardian perspective calls the "double-bind." On the one hand, the model/mediator acts/lives in such a way as to suggest "desire this object." On the other hand, the model/mediator acts/lives in such a way as to say "you can not have this object." Girard writes, "To imitate the desires of someone else is to turn this someone else into a rival as well as a model. From the convergence of two or more desires on the same object, conflict must necessarily arise."[13] The model/mediator serves as the basis for showing the subject what to possess while at the same time preventing the subject from possessing what is desired. The model, while remaining in that capacity, becomes at the same time the obstacle to that which is to be possessed.[14] Raymund Schwager highlights well the rivalry that develops in his *Must There be Scapegoats?*[15] In his earlier work Girard refers to the subject as *vaniteux*: "A *vaniteux* will desire any object so long as he is convinced that it is already desired by another person whom he admires. The mediator here is a *rival*, brought into existence as a rival by vanity, and that same vanity demands his

---

penetrate each other more or less profoundly" (Girard, *Deceit, Desire, and the Novel*, 9; italics original).

13. Girard, *To Double Business Bound*, 140.

14. Girard, *Things Hidden*, 3–47. See especially 296 and 321 for descriptions of how the model-obstacle works.

15. Schwager, *Must There Be Scapegoats?*

defeat."[16] Describing metaphysical desire in *Things Hidden Since the Foundation of the World* Girard says that "the subject will always manage to track down the obstacle that cannot be surmounted ... and he will destroy himself against it."[17]

TRIANGULAR DESIRE, CONFLICT, AND VIOLENCE

We have seen the subject who seeks to imitate the model by seeking the same object. This is usually classified as triangular desire. The subject might even structure their life around the rivalry over control of the object in order to become the model/mediator. The imitator and the imitated become "doubles" in their metaphysical desire and as they become more proximate/closer to one another in their triangulation, the possibility for violence to emerge from the conflict becomes greater. In *Violence and the Sacred* Girard uses an example from the Greek tragedy of Euripides' *Phoenician Women* that explains the nature of conflict and violence that emerges in this triangular desire. What is more, the desire he describes between the brothers Eteocles and Polyneices is precisely a feud over the throne of Thebes, not far removed from our throne battle in Judges 9 where brothers and Gaal contest for control. In *Phoenician Women*, Girard notes that even the death of both brothers fails to bring resolution as the tale itself states, "They hit the dust and lay together side by side; and their heritage was still unclaimed."[18] Girard chronicles how the physical conflict of the brothers now escalates into a verbal feud between each man's armies leading to what Girard calls a "tragic dialogue ... a debate without resolution."[19] In the struggle narrated by Euripides, the city of Thebes is nearly destroyed.[20]

As detailed thus far, the result of triangular desire escalating into violence seems to cure the issue by removing the model/mediator, but it solves the problem of mimesis only at the cost of great violence, usually

---

16. Girard, *Deceit, Desire, and the Novel*, 8 (italics original).
17. Girard, *Things Hidden*, 298.
18. Girard, *Violence and the Sacred*, 44–45.
19. Ibid., 45.
20. It is not within the scope of this study, but it deserves further attention elsewhere. The near destruction of Thebes in Euripides tragedy as a conflict between brothers escalates is close in storyline and in phonology for the city of Thebez in our Abimelech narrative of Judges 9.

Assessing a Girardian Hermeneutic within this Study

murder of the model/mediator. Even then, however, resolution is not afforded as violence itself now becomes imitated. As Girard states:

> At the level of the blood feud, in fact, there is always only one act, murder, which is performed in the same way for the same reasons, in vengeful imitation of the preceding murder. And this imitation propagates itself by degrees. It becomes a duty for distant relatives who had nothing to do with the original act, if in fact an original act can be identified; it surpasses limits in space and time and leaves destruction everywhere in its wake; it moves from generation to generation. In such cases in its perfection and paroxysm mimesis becomes a chain reaction of vengeance, in which human beings are constrained to the monotonous repetition of homicide. Vengeance turns them into *doubles*.[21]

VIOLENCE RESOLUTION THROUGH SCAPEGOATING

For Girard, virtually every culture has a history of rivalry. For culture to emerge from its violent origins something must happen—some difference must be made. Conflict does not always lead to violence resulting in murder of subject or model/mediator. While the rivalry is present, there are times and ways by which the violence can be curbed or redirected. Rivalry is real and the rivalry needs to be cured. The need is for a cure to the violence that does not just produce more violent reciprocity. This often comes, in the literature that Girard reflects on and in the myths of many cultures and in their sacrificial ritual, when the violence is redirected from all-against-all to all-against-one in scapegoating.

Girard posits the original act of murder begetting murder.[22] As murder begets murder, all become rivals and hostility passes through families, clans, groups to the point of infecting all persons to see others as enemies. This can result in outbursts of violence followed by periods of calm or outright anarchy. Unanimity among social groups/families turns to enmity as they become enemies of one another. Girard describes stories of famine or plague where differences break down resulting in doubling where competition increases leading to mimetic crises. The

---

21. Girard, *Things Hidden*, 12 (italics original).

22. In biblical texts, Girard and others narrate the murder of Abel by Cain in Genesis 4 in these categories. In that story, Lamech is the seventh generation removed from Adam; Lamech has in his own poetic testimony become accursed "seven times seven times" more than Cain.

issue of "difference" has been important in the biblical stories we have reviewed in our study as we have detailed. The non-differentiation of persons leads each member of the social class to be against one another without a means of cooperation. Each member of the social class existing as rivals leads to the possibility of anarchy and total dissolution in self-destruction.

Girard proposes that it is in the midst of this crisis that the possibility for culture emerges. This possibility occurs not as violent rivalry leads enemies to a table of peace and unanimity with one another but as the violent rivalry is redirected against a different agent/person/character—who becomes the scapegoat. The full scope of Girard's hypothesis is that the scapegoat mechanism is at the foundation of cultural origins.

To understand the means by which the scapegoat "achieves" the resolution of violence we must imagine the violent, mimetic crisis of the crowd. In the midst of this violent imitation, so Girard hypothesizes, one person caught up in the rivalrous reciprocity turns his hostility from his rival to an-other person. We could use "another" person here but the "an-other" helps characterize how this "another person" quickly becomes "other" and serves as the basis of differentiation that is needed to quell the contagious violence that Girard describes. If the rival follows the lead and turns to an-other person—the same other person—the direction of the violence now turns from the two that are indistinguishable in their rivalry to this other, different, third. Girard hypothesizes that in such moments of intense animosity at the verge of chaos, others follow the two and the enmity of the entire group/clan turns now against this single "Other." This "Other" now appears to be different from the crowd and all of the blame for the rivalry is redirected to this one. What happens next has been characterized as a lynch mob. The violent conflict of all turns against the one who has now become perceived as the sole cause of all trouble and all conflict. This one-other is killed and, as Girard hypothesizes, by the death of this "other"—the different one now called scapegoat—the violent conflict is resolved. Resolution has come using violence but not through the chaos and death of many, but through the sacrifice of one.

Girard has written most specifically at length on the role associated with the scapegoat in a book by that title, *The Scapegoat*.[23] In his analysis

---

23. Girard's positions have generally been framed in a single book and then clarified and reframed in numerous interviews. So subsequent interviews and responses

Assessing a Girardian Hermeneutic within this Study 165

he notes the relative arbitrary choice of the scapegoat but also characterizes the unique features of the scapegoat. We might call this unique characterization the caricature of the scapegoat. The scapegoat might have an illness or deformity or perhaps have status as an insider that is somehow a foreigner or "different" from the crowd. Even being chosen by lot can mark one as different/other. In *The Scapegoat* Girard proposes the "marginal insider, the rich and powerful" as possibilities for becoming "other" as well.[24] This difference fits precisely with our texts dealing with Saul as Girard goes on to note that "the monarch and his court are often reminiscent of the *eye* of the hurricane."[25] The arbitrary victim takes the violence of all and as a result, the rivalries are redirected to this one who, in becoming the victim, resolves the crisis in being murdered. Often the victim is characterized as an outsider, even decisively innocent.

Once scapegoating has been enacted, the violence of all-against-all which led to all-against-one now leads to peace for all. The victim upon whom all the animosity is channeled at one and the same time is the victim, but also is the agent who rescues "all" from becoming victims themselves. The victim—the scapegoat—reconciles the community by being victimized.

SCAPEGOATING, SACRIFICE, AND CULTURE IN RITUAL AND MYTH

Central to Girard's insight is the idea that human persons do not forget the event that brings social order from the chaos. In fact, so important is the event that it must be remembered. But Girard suggests that it is not remembered in precisely the way it happened. Reviewing the literature concerning the Greek god Dionysius in *Violence and the Sacred*, Girard writes that remembrance without exact recognition is important so that new suspicions may not arise which would lead to renewed violence.[26] In order to frame this idea of 'memory that is imprecise,' Girard uses the

---

become the means by which Girard helps to articulate his position(s). Here we refer to the earliest works of Girard, aware that he nuances his positions in later works. This study is aware of and uses all these interviews and clarifications in discerning Girard's perspective as it applies to the biblical texts we have studied.

24. Girard, *The Scapegoat*, 18.
25. Ibid (italics original).
26. Girard, *Violence and the Sacred*, 134–35.

French word that we might translate as misapprehension, misrecognition, or misunderstanding, "*méconnaisance*."[27]

In the first part of *Things Hidden Since the Foundation of the World*, Girard with Jean-Michel Oughourlian and Guy Lefort details what he understands preserves the experience of sacred that takes place in response to the act of scapegoating that brings peace: ritual, and myth.[28]

RITUAL

In order to recreate or re-live this resolution of conflict, so Girard hypothesizes, communities create a process or processes whereby this victim is remembered—and at the same time hidden—in the telling of a myth associated with the creation of ritualized sacrifice. The function of the sacrifice is, at some level, to recreate the cathartic event whereby the victim cured the community of its violence and thereby saved the community. This is vital to resolving violent desire and rivalry that might result in the death of many persons. Violence is enacted, but by scapegoating one, further violent resolution is prevented. The scapegoat becomes the means of salvation for the community. The scapegoat is the means for achieving atonement within a community.[29] Social groups, now unified, replay the founding event that brought peace in order that they might achieve the same unification brought about by the original violence. Now though, in ritual, they substitute an animal in the act of sacrifice for the original human victim. They divert the violence from the community while still achieving its cathartic benefits.[30] A strong proponent of a Girardian hermeneutic, James G. Williams, characterizes ritual in this way:

> My understanding of ritual is that it originates in the sacrifice of a victim. Ritual reenacts and thus represents to the group the

27. Ibid., 103–4.

28. Girard, *Things Hidden*, 1–138. Robert G. Hamerton-Kelly does a succinct job of laying out the basic framework used here, itself deriving from the Girard text. Hamerton-Kelly, *Sacred Violence*, 29–39. See also Hamerton-Kelly, "Biblical Interpretation," 31. In *Things Hidden* Girard also deals at length with issues of prohibition, but that is outside the scope of our focus.

29. Here our use of atonement is not meant to invoke any Christian categories or christological connections, though we recognize the possibility of such reading. Girard can and has been used to describe Christian atonement, but that is not our function here.

30. Girard, *Things Hidden*, 19–30.

unifying energy of the founding 'moment' when all turn against one, when the embryonic group lynched a victim (or victims). Ritual reenacts the crisis in such a way that it is emptied of all real violence in order to arrive at the resolution, the production of peace through the death or expulsion that produced peace in the first place. Ritual is a process in which a community goes into a mock mimetic crisis, representing to itself the disorder caused by putative transgressions that are transferred to the victim. It differentiates sacred time—the occasion of the festival or observance—from ordinary time, and within the reenactment of sacred time it represents the necessary differentiations, the threat to these differentiations, and the overcoming of this threat. One way to describe the mock crisis is to say that ritual undoes prohibition and then reestablishes it. The danger lying behind the prohibition, mimetic desire and mimetic rivalry, is embodied by the victim, whose divine or sacred status validates the community and conforms its identity.[31]

In the moment of redirected violence of all against one, the other who is the scapegoat becomes the "bivalent" character who brings the differentiation of sacred.[32] The peace that results from the destruction of the scapegoat cures the crowd of its violent rivalry and the other who is the scapegoat now is seen not simply as other, but as having been beneficent and good. This other has become the bringer of peace and stability for a social order at the brink of anarchy. This other is then, as Girard demonstrates, characterized as good, even as god. In a moment, the victim who received violence becomes the salvation from further violence. This moment or event is characterized by Girard as "double transference, the aggressive transference followed by the reconciliatory transference. The reconciliatory transference sacralizes the victim and is the one most fragile, most easily lost, since to all evidence it does not occur until the mechanism has completely 'played itself out.'"[33]

Girard's full exposition of this double transference from victim to god is detailed more fully in *Things Hidden Since the Foundation of the World*. While the scapegoat is murdered, the victim is not fully dead to the community in the sense that the act of destruction that does lead to the physical death of the scapegoat brings to life the spiritual and sacred.

31. Williams, "Sacrifice and the Beginning of Kingship," 75.
32. Girard, *Violence and the Sacred*, 136.
33. Girard, *Things Hidden*, 37.

The sacred emerges as the point where violence and resolution meet. By means of the scapegoat the group/clan has passed from violent mimetic crisis of all against all to reciprocal mimetic peace as all unite against one. With reference to Greek literature, Girard notes that the scapegoated other is seen as the poison that is set upon, but also becomes the antidote to the crowds violence and is thus the *pharmakon*.[34]

Girard hypothesizes that it is from this violent scapegoating mechanism that culture emerges. Culture exists with rules that govern differentiation, laws for prohibition, pure and impure, clean and unclean stipulations in rituals and in myth. At the end of *Violence and the Sacred* Girard writes: "All religious rituals spring from the surrogate victim, and all the great institutions of mankind, both secular and religious, spring from ritual. Such is the case, as we have seen, with political power, legal institutions, medicine, the theater, philosophy, and anthropology itself. It could hardly be otherwise, for the working basis of human thought, the process of 'symbolization,' is rooted in the surrogate victim [the scapegoat]."[35]

Most specific to this study is Girard's suggestion (as cited in the introductory chapter of this study) that the process of scapegoating might be connected to the emergence of monarchy as the means of bringing social/political/religious (priestly) differentiation.

The violent crowd can kill the agent of reconciliation a second time if violent rivalry should break out again. The crowd must have, then, a surrogate victim, an-other victim. Instead of finding a new victim to quell their violence, Girard hypothesizes that ritual begins for the community as they redirect violence now not to the one victim, but to a *representative* victim that represents the original act of reconciliation of the original "other." That is, the people begin the ritualized/priestly practice of sacrifice—now redirected towards an animal as a remembrance of but masking of the original violence that broke forth in and upon the crowd.

Ritual develops around the act of the murder, by means of those who can recreate the moment of reconciliation through differentiation. But the ritual need not be focused on the murder of an-other human.

---

34. Girard, *Violence and the Sacred*, 95. In this same work, Girard gives substantial review of Euripides's tragedy, *The Bacchae* as an example of literary record of this kind of event. See 126–39.

35. Ibid., 306.

An animal sacrifice can serve as the substitute for the human death that brought reconciliation. Ritualized animal sacrifice replaces the violent origins of cultures nascent start in rivalrous homicide. In ritual, the one who creates the opportunity for the scapegoat to work becomes viewed as the one who brings differentiation. This one can then be viewed in an exalted position as priest or king, or both.

MYTH

Subsequent to the sacrifice is the myth.[36] The function of ritualized sacrifice is to relive the violence without causing social breakdown. As ritual remembers the violence but redirects it, so myth remembers the event but in a hidden way for, so Girard suggests, communities need not know exactly about the violence that has unified them. Robert North characterizes myth as the "*rationalized* . . . poetic expressions of how the built-in human aggressions really *demanded* a victim."[37]

Girard argues that myths tell in their own way about the lynching of a victim who deserved to suffer.[38] "The particular combination of themes that we find in mythology, the signs of crisis and the signs of reconciliation against and around the victim can be explained, perfectly and completely, only by the presence of a necessarily real lynching behind the myth."[39]

We need to say little more about myth here, because in our analysis of the stories that will follow we will lay out the myth that has been cre-

---

36. Here we will not deal with the Christian or gospel unmasking of myth that is a significant part of much of Girard's work since it lies outside the scope of our project. But we mention here that for Girard, the texts of the Bible are not myth like those of other cultures: "The Bible is more concerned with victims than mythology is and with the possibility that individuals might be unjustly victimized" (Girard, "The Bible Is Not a Myth," 10). Much of Girardian theory about myth is framed in his conversation with his friend Mircea Eliade.

37. North, "Violence and the Bible," 5 (italics original).

38. Girard's early optimism for understanding all myths as pointing toward some form of lynching as demonstrated in *Things Hidden* is more restrained later. See the "Discussion" in Hammerton-Kelley, *Violent Origins,* 136.

39. Girard, *Things Hidden*, 118. See the context where he deals with the work of Lévi-Strauss and Paul Valéry, when he states for his own position: "To reject my hypothesis on the grounds that *structuralism has taught us not to confuse representations with their referents* is to misunderstand completely the reasons that necessitate my postulating the reality of lynching behind mythology" (ibid., 119, italics original).

ated in moving from chaos to conciliation through violence in Judges 9, 17–21, then 1 Samuel 9–11.

SUPPORT FOR A GIRARDIAN HERMENEUTIC

We depart from our controlled Girardian hermeneutic temporarily to point the reader of this study to non-Girardian readings of our Biblical texts. We make the departure, though, with the intention of strengthening the Girardian ideas expressed in the Biblical texts themselves, thus supporting the argument of this study. We cite here the works of Walter Brueggemann, Corrine Patton and E. Evans Pritchard.

WALTER BRUEGGEMANN: MONARCHY AND IMITATION

Our argument, which will continue to be extended here, is about Abimelech and "pseudo-kingship," the Levite and "priests and sacrifice," and Saul as the "king" who bring together kingship and sacrifice, priest and power. Walter Brueggemann has studied the united monarchy after Saul in the person of David. Brueggemann's analysis is not framed as a Girardian study but his analysis demonstrates resonance with Girardian insight. "The innovations and inventiveness of David and Solomon (expressed, e.g., in temple, bureaucracy, harem, standing army, taxation system, utilization of wisdom) embody an *imitation* of urban imperial consciousness of Israel's more impressive neighbors and a radical rejection of the liberation consciousness of the Mosaic tradition" (*emphasis mine*).[40] Noting the work of Frank Moore Cross, Brueggemann writes, "By carefully piecing together the fragmentary evidence, Cross concludes that David held together the priestly *rivalry* to serve his dominant interest of political unification."[41] Striking to us in these assertions is that Brueggemann makes an argument consistent with the argument we will proceed to make here. But our argument will be informed by the critical terminology and theory of René Girard. Brueggemann uses "Girardian" terminology with, it seems, no critical awareness of the work of Girard. This is not to imply any failure on his part, but to note prior to the rest of our argument that Girardian connections can be made by others without an awareness of their congruence with Girard's thought. This, I believe, strengthens the argument of this study. Issues of desire, imitation, rivalry

---

40. Brueggemann, "Trajectories in Old Testament Literature," 169.
41. Ibid., 170.

Assessing a Girardian Hermeneutic within this Study 171

alongside issues of priestly and political control are apparent to others scholars. Others have seen similar connections in the framework of the Deuteronomistic History.[42]

CORRINE PATTON: THE LEVITE'S CONCUBINE

We have given careful attention to issues of the story in the biblical texts in our literary review. To a serious degree we have introduced a Girardian framework for understanding and perceiving the story as it has unfolded before us. At the same time, though, we have attempted to be careful to try to read the text closely for what the text says "on its own" apart from any notions of what happened "behind" the text in some sense. Obviously our reading is always privileged and shaped by some hermeneutic and some framework and that has been revealed in comments throughout the preceding chapters. Most specifically and explicitly I want to cite here a lengthy section from a fairly recent work by Corrine Patton. Her contribution to the *festschrift* for John F. Priest begins with a footnote showing how her work is a contribution to the "burgeoning field of sociological criticism" investigating the "intersection of sociological and feminist studies."[43] Patton's short work examines the lives/stories of Deborah and Jael, Jephthah's daughter and the Levite's concubine "to 're-relativize' the stories of these women as portraying the inherently essential nature of social change on the micro-level effecting macro-political upheaval."[44] Patton's work attempts to understand how the insignificant or unnamed characters can affect any social situation or outcome, specifically any major social situation or outcome about Israel's body politic. While her work is intriguing in its own right, I comment on it in an extended way here for the manner in which Patton deals with the Levite's concubine. What is worthy of note for our review is the fact that in none of her explicit statements nor in her footnotes does Patton

---

42. No doubt others have more specifically used Girardian insights to speak to issues within the Deuteronomistic History and those persons and their work can be reviewed in numerous references listed in the bibliography to this study. What makes the use of Brueggemann unique for us here is that from all the data gleaned from Brueggemann, he seems to not be informed by a Girardian framework, hypothesis, or "method." His use of the same verbal ideas, though, demonstrate the same "sense" of what is going on in this passage, even though Brueggemann does not frame it from Girard, it has consonance with Girardian theory.

43. Patton, "From Heroic Individual," 33.

44. Ibid.

use or incorporate a Girardian reading in her discernment of the characters and political happenings in these stories. But, her rendering of what happens in the story, specifically in the story of the Levite's concubine is framed in such clearly "Girardian categories" that it can and does read as if it were an excerpt from a Girardian reading of this text. In that sense, then, I use Patton's extended quote here because it indeed *does* fit the Girardian reading I am trying to apply to this story. And, the fact that she does it apart from any acknowledgment or hint of a Girardian reading, demonstrates in my view the clear perspective that my reading of Girard for these texts is not forced. The fact that Patton reads the text in a Girardian way, apart from the use of Girard, in my estimation shows the power and import of how a full understanding of Girardian issues will allow us to read this text better than Patton has done without our controlled hermeneutic.

Patton starts her discussion of the Levite's concubine noting that the social world of this story is more complex than Jephthah's. She notes that the danger comes not from pastoral disaster like drought or famine, but "in the form of urban danger with the aggression by male citizens against an 'outsider.'"[45] She continues:

> The social structure is more obviously hierarchical [compared to Jephthah's story]: the Levite has a servant, and there are degrees of marriage. There is more overt attention paid to who is the insider and who the outsider, preparing the reader for the chapters that follow in which the Benjaminites define Israelites not belonging to their tribe as "outsiders" or sojourners. This increasing social complexity leads to decreasing autonomy for all the characters, including the women. Here not only is the concubine anonymous, but even her father and husband are unnamed. She is not only a nobody, but she is the daughter of a nobody and the secondary wife of a nobody. She is raped by a nameless crowd, and her dismembered body is sent to nameless tribal leaders. She has no status, no rights, because those who should defend and protect her, i.e. her husband and father, fail to do so. Her situation brings the message of the text to the fore: the need for the monarchy. One of the primary duties of the king was to protect the rights of the "widow, orphan and resident alien." As is known these categories refer to those elements in society who have no one to plead their case in Israel. I would content that, functionally, the Levite's concubine fits all three categories. First, the

---

45. Ibid., 43.

> Benjaminites would surely view her as a resident alien. Second, since her father has sent her out of his house, she is no longer under his protection, rendering her an orphan. Finally, her status as concubine, rather than wife, limits the Levite's responsibility toward her. Like Ruth, without a king to guarantee her rights, this woman is completely vulnerable. In this way the text clearly reflects the monarchic view.[46]

I will come back to comment on Patton's position, but let me continue with her statements un-edited or un-reflected upon for the moment.

> In addition, the text projects the clearest veneer in the book of pan-Israelite activity. All eleven tribes gather to decide the fate of Benjamin. They all act in concert, displaying military effectiveness at a time when it is most self-destructive. The overlay of pan-Israelite activity clearly reflects a later time period, a period that idealized Israel as a unity of twelve, and only twelve, tribes. If this story retains any social *Kern* [sic] it would be of the period immediately preceding the monarchy. The increased urbanization, the loss of individual identity replaced by simple tribal designation, the increased specialization, the level at which decisions are made all point to a complex society in need of strong central leadership. There is ample evidence, however, that the story in its current form displays signs of at least heavy redactional activity, if not outright authorship by the final redactor. Overt parallels to Genesis 19 require a date post-dating the text. Further parallels with the Saul narrative suggest either the activity of a single Deuteronomic redactor or an author later than the traditions now contained in 1 Samuel. The book of Judges portrays the growing social complexity as spontaneous, natural, and uncontrolled. Yet it is this very complexity, with its inherent abuses, that inevitably leads to the necessity of central authority yielded under God, i.e., the monarchy. The redactor casts the final story of the rape of the concubine and the subsequent inter-tribal wars against the background of the complex social structure that closely mirrors monarchic Israel: this casing of the story expresses the inevitability of monarchy, not as an ideal in and of itself, but as a necessary evil in a society unable to protect its citizens or adjudicate inter-tribal disputes.

---

46. Ibid., 43–44.

> The final redaction of Judges then expresses the theme of the need of a king within an ever-increasing complex society.[47]

It will not be my intent to respond to every statement made in the lengthy section I have quoted from Patton, but I need to comment on several items. First, note how Patton uses Girardian language to talk about the rise of aggression and rivalry among persons. The rising aggression leads to a loss of identity of all against one. Patton argues that the Levite's concubine begins as insider in the story but emerges as outsider in several ways, specifically for Patton as each and every kind of outsider "widow, orphan and resident alien." Note as well that Patton sees the complexity of this story as preceding the monarchy in a "complex society" where we might note in Girardian categories the complexity is burgeoning as culture is developing.

While Patton discerns the story in decidedly Girardian ways she is not Girardian and I suggest that by not being Girardian, her final reading of the text is in error. Here, then, I note clearly my bias toward the Girardian reading as speaking to complexities of the social situation that persons like Patton miss. Patton suggests that the increasing complexity points to a need for "central authority" and the "inevitability of monarchy." What Patton fails to demonstrate, though, is how and why a group of persons in their greatest time of "social complexity" could come together in solidarity to choose anything for their own good. I suggest Patton projects her own wrong bias on the story and situation of Israel. Her reading suggests that the collective whole of this massively chaotic body of persons all united together in solidarity and "inevitably" to choose a Monarch.

I disagree and instead, with Girard, I suggest that there was no "inevitable" thing and certainly no "institution" that beckoned their coming together. Instead, one of the group pointed to an outsider as the source of rising aggression and social complexity and in pointing to the one, violence was channeled to and against that one—purged—and the victim became seen as a sort of savior, as did the person who redirected the collective aggression. It is unlikely the case that a violent crowd chose a new form of institutionalized government. Instead, an event of scapegoating purged their desire and brought reconciliation.

---

47. Ibid., 44–45.

EVANS-PRITCHARD: PRIEST AND KING

While the focus of E. Evans-Pritchard does not follow from the same literary categories that informs a Girardian reading, we note that E. Evan-Pritchard's other work has called attention to the sacred and regnal functions of a king in recent anthropological study. The sacred and regnal practices of the king functioned in order to settle feuds. Evans-Pritchard writes about the Shilluk people in Africa concerning the "settlement of a feud" where; "it is evident that the king could not have imposed a settlement had the disputants not been ready to accept one, that the part played by the king was that of peacemaker and not judge, and that his participation can better be described as sacerdotal than as governmental. The king of the Shilluk reigns but does not govern."[48]

Quoting several other sources of study on the Shilluk, Evans-Pritchard notes that the sacral position of the king is recognized by titles associated with the king including: of 'the royal and priestly line' and of its "priestly function' and the king as "high priest of the tribal religion."[49] While our study here is not of the anthropological cast that Evans-Pritchard examines, it is important to note that the kings for a people like the Shilluk are not just government officials, but priestly officials. And, while we do not have the space or need to examine it here since Pritchard does it in his work, it is important to note that the king for the Shilluk must also be invested by the "collective participation" of the entire country "for the kingship represents the whole country and a king can only be made by rites in which the whole country takes part."[50] Pritchard notes that the kingship for the Shilluk means "a king symbolizes a whole society and must not be identified with any part of it. He must be in the society and yet stand outside it and this is only possible if his office is raised to a mystical plane. It is the kingship and not the king who is divine."[51]

---

48. Evan-Pritchard, *The Divine Kingship*, 16.
49. Ibid.
50. Ibid., 25.
51. Ibid., 36.

GIRARDIAN THEORY AND JUDGES 9, 17–21, AND 1 SAMUEL 9–11

What we have yet to demonstrate is how Girard can be used to help us understand the stories of Judges 9, Judges 17–21 and 1 Samuel 9–11. It is therefore our aim now to demonstrate how Girard can help us make sense of these stories.

The function of all that has been said to this point in the study is to demonstrate that in the Book of Judges there is no monarch even though it is clearly the case that Abimelech tries to become one after Gideon's refusal to be one. In 1 Samuel 11, kingship is finally and fully a reality. In Judges there is fratricide, rivalry, mayhem, theft, shame, rape, dismemberment, genocide and anarchy. In 1 Samuel 11 there is dismemberment that leads to salvation and life and monarchy. The literary hinge upon which these chapters swing is the four-time repeated expression in Judges that "There was no king in Israel."

We will show how each subsection of our texts can be understood in Girardian categories. We will suggest how kingship emerges alongside of and participates with sacred priesthood in Israel. This serves as the foundation of culture for Israel, but also the ambivalent basis of this foundation because it is founded in the memory of ritualized murder.[52]

JUDGES 9

We have already attended to our close reading of the story of Abimelech. Additionally, we have demarcated some of the issues of rivalry and violence that frame the story. In many ways we have laid the foundation for understanding this story through a Girardian lens.

Now with our Girardian lens, we can see more clearly the issues of rivalry that operate in the story of Abimelech. The very naming of Abimelech in the story narrates for us the person with whom he is associated and the nature of the rivalrous relations that will operate within the story. Abimelech, as the son of the "king" Gideon is introduced to us

---

52. Girard maintains that the ritual is unmasked through the revelation made known in Jewish Scriptures. The unmasking of the violent basis of human culture and the origin of cultural institutions is finally revealed in the cross and resurrection of Jesus as the Son of God in the gospels. For the full understanding of this larger reading of the biblical story from the Hebrew Scripture to the Christian Scripture, numerous works can be consulted from these scholars: Raymund Schwager, James G. Williams, Robert Hammerton-Kelly, Paul Neuchterlein, et al.

Assessing a Girardian Hermeneutic within this Study

as insider and outsider in the ways already detailed. He shows up in the town of his mother's kin and asks for the opportunity to gain control. But the justification for his quest for control is rooted in the desire to be like his father who had control over the people who sought his "rule." While Abimelech desires the "rule" that his father had possessed, he recognizes that in order to rule it would place him in rivalrous relations with his brothers.

He mimetically desires the "rule" of his father against the rivalrous impulses that he fears with his brothers, all seventy of them "perfectly" weighted against him. That the brothers can not dwell together seems to be clear to the lords of Shechem for they empower and enlist the murder of the brothers.

Abimelech, claims Fokkelman, "is inspired by his father in the *desire (emphasis mine)* to be king, but at the same time he rejects and hates his parents. He divides the family into one-half on his father's side, which is killed by him, and for that he uses the half on his mother's side, which is pampered by him."[53] Fokkelman goes on to cite issues of rivalry—an important Girardian term—that are created in this narrative by the narrator's story of Abimelech, "one can and should trace all references to mother and father, to men and women in this chapter in the light of Abimelech's pathological polarizing."[54] Abimelech—in name, in speech, in action—is the *vaniteaux* who molds his decisions based on the competing desire he has with others to "rule."

Jotham alone escapes the fratricide. In poetic voice he castigates what he recognizes as the problem of the inhabitants of Shechem. They want non-differentiation by having someone like themselves to rule over them. But, in a curious twist Jotham's fable recognizes the place of the king—the other or the different. The "trees" seek out one to rule over them—from among other fruit bearing plants, from other trees—but they finally settle on "the thornbush." That which is selected or chosen to rule is that thing which is different. This recognition of the differentiating function that takes place as rule is established.

---

53. Fokkelman, "Structural Remarks," 38. While Fokkelman's reading is informed by Freudian categories of desire that are different from Girard's, categories of desire that lead to conflict have similarity for both thinkers. Both Freud and Girard understand desire to lead to rivalry as well.

54. Fokkelman, "Structural Remarks," 38.

What is striking even in the fable is the claim of Jotham that the thornbush says, "If you really want to make me king, take refuge in my shade—but if not, then let fire come out of the thornbush and consume the cedars of Lebanon." Jotham's fable hints at the fact that, if aligned with or towards this "other" the people will have unanimity. If, however, they fail to align towards this one other, then fire will come out and consume the cedars of Lebanon. What the Jotham fable recognizes is not that violence will emerge "from the thornbush" itself but by failing to align around the one figure. The image of fire consuming the cedars of Lebanon suggests the destruction that comes by *not* rallying around this one that is chosen. The escalating rivalry can be all consuming unless persons unite against a single victim.

One of the interesting aspects of the Gideon/Jerubbaal story that we intentionally passed over when he was asked to become "king" and to "rule" over the people is the unique fact that Gideon set up from among the people, in the midst of the people an ephod. The ephod was created from among the people and is later associated with the priest specifically who officiates over sacral functions. The priest in the stories of Judges 17–21 established an ephod as well. The Gideon story associated with rule and kingship is mediated with the placement of sacral/priestly functions alongside it. In the narrative, Gideon refuses kingship and rule politically while embracing its sacral functions in the use of the ephod. The act of any sacral functions is missing in entirety of the story associated with Abimelech. Gideon is no king but he has an ephod. Abimelech has no ephod, but he wants to reign.

When Abimelech forces his mimetically rivalrous violence in the narrative, he sets up and contributes no sacral functions. Seventy brothers are murdered by the one outsider on one stone, but it is not the case in the narrative that the persons are mobilized around one victim as a Girardian reading might suggest for us. Instead, they mobilize around the one in order to murder the many. With their actions complicit in the murderous rivalry, violence is not quelled but actually swells.

The story continues to tell us that the lords of Shechem are displeased with the rule of Abimelech. The text narrates it to us as an "evil spirit" that existed between the persons and Abimelech. Rivalry has not been quelled by Abimelech's activity for there was not a single victim around which the members united and found their peace. Instead, the rivalry that Abimelech had insinuated against his brothers

Assessing a Girardian Hermeneutic within this Study 179

is now spread. A sense of lawlessness and non-differentiation presides.[55] Resident bandits take to the hills in the days when Abimelech is supposed to provide peace. But there is no peace. There is no union around this one who rules.

The narrative moves through other rivalrous relations, specifically in the person of Gaal. His speech clearly sets himself over against Abimelech as desiring the same rule that Abimelech had possessed. Gaal mimetically desires to rule the Shechemites, and like Abimelech before him, he makes a case for his rule.

The clear fact of this conflict inspires Abimelech to action. He had been the *vaniteaux* and he now seeks to remove his *vaniteaux* to Gideon's sons. Conflict and violence dominate the story. And in the midst of this story there is no sacral function that operates. There is no priestly order. There is no sacrifice. There is no Levite. There is no ephod. There are only rivals in conflict meting out violence. In order to demonstrate the extent of escalated violence to us, even after conquering Shechem, the extreme of Abimelech's unmediated rule, carries itself to violent extreme.

The thornbush king of Jotham's fable had promised that if the people would unite around his rule, then they would receive refuge. If they rejected the rule of the thornbush/king then fire would break forth. But in the events of Abimelech's actions we see revealed that which was concealed in the myth of the way of the king. The king, in the fable, promised security. But in fact, this king's violent way of rivalrous action does not bring peace, but only murder, destruction, and death. The "trees" had listened to the "thornbush" and had chosen him to be king but instead of refuge, in the events that play out in Abimelech's life they get what is revealed, fire breaking forth. Quite literally, after having joined in the rivalrous, non-differentiating actions of Abimelech the inhabitants and city of Shechem are destroyed by fire.

55. Richter characterizes the bloody, evil, violent nature of Abimelech's rule in distinction from Jerubbaal throughout the framing of Judges 9. Richter writes: "An Aussagen, die den Bearbeiter interessieren, ist zunächst die in V. 6 zu nennen: das Königtum, un zwar nicht nur das des Abimelek, sondern darüber hinaus auch eines anderen, das auf ältere Institutionen zurückgeht, die an Gideon gezeigt sind. Dieses Königtum interessiert nicht neutral, sondern ist gewertet einmal dadurch, daß Giden es ablehnt 8, 22f, dann durch die blutige Art, wie es errichtet wurde 9, 1–5. 24. 56f, die als Gewalttat V. 24 und Böses V. 56f bezeichnet wird, ferner durch den blutigen und vollständigen Untergang des Königs und seiner Stadt, weiter durch die halbheidnische = kanaanäische Art, schleißlich durch Betonung des Unrechts, das an Jerubbaal geschah" (Richter, *Traditionsgeschichtliche*, 315).

What is curious in the narrative is the means by which Abimelech's violence continues after having destroyed Shechem. I suggest that we might expect that the violence of Abimelech should have ceased with the destruction of Shechem. Curiously, though, it does not. The story seems to know something important about the extent of rivalry that is hired and financed, it spirals fully out of control. Commenting on uncontrolled rivalry viewed in another narrative later in the Deuteronomistic History, Hans Jensen writes, "Mimetic reactions—or mimetism—running wild will make everybody the enemy or everybody else."[56]

Abimelech's violent conflict moves from Shechem to a new city introduced in the narrative, Thebez. Curiously there we meet a woman. This woman is not in rivalrous conflict with Abimelech. She does not seek to possess what he possesses nor rule as he rules. She speaks no words in the narrative. But she does move to action. Moved to action, she symbolically acts against the rivalry that had shaped Abimelech's narrative. Abimelech used one stone to kill many, the 70 brothers with whom he was in mimetic rivalry. The murder of the many did not quell violence but only fostered its growth among the Shechemites and Gaal, all of which are in triangular conflict with Abimelech. This one woman, though, as it were, goes to the root of the problem with this thornbush/king. Not by killing many, but by killing the one, with the one stone, violence is ended in the narrative.

The narrative does not say that the woman "sacrifices" or "makes a sacrifice" of Abimelech. And there is no specifically priestly or monarchial object here. But, narratively she uses the "one stone" that had inaugurated his reign as the "one stone" that crushes his head and his headship over Israel. Narratively speaking, the peace that the people wanted does not come with the rivalry of Abimelech against his brothers. Narratively speaking, the peace that the people wanted comes when the one who causes the rivalry is removed from causing the rivalry to take root.

The narrative ends with an editorial note we had passed over in our earlier assessment of this narrative. The editor tells us that

---

56. Jensen, "Desire," 39. Jensen's article is not too far removed from our analysis. In fact, it could be argued that his analysis of the Succession Narrative, which follows the rule of King David, shows that the problems of mimetic rivalry continue even after kingship and sacrificing functions are set up. Girardian thought suggests that apart from a scapegoat, communities exist not too far removed from the brink of contagious violence.

both Abimelech and inhabitants were "repaid" for their "wickedness." In this narrative, the wickedness that operates is unmitigated rivalry that leads to conflict and rivalry. All of which is in a time when there is no Levite, no priest, no ephod, no ritual, no sacrifice, and no sacrificer to bring peace.

Girard would suggest for us, I believe, that the narrative of chaos associated with the Abimelech narrative is what we would expect when there is no scapegoat mechanism that can channel the rivalry away from internecine conflict.

JUDGES 17–21

As detailed in the opening two chapters of this study, scholars are agreed that there is ambivalence about the issue of kingship in Israel. That ambivalence, it is argued, is manifest in two dominant themes of this literature; that which is anti-monarchic in tone and that which is pro-monarchic. The final chapters of Judges are often characterized as being positive towards kingship in their presentation of the anarchy that dominates these stories. Martin Buber has argued that these final chapters of Judges serve as the counter-balance to anti-monarchial tones or the "romantic error" of the earlier material.[57] We agree that there exist issues of pro-monarchy and anti-monarchy in these texts but suggest that their import is essential for other reasons than simply what source critical scholarship would aim for us to believe.

Some scholars see a break between Judges 17–18 and 19–21. This perspective is based on several issues, not the least of which is the sense that at the end of 18:31 and at 19:1 we hear the "there was no king in Israel" refrain that punctuates our text. And while it may be the case that the Levite in 19–21 is a different Levite than the one of 17–18, it is the contention of this study that this position cannot be solidly maintained and that narratively the person of the Levite is not what is important to the narrative but the office of the Levite. In 17–18 it is clear that there is desire and rivalry that takes place for control of the Levite. In the midst of this rivalry he embodies textually and spatially the office of priest. This is clear in the attempt by the Danites to entice the Levite away from Micah and then by kidnapping him. The story of Micah's Levite begins with the need for a "priest" (17:6) who presides over activities

57. Buber, *Kingship of God*, 86.

of worship. It centers then on the rivalry over this priest by the Danites (18:1) but it ends where it begins, with Micah's image and the Levite in 18:31. In both stories of 17–18 and 19–21 the geographical identity of the Levite—coupled with the anonymity of the Levite—suggests that the author sees the stories acting in the same ways. The Levite of 19:1 is like the Levite of 17:8 and appears in the hill country of Ephraim. The journeys of the Levites are from Bethlehem in Judah to Ephraim in both stories. Curiously the first story ends with the Levite who has been fought over with a joyful heart (18:20) whereas the second story only pictures a joyous Levite while he feasts and drinks with his host (19:6, 22) prior to the violent rape of his concubine.

There are many issues which play into our Girardian perspective on the story that takes place between Judges 17–21. Some of the issues have been outlined in the narrative of the text itself as it was outlined earlier. Our goal here is to explain what happens in Judges 17–21 in a way that Girard will help us make sense of these stories. Having detailed the connections in the stories here with that which takes place in Judges 9 and 1 Samuel 9–11, we will recount some of those details again. But our focus will not be on re-narrating what has already been said, but instead on framing this story in Girardian categories.

We have already noted that the inclusion of kingship in these stories is specifically and clearly narrated. What we have been less clear to demarcate to this point is the fact of sacral/priestly functions that clearly make up this story. The fact that Levites are central in these stories is important. The Levites make up the priestly class in Israel. We have noted already the fact that when the Levite cuts up his concubine, the narration of the dismemberment makes her out to be, verbally, a sacrifice. We have paid less attention to this point in the study to the stories of Judges 17–18 that set the important tone for what we read in the full context of Judges 17–21. And it is urgent to this study that the issues that make up the narrative in Judges 17–18 are issues of mimetism, rivalry, violence, control over sacred functions, sacred offices, and sacred duties effected by a priest.

The story introduces us to Micah and his unnamed mother.[58] But in the story we are introduced as well to how the silver is "solemnly con-

---

58. Amit sees Micah as a "negative personality" that is " a ludicrous character rather than one who arouses pity" (Amit, "Hidden Polemic," 7). In this way, Amit, like us sees the character of Micah as important, but not central to the larger issues that she calls the "central plot axis—the conquest of Dan and the establishment of its sanctuary" (ibid.).

secrated" for the son to make an image, an idol, a shrine and an ephod. The stories associated with Micah here begin in ways similar to our introduction to Abimelech. The story in Judges 17 clearly tells us that a "priest" had been put in place to officiate, but the priest seems not to have been sufficient. When the "young Levite" begins to wander to look for "some other place to stay" (Judg 17:8) he replaces the unnamed, non-Levitical priest. In the story we have no narrated reason for the Levite's departure, but we recognize the significance of priestly issues that take place in this text when we are told of the priest in Judges, 17:5, 10, 12 and 13.[59] The Levite becomes, textually stated five times, the "priest." And verse 12 states that the young Levite had become "his priest." This is of importance to us in the narrative because the priest becomes the issue of mimetic rivalry and control in the story.

As the story moves into chapter 18 we are introduced to the repeated refrain about the fact of their being "no king" in Israel. These stories then are clearly, definitively about issues of priestly concern alongside issues of monarchial concern. "In Judges 17–21 interest in foreign powers dissipates, being replaced by an internal analysis of cultic and moral problems which plagued Israel [when there was no king]."[60]

When the Danites show up on their way to sack Laish, which they have mimetically desired, they hear the voice of the Levite and ask him who he is and what he is doing. "He has hired me, I am his priest" is how the Levite understands his office.

The Danites desire the land of the unsuspecting people of Laish as they attempt to set up their identity. They spy out the land, desire it, and commit to enact violence to obtain it. But, they want not just the land, they desire to possess the priest as well. As they establish themselves, they want to be like Micah, with a priest over them. The priestly con-

---

59. About this wandering Levite Wilson writes, "The Levite should not inspire such overweening confidence. His domicile, Bethlehem in Judah (17:7, 9), raises misgivings—why was he not in one of the cities designated for a Levite (Lev. 25:32–33; Num 35:2–8; Josh 21)? His search for a place to stay (vv. 8, 9) also introduces a disturbing note into the narrative. His apparent search for a livelihood implies that Israelites had not supported him as required by the law (Deut. 12:9; 14:27–29; 18:8, 26:12–13). What irony we are dealing with in Judges 17! The Levites begin as a people so implacably opposed to idolatry that, to stamp it out, they kill loved ones (Exod. 32:26–29). But now things are so topsy-turvy that a Levite is prepared even to serve in an idolatrous cult in the home of a relative stranger in a remote area." Wilson, "'As You Like It,'" 82–83. Indeed, the situation of the story seems "remote" and "strange" and "topsy-turvy" for us.

60. Ibid., 73.

cerns are replete in virtually every conversation that involves the Levite. He claims to be a priest and the Danites want him to become their priest. References to the person or office of priest are made in Judges 18:4, 6, 17, 18, 19, 20, 24, 27, and 30. That this narrative is about the attempt to control the priest(hood) is clear. The Levite, himself, protests his being taken by the Danites and they reply to him, "Is it not better that you serve a tribe and clan in Israel as priest rather than just one man's household?" (Judg 18:19). Micah protests the theft of his priest and is met with the threat of violence over the person that is mimetically desired and the office that has given rise to rivalry in their midst. The justification of the Danites for taking the priest is rooted in rivalry. They understand that the purpose of the priest is to serve community issues—over a tribe and clan and not just one man's household. And in the narrative the Danites are trying to establish their identity, their cultural place, and the priest is perceived by them in the narrative as a necessary ingredient, along with his ephod, for their community formation. Violent physical conflict is avoided in the narrative for Micah's household, but narratively and in dialogue it is present. Amit sees the characterization in this story as "negative" but not rooted so much in the characters or persons as much as in the circumstances. Amit argues that "the reader becomes convinced that had there been a central government, one could reasonably assume that the personalities involved would not have degenerated to the level of the actions described."[61] But violent conflict is acted out against what had been the "peaceful and unsuspecting" inhabitants of Laish. Intertribal violence over priestly and communitarian concerns is nascent. We suggest that the issue is not about central government to curb violence, but sacral kingship.

The Levite who is involved in the stories of Judges 19–21 is not necessarily the same person of the narratives of Judges 17–18. But it is not clear that he is necessarily another Levite. Further, the function and role of priest/priestly office is what has been introduced to us as central in the story, not necessarily the person of the Levite himself.

In the story of the Levite and his concubine we continue with the concerns of priestly office, though they are not as central here. What is important though is that here in Judges 19–21, like in 17–18, the possession of the Levite is the reason for contention. The mimetic desire for the priest is what spurs the rivalry and the violence. When the priest in this

---

61. Amit, "Hidden Polemic," 8.

narrative is not given over, as had been the case in Judges 17–18, violence is enacted against a helpless concubine that was by extension the property of the Levite. And as we have already seen in the speech of the Levite after having dismembered the concubine, he clearly feels that his life had been the issue and he had been the person who had suffered the unjust violence of the sons of Belial who had come in the night. What is striking to us in these stories then is this; the priest—in a way—dismembers his concubine as sacrifice but it is not in order to quell violence. In fact, in these days when there was no king and only this Levite/Priest the "sacrifice" that is cut up escalates the violence. To be clear, here, let us restate. The Levite does offer a sort of sacrifice in this narrative. But, the sacrifice of his concubine does not cease the violence. There is no king. There is no king alongside the priest or there is no connection between the sacral and monarchial roles here in Judges 17–21. The sacrifice that the Levite offers is ineffective to quell violence and instead, only escalates it.

We have already noted the rising anarchy that makes up the story of Judges 19–21, particularly 20–21 so we will not recount the details here. But in the midst of these stories we see nothing but the wholesale violence of brothers against brothers in a time when the person in the functional office of priest, the Levite, fails to curb violence. The sacral function does not work here when there is no king.

The concubine is not the cause of ceasing violence, but is the contagion for violence. In 21:3 though, violence is nearly at its end with the weeping of the people. They weep because they recognize what has happened in their midst, or what they fear to have happened. Their intertribal, brotherly conflict has left "one tribe missing." One tribe has become the victim in the violence. One tribe has been scapegoated. Even though it clearly had not been the entire tribe that had lynched and raped the concubine, the entire tribe received the brute force of being scapegoated. And it is important that it is not a collection of individual persons that are viewed as scapegoated here, but only one tribe.

When it is recognized that this one tribe has been cut off and weeping takes place (Judg 21:3) they offer sacrifices (21:4) and we are told again they recognize that "one tribe is cut off from Israel" (21:6). The Benjaminites have been scapegoated. But it is discovered that they are not completely dead, thought to be lost and grieved as dead, but still alive. The recognition that some men of this tribe are still alive allows for prohibitions to be violated. The scapegoated "one tribe" is allowed to break the prohibitions as they hide and steal the women of Shiloh. The scapegoated tribe goes home. But, the author does not narrate "peace" for us. There is no mention of safety. We only hear the final word of Judg 21:25, "In those days Israel had no king, everyone did as he saw fit." Now the people are without a king. Now there is no rivalry as they act in ways seeking to possess the same thing. The scapegoat is not *finally* the dismembered concubine, though she is clearly a victim in the narrative. Rather, building upon the narratives obfuscation of persons in the anonymous characterization in the story, and then the narratives clear label and principal naming of the tribe of Benjamin, the focus of the narrative centers on the victimized tribe, the scapegoated tribe of Benjamin. Hudson notes that this narrative "communicates a savage world that inflicts pain on the victim; integral to the plot-line is the scapegoat ritual usually centered around mob violence; and the violence of the narrative is symbolic of the society's 'viciousness' rather than the individuals."[62]

The narrative is aware of individual persons, no doubt. But, the named character finally victimized is the social group and the tribe of Benjamin. They, ultimately, are victimized by the narrative's end.

Don Michael Hudson's work on Judges 19–21 is important for the scope of this study as he will go on to state in harmony with our reading: "Judges 17–21 is a dialectic to the introduction without the possibility of any synthesis, wholeness or individual or national identity ... Judges 19–21 is about a loss of leadership, a loss of boundaries, a loss of identity, a loss of names and naming. It is about chaos, disorder, obscurity and dismemberment. It is also about the obliteration of memory, lineage, genealogy."[63]

In this study we agree and disagree with Hudson. We agree that Judges 17–21 frame the story of Israel in such a way that there is loss of synthesis, wholeness and identity. However, it is principally the argument of this narrative that the intention of this deliberate construction in Judges and 1 Samuel is not to demonstrate that the story is "without the possibility" of any synthesis or identity. Rather, the argument of this study aims to show that the loss of identity here in Judges emphatically sets the stage for the need for synthesis, wholeness and identity to be framed in a way that redeems or reconciles what happens here. Further, with Hudson, we agree that here in Judges 17–21 there is loss of names,

---

62. Hudson, "Living in a Land," 52.
63. Ibid., 53.

Assessing a Girardian Hermeneutic within this Study

identity; there is chaos and disorder; there is an obliteration of memory, lineage and genealogy. However, the argument of this study has been and continues here that in the person of Saul, particularly in his introduction in 1 Samuel 9 we are reintroduced to the significance of memory, lineage and genealogy that sets the state for his ordering and reconciliation from chaos the principal tribe that was scapegoated in Judges 17–21. The loss of Judges 17–21 then sets the stage for a different, though similar act of dismemberment in 1 Samuel 11 but where this new act does not cause loss without the possibility for synthesis, wholeness, or individual or national identity but where, in fact, synthesis, unanimity, and national identity is heralded in the people's uniting as "one man" around Saul and then crowning him as king in what is clearly a reconciliation of national identity for this people fractured here in Judges.

The scapegoated tribe allows for the people to move out of anarchy, towards monarchy when one person of this scapegoated tribe will recall these moments of anarchy when he dismembers his oxen.

Important here is our ability to line up Girardian understanding with the story by authors who are not intent to use Girard for their analysis. Mieke Bal has done significant work with the narratives in Judges in general, and particularly with issues related to women in the narratives. She views the death of the concubine in Judges 19 as "The moment in the biblical 'pre-text' in which language and violence are intricately related . . . the moment where the woman is no longer able to speak her truth of life and death where her body is *seen*, misunderstood both by her husband and by subsequent critics, addressed, and ultimately, misused in a radical perversion of speech."[64] Bal goes on to say about the moment of death that "In Judges, moreover, the agents of the woman's death are as unclear as is its moment; the act keeps being displaced from one man to the next. This contamination by collective guilt is obviously problematic to all readers."[65] Clearly it is not the case that Bal understands Girardian categories for her reading of the story, and her reading is important in and of itself. We highlight her reading though for what it understands to operate in the text. The text is complicit in violence. Further, the responsible "party" or "person" for the violence is not clear and remains, as it were, hanging there in the story, for all to be responsible for. All persons in the narrative cycle through violence that escalates and explodes be-

---

64. Bal, "A Body of Writing," 221. Italics in original.
65. Ibid., 223.

cause there is no means to remove or redirect the guilt associated with the violent rape and murder of this victim precisely because she was a human victim of violence. "Before her death by the gang-rape she is surrendered linguistically, and after her death she is dispatched as language, when her body is cut into pieces and sent to the tribes of Israel, as a *letter*—a piece of writing not containing but embodying a message—and as a slaughtered piece of meat. Butchering equals writing here; and death equals vision."[66] What can be understood from Bal then is that she, too, understands the nature of sacrifice operating in this text.

While describing the "scapegoat resolution" Girard writes, "In many instances, the victim was lynched, torn apart, devoured by the entire community."[67] With this we might note that the concubine was lynched at the home, torn apart in rape—but her being devoured by the entire community was again effected in her dismemberment. But it is not just in this moment of dismembering the concubine that we see the atrocity of the situation. It is, in effect, when the community, as a community, functionally dismembers itself by cutting off one of its own tribes. With greater vengeance and retribution than we have seen in any story in Judges or in the Biblical text to this point the Israelites seek to cut off this brother tribe—concluding with the war against insiders and coping with the consequences of such atrocity by taking and raping the daughters of Shiloh "thereby committing a greater atrocity than the original crime which they have been striving to revenge!"[68]

1 SAMUEL 9–11

In the stories here of 1 Samuel 9–11, we have the start of kingship. But the stories are equally about sacrifice and priestly matters. Apart from the laws governing cultic obligations in the Torah, James Williams points out that in 1 Samuel texts which he examines, which include our text in 1 Samuel 9–11, we have the section of the Hebrew Bible that "recounts the greatest number of sacrificial occasions of any narrative portion of the Hebrew Bible, yet it is not obvious at all that priestly narrators composed the text."[69] In another article by Williams, he writes that "the book

---

66. Bal, "A Body of Writing," 224. Italics in original.
67. Lefebure, "Beyond Scapegoating," 374.
68. Guest, "Dangerous Liaisons," 265.
69. Williams, "Sacrifice," 81.

of 1 Samuel recounts the greatest number of sacrificial occasions of any narrative portion of the Hebrew Bible."[70] The story of Saul's being chosen by lot, anointed, and inaugurated is squarely about monarchy alongside stories of priesthood and sacrifice.

When we meet Saul in the narrative of 1 Samuel 9, we are squarely back with the stories of Judges. In the context of geography, we are back in Ramah and soon to be in Gibeah and Jabesh-Gilead. In the context of lineage, we are with the Benjaminites.

We meet Saul on his quest for his asses, conversing with his servant, and we think back to the Levite with his asses also traveling with his servant. We watch in the narrative how Saul meets the prophet who selects him for a new role in Israel as נָגִיד. We are aware that Saul participates in a sacrificial meal and then is chosen to be anointed in a private ceremony. Private ceremony leads to public recognition, but only when Saul is chosen by lot. He hides from this "chosen" status, perhaps fearing for his life as having been "picked" out for being picked upon.

Saul goes back to his private life and attends to his personal duties, so it seems. He has been called forth from the scapegoated tribe of Benjamin in Judges 19–21. When a threat emerges for Israel, squarely back in "besieged" Jabesh-Gilead (1 Sam 11:1), Saul comes up from his field. He shows up on the scene here like the old man in Judges 19 who came to meet the Levite. In that scene, neither the old man nor the Levite knew how to quell the violence that besieged the house, so the concubine becomes the victim of violence. That violence escalates to all the inhabitants of Benjamin. The Levite there who could have redirected violence away from human and internecine conflict, exacerbates it.

But here, unlike the Levite or his host, this one who had been chosen from Benjamin redirects violence on behalf of saving lives. What is more, it creates the moment of differentiation as Israelites and those with them are distinguished from the Ammonites. Saul slays the oxen and calls to mind the threat of violence that had earlier existed in the anarchy of Judges when there was no king. And, in response to his action of redirecting violence, Saul is inaugurated as king. E. H. Scheffler argues that Saul was the first king of Israel who was the father of the

---

70. Williams, "History-Writing as Protest," 105. Williams comments include texts that precede those in the focus of this study. Williams details sacrificial activity in several places in 1 Samuel 1–8, but the focus on issues of sacrifice and priesthood is important here in this narrative of our concern.

Israelite state and nation who would go on to die a heroic death after leading a people whom he did not exploit. He founded Israel as nation and he "gave the Israelites their religion."[71] Scheffler is not alone in his assessment that with Saul politics and religion find their genesis. "As the founding father of the Israelite state, [Saul] laid the foundation of a national religion. It was, in a sense, impossible not to do so."[72] Karel Van Der Toorn goes on to note that it was "state religion" that began to symbolize the unity of the nation, transcending the divisions of families and clans that had previously existed. Saul would later take priests with him into battle and, it appears, housed a central temple in Nob (1 Sam 22:19.) Kingship emerges in Israel alongside the offices of "priest." Both are understood as involved in sacrificial activity.

Stuart Lasine notes the contrast, but fails in any convincing way to demonstrate what it is that Saul does. And, in fact, the one point of significance that Lasine makes actually fits within the purview of a Girardian reading. Lasine writes that "the deliberate contrast between the Levite dismembering his concubine (Judg. 19.29) and Saul's dismembering the oxen (1 Sam. 11.7) demonstrates the difference between the way a disaster is prevented by a newly chosen king and the way a disaster is avenged by an irresponsible, callous, and self-absorbed man who lives at a time in which there is no king in Israel."[73]

Lasine goes on to suggest that the Levite models his action after Saul, thus confusing why he suggests this man acted in the days when there was no king. Lasine states that, in his reading, the reason for the carnage with the Levite is because "the Levite is lying" and "the reader is meant to notice this and react to it."[74]

Robert Polzin's analysis of the story of Saul as presented in this chapter could have easily fit in the preceding chapter of this study, but I have left his analysis for this chapter on Girardian perspectives because it helps pull together thematic issues for us here. Polzin believes Chapter

---

71. Scheffler, "Saving Saul," 270. Scheffler's article begins, "It is contended in this article that the Deuteronomist's negative view of Saul has influenced subsequent Bible readers to such an extent that even today the Saul of history is obscured" (ibid., 263). Scheffler then proceeds to read the Deuteronomist with a "hermeneutics of suspicion" that among other things, reads David's Song of the Bow (2 Samuel 1) closely and recognize the good, non-exploitive characteristics of Saul's kingship.

72. Van Der Toorn, "Saul and the Rise," 527.

73. Lasine, "Guest and Host," 37.

74. Ibid., 48–49.

Assessing a Girardian Hermeneutic within this Study 191

11 to be a "hybrid account ... in chap. 11 [which] confusingly pulls us backward in time toward the charismatic leaders of the Book of Judges even as it proceeds forward with the story of Saul's kingship."[75]

Noting several issues in the text that are important, Polzin narrows his focus to verse 12 of chapter 11, which its claim about Saul's kingship. Polzin states the obvious need for textual emendation to help the redactor's confused story make sense. "No sooner does Saul lead Israel to victory over the Ammonites than the people demand to put to death those who had promoted kingship."[76]

With reference to Alt, Polzin notes how Saul's charismatic leadership in this chapter would make one think they are "confronted with a story from the Book of Judges, except perhaps that the circle of people who were born along by the enthusiasm of the leader is wider here than elsewhere. But in the final terse sentences comes the unexpected twist: the victorious tribes bring Saul to their sanctuary and by their act of homage make him what no charismatic leader ever was before him: the king of Israel (1 Sam XI.1—XI.15)."[77]

Polzin goes on to note that this passage is clearly connected to the stories of Jabesh-Gilead and Gibeah as we have noted in this study. And with this reference Polzin writes, "It is as if the chaotic situation described at the end of the Book of Judges—when there was no human deliverer, be he judge or king, to set Israel on the right path—deliberately looks forward to a sequel here in 1 Sam 11 involving these same towns. This time, however, a newly acclaimed king from Gibeah turns out to act, in Jabesh-Gilead's behalf and at God's behest."[78] Saul, as we have noted, refuses to put anyone to death. In this, then, Saul has used the violent sacrifice of the oxen to replace the need for violence to break out in rivalrous ways in Israel. The people want there to be a rivalry between those who have anointed Saul and those who had rejected his rule. But Saul refuses to allow this to form a rivalry that divides in the narrative. Saul's refusal to execute is what heralds his kingship.[79]

75. Polzin "On Taking Renewal Seriously," 494.
76. Ibid.
77. Ibid., 499. With reference to Albrecht Alt, *Essays on Old Testament History,* 253.
78. Polzin, "On Taking Renewal," 501.
79. Ibid., 506. Polzin writes, "For Saul, his unwillingness to kill those who deserved to die will come back to haunt him in chap. 15, when he is again unwilling to put someone to death. Which chapter's account of the king's refusal-to-execute is more fundamental

In the moment of dismembering the oxen and sending the pieces out, Saul called to mind the moment of escalating violence from Judges. In effect, he used violence against the oxen to call the people to arms not against their kinsfolk but in defense of and on behalf of their kinsfolk.[80] Girardian theory articulates that the one who creates the difference (himself or herself) becomes a victim with an extended sentence.[81] With reference to what is operating in this passage, we turn to Gil Bailie's review of "violence and violation" that operate here.[82] In this narrative Saul is like the man who has come up from his fields in Judges 19 but here, instead of a helpless concubine becoming victim and inter-tribal warfare breaking out, Saul takes action to redirect violence towards the oxen in order to work to save tribal brothers. Saul evokes an image of violent encroachment from the past in order to work against the destructive violence that could break out. About this kind of activity Bailie writes,

> If, on the other hand, an encroachment on the sacred domain were to be made with sufficient boldness or reverence for authority, the community might be too stunned and fascinated by the brazen audacity of the transgression to converge on the transgressor immediately. In that moment between the "violation"—the touch of the corpse or the entering of the sacred precinct—and the new outbreak of violence, the mob regards the violator with the same combination of horror and deference with which it regards the sacred corpse or sacred space he has dared to approach. For the moment between the transgression and the violence, the sacred

---

to his failures as leader of Israel is not difficult for the reader to decide: the first refusal foreshadows and forms the basis for the second." But Polzin and I disagree. I would not suggest that in chapter 15 Saul fails to avoid violence, because he does fail to execute. But, I would suggest in Girardian categories, and in line with the kings of Disaster that Simon Simonse has described, that the king in chapter 15 has failed to bring the people towards an appropriate scapegoat and in the process, he becomes scapegoated himself. Here we disagree with Polzin who states that this unwillingness to execute foreshadows the failure of Saul's kingship later in the story, in 1 Samuel 15.

80. "By linking violence to the practice of offering sacrifice, Girard has demonstrated the inner connections between sacred ritual and political order. In fact, it is the violence inherent in the status quo, enacted in and legitimized by periodic sacrifice of the leaders, which forms the subject of conversations between Girard and his psychoanalytic colleagues in *Des Choses cacheés*" (Burrell, "Rene Girard," 443).

81. Girard, *Things Hidden*, 51–56.

82. Bailie, *Violence Unveiled*, 123. Bailie here picks up on a Girardian idea discerned etymologically in Latin. "'Violence' and 'violation' have the same Latin root, and apprehension about the violent consequences of taboo violation is a driving force in primitive religion."

Assessing a Girardian Hermeneutic within this Study 193

aura enjoyed by the transgressor endows him with an immense social prestige. By deftly exploiting this prestige, the transgressor might be able to postpone indefinitely the violent repercussions of his transgression . . .[83]

About this same narrative, Williams writes in agreement with our assessment:

> When Saul cuts the oxen: "The verb is used otherwise in the Bible only with reference to severing an animal for an *'olah* or burnt offering (Exod 29:17; Lev 1:6, 12; 8:20; 1 Kings 18:23, 33). The act of cutting in this case amounts to an indication of what will happen not to the enemy but to the Israelites if they do not respond positively to the summons. This is clearly stated by Saul (11:7). The animal parts substitutes for the people, but the sacrificial exchange cannot be completed until the enemy is defeated.
>
> Saul had earlier been prepared for kingship by experiencing prophetic rapture as he encountered the groups who were going to and coming from the places of sacrifice. Now he is caught or seized by the spirit and consequently engages in a sacrificial act to demonstrate the charisma of leadership. This episode is extremely important, for it shows Saul as the *divide*, as the one who makes the difference—the differentiator who brings order to Israel in its time of crisis.[84]

George Pattison also comments on the effectiveness of Saul's dismembering the oxen, noting as we do that the oxen replace the human body or bodies of his own tribe that had been scapegoated in the crisis of Judges 19–21. Commenting on the effectiveness of the substitution, Pattison writes, "The extent of substitution is further indicated in this story by the fact that the enemy against whom the collective act of violence is to be directed is conceived of as external."[85]

---

83. Ibid., 123. The focus of Bailie's work allows him considerably more textual space than we have here to present the anthropological evidence that supports Girard's claim that originally the king was a victim with an extended sentence. His work can be consulted where he builds his case based on the nineteenth-century work of Elias Canetti with the new king in Gaboon. Additionally, a much more recent work by Simon Simonse validates in many other ways the anthropological support for understanding the king as sacrificer and potential sacrifice. See Simonse, *Kings of Disaster*. See especially chapter 10, "The King as Unifier of the People" and chapters 16 & 17, "The King as Victim in Suspense" & "The King as Victim." Simonse offers his own conclusions on the scapegoat mechanism in Nilotic kingship in his summary conclusions, especially pp. 421ff.

84. Williams, "Sacrifice and the Beginning of Kingship," 85.

85. Pattison, "Violence," 138.

In the scope of these narratives, J. Cheryl Exum and J. William Whedbee write in ways similar to this study, "In the Saul narrative the portrayal of the deity is uncomfortably ambiguous (see chs. 8 and 9). Any way you look at it, Yhwh has an ambivalent attitude toward kingship."[86] She later comes to the assessment of David Gunn when she writes, "To use Gunn's phrase, Saul becomes kingship's scapegoat."[87]

GIRARDIAN INSIGHT

"The beauty of interpreting biblical narratives, as some literary theorists have pointed out, lies in the fact that behind their apparent simplicity lingers a background full of ambiguity and complexity which challenges our imagination."[88] And so with our narratives, we have seen ambiguity and complexity.

We have seen that it is possible to take the terminology and the framework of Girardian thought and discern in the individual narratives of this study Girardian insight. That is to say, Girard helps us read Judges 9. Girard helps us read Judges 17–21. And Girard helps us read 1 Samuel 9–11. But what is most urgent to our exposition is that Girard helps us understand the confluence of these stories, demonstrating their move towards kingship for Israel. At the start of our study we noted that the Deuteronomistic History seems ambivalent about kingship with pro- and "anti-monarchial sources. Our exposition demonstrates that this ambivalence is intentional in the presentation of kingship as kingship masks the myth of how harmony is achieved. Kingship masks that myth by remembering through sacrificial cult the murder of the one for the many. The monarchy then is welcomed for the peace it effects, but is disdained for the homicidal history of how peace is achieved.

As we have seen in Judges 9, the mimesis of Abimelech leads to his own destruction. Rivalry operates in the story and the one who sought to be like his father "as king" effects only destruction. Gaal is the direct rival, but in the absence of a scapegoat upon whom they can redirect their violence, Abimelech and Gaal together effect the destruction of Shechem entirely. And the movement of the story goes beyond the destruction only of Shechem to demonstrate how Abimelech is murdered

---

86. Exum and Whedbee, "Isaac, Samson, and Saul," 31.
87. Ibid.
88. Krondorfer, "Re-Mythologizing Scriptural Authority," 103.

not by a rival—the stone-throwing woman—but by an anti-rival who, with "one stone," effects his anti-kingship. There is nothing effective in a positive way about Abimelech's kingship. It is entirely void of "saving" value. Though there is "burning" that takes place by the fires Abimelech sets, these are not akin to burnt sacrifices that bring peace or harmony or release a scapegoat for salvation—there is only destruction, a city and memory sown with salt, to be unfertilized and unused in Israel's history. At the end of this story there is no ritual, there is no king, there is no peace, there is no unity.

Moving through the start of the stories in Judges 17 we begin to see marks of the priesthood but there is no sacrifice by this unnamed Levite. Sacrifice, we argue, is the means of effected violence for unification has not become operative in Israel's history yet. The Levite, a reader of the Biblical story might know, will function in the role of the one who offers sacrifice in the Temple of Israel, but it is not a part of this story, at least not on the clear surface of the story. The Levite in the first portion of the stories of Judges 17–21, specifically in Judges 17–18, is at the whimsy of those who move him around, be it Micah or the warriors of Dan who prey upon unsuspecting people. And perhaps that is what the reader is meant to see in this narrative, the unsuspecting victimage that takes place in this story. It is not only the people of Laish who are overrun by the Danites, it is the false notion of the Levitical priesthood that is overrun in this weak, ineffective, un-sacrificing Levite who does not function as a sacrificial priest.

Though it could be a different Levite in Judges 19–21, the lack of name for the Levite leaves us with the continuing ambiguity regarding the role and place of the Levite and priesthood in Israel.[89] The fact of so many characters in this story who are unnamed for us moves the reader to perceive the unnamed characters as representative of any persons living at anytime, but no doubt also hides the identity of the "real" characters of the "real" story that lie behind the events that are narrated to us here. It is upon the Levite that the threat of violence is evoked but it is upon the concubine that violence is enacted by all. Quite literally in the story, there was no one who provided safety for the concubine. The host did not save her in offering her to the sons of Belial. Whether we

---

89. We have already cited the fact that Judges 17–18 and 19–21 are read as two separate stories by some, but for us they function together about the ineffectiveness of priests who do not or a priesthood who does not offer sacrifice for quelling violence.

presume the Levite to have been the one to have thrust her out or the host, the Levite does not save her and, in hacking up her body, he violates and violently treats whatever semblance of being she was. And of course the sons of belial in having their way with her through the night violate her in every way. The concubine becomes the victim of the violence of the entire community. But, she is not in this story the scapegoat that curbs violence, and that is urgent to our reading. The concubine is not the scapegoat. In fact, in this story the murderous rape and heinous dismemberment of the concubine led to the genocide not of "all-against-one" in the anti-scapegoat of the concubine, but to all-against-one when all the tribes come out as "one man" to take on and to take out by genocidal warfare the tribe of Benjamin. In the story that has been created for us, there is more than one victim, there is the concubine as victim, but there is the tribe of Benjamin as scapegoated victim as well.

When all the tribes come as "one" against the one tribe and functionally annihilate them in the narrative, then Benjamin has been made the victim. And while it is the case in the narrative that some 600 men reside safely at the Rock of Rimmon in the narrative, so they are not fully "sacrificed" by the mob violence, the fact that they are "wept over" as though "one tribe has been cut off" helps the reader to see the scapegoating role they play.

Turning from this story to the story of Saul, then, in 1 Samuel we have seen how Saul comes from the very tribe that was seemingly cut off. Saul in the narrative represents then the victim. "The original violence took place within a single, solitary group, which the mechanism of the surrogate victim compelled either to split into separate groups or to seek an association with other groups . . . Ritual violence is intended to reproduce an original act of violence . . . [but] it conceals the site of original violence, thereby shielding from this violence, and from the very knowledge of this violence, the elementary group whose very survival depends on the absolute triumph of peace. . . Ritual violence invariably takes place between already constituted groups."[90] Saul, we might say, as one of the tribes of Benjamin in the narrative is the victim of the constituted groups. Using terminology that fits within our perspective specifically, David Gunn writes at the end of his review of Saul's reign; "Saul, therefore, is kingship's scapegoat."[91]

90. Girard, *Violence and the Sacred*, 249.
91. Gunn, "A Man Given Over to Trouble," 110.

But in our narrative of Saul, it is not the case that Saul is killed as Benjamin functionally was in the narrative. Instead, Saul is not cut-off and destroyed but is exalted. And Saul is exalted and brings kingship to Israel. By calling to mind the earlier victims that he and the concubine represent. He, from the tribe of Benjamin, represents the victim cut off from the others. He, as the one who effects the dismemberment of the oxen, calls to mind the victimage crisis of the concubine in Judges 19. In the narrative then, Saul brings together the two victims whose situation leads to anarchy in Judges 19–21. He is both the victim—Benjamite, and the one who remembers the first victim—the concubine who was dismembered. As this singular victim is recalled in the narrative, the violent tendency of Israel to turn their violence of all against themselves is redirected not towards themselves—but outward, against the threat to the city of Jabesh-Gilead. They effectively then, in 1 Samuel 11, save the persons who had effected their near annihilation in Judges 19–21. And what is more, instead of proclaiming destruction for this new way that kingship brings in Saul, Saul proclaims their lives are to remain—the naysayers will live.

At the end of this study, then, we return to where we began in chapter one. Girard writes specifically, "At first there is neither kingship nor any institution. There is only the spontaneous reconciliation over and against the victim who is a 'true scapegoat'... Like any human institution, monarchy is at first nothing but the will to reproduce the reconciliatory mechanism."[92] And more from Girard, "The king is at first nothing more than a victim with a sort of suspended sentence [even as we saw Saul chosen by lot], and this demonstrates that the victim is made responsible for the transformation that moves the community from mimetic violence to the order of ritual. In reality the victim is passive, but because the collective transference discharges the community of all responsibility, it creates the illusion of a supremely active and all-powerful victim. Kingship stages this metaphysical and religious illusion of the victim and the founding mechanism."[93]

Saul represents in his person and action the victim, who quells violence and brings peace. Saul is the scapegoat of the narrative.

---

92. Girard, *Things Hidden*, 51.
93. Ibid., 52.

7

Summary and Conclusions

THE LOGIC AND THOUGHT of this study has reached its full hearing. We have attempted to construct an idea of kingship and its emergence in the story and history of Israel. Our literary reading has allowed us to see how in the story of Abimelech, the Levite and his concubine, and in the anointing and inauguration of Saul, kingship emerges in Israel's story. It comes tenuously, falteringly, with conflict. But through chaos it emerges as sacred and the inauguration of kingship does happen with Saul. The narrative itself constructs fully named and unnamed persons who build our understanding of kingship in the Biblical narratives.

Our reading of these texts has also allowed us to construct an understanding of the emergence of kingship in the history of Israel's culture, passing through the myth and magic of this story understood in Girardian categories—we see a different construction. Using Girard we have seen that in these stories there may be a concrete past, now hidden in the myth of these stories, that harkens back to an originary sacrifice that quells violence and heralds sacral kingship.

Our construction from the narratives has been grounded in story and Girard's thinking. Two constructions seek to build the whole. And, it is believed, the constructions of this study establish a fortified reading of these stories.

But, lest we forget, when kingship was emerging in Israel's history, Abimelech tore down one constructed tower, and when he laid siege to the second, a single woman cast a stone on his head, and crushed his skull. Perhaps the argument created in this story constructs a sort of fortified tower, but a tower that can be burned down or led to a shameful end.

Our assessment is near its end. We have examined closely three separate texts/stories in the Hebrew Bible. We have discerned the weave of these individual stories into a larger whole. We have reviewed and assessed how Girardian theory helps us read these texts in a particular way. If this argument is fortified and holds firm, the implications for kingship in Israel and in the story of the Deuteronomistic History stand in a new light for us.

CHAOS TO CONCILIATION THROUGH VIOLENCE AND EMERGENT KINGSHIP

In the course of this study we intentionally read the Abimelech narrative for what it is most clearly about, the fact that the Shechemites—the people of the shoulders—lifted up over them and "kinged 'my father is king' king." But, this kingship story is bound up at every level with desire, rivalry, greed, mimesis, conflict, death (for persons), destruction (for towns), and ends in shame The kingship narrative then, with the conflict this king brings, mocks his kingship and shows the futility of this kingship. Unlike Gideon who has sons whom the people request to rule over them, Abimelech leaves nothing behind but, almost literally, a scorched earth. This pseudo king brings conflict. Conflict operates at every level in the story. Conflict within Abimelech's rivalry, conflict with his brothers, conflict with the Shechemite raiders, conflict with Gaal, conflict with Shechem and the Shechemites themselves, conflict with Thebez, and, perhaps we might even say, Abimelech's conflict with his own demise—trying to renounce its reality by saying "lest they say of me, a woman killed him." When "they king 'my father is king' king" they received not a king, but conflict.

We moved to the narratives concerning so many unnamed persons in Judges. There is no king to be named, for no one exists as king as we are told. And there are many persons acting "as they saw fit" but they are not named for us, just the general mass of unnamed persons at a time when no leadership or kingship is named. The primary characters and actors in the narrative that we read act in decisive ways, travelling, having conversations, eating, calling a war-tribunal and calling to war, weeping, destroying, raping, sacking, kidnapping and finally going home. But none of the characters are named for us. We read a horrific story of rape in the night after the primary unnamed Levite went to speak "kind words" to his unnamed concubine, but the unnamed old man, his unnamed virgin daughters, the unnamed servant, and the unnamed men of the house do nothing to bring kindness to this unnamed concubine. The lack of names for us causes us to recognize that not only are the actions narrated in this story full of chaos for all their violent destruction, the very characterization of person in this narrative leaves us as readers in a certain amount of chaos as well. If we were forensic investigators intent upon hunting down leads to quell the violence prevalent in all these stories, we would find ourselves unable to investigate much of anything for the sake of bringing persons to justice—or giving fair trial to either the accused or the abused. We know not any of the characters in this story. The violent chaos of destruction at so many levels in this story is matched by the virulent chaos of non-identified persons in this time when there is also no king to identify.

And finally, we moved to a story that introduced for us at several levels of detail, a person bound to use violence in one scene, and in one scene only—not for rape, pillage, dismemberment, fratricide, not even as a challenge to the threat of his would be rivals—but against a yoke of oxen for the sake of calling the people together as one in order to save brothers and, in the end, not even punish those who do not come together as one in order that they might finally all be alive as one. This one who is bound for kingship has several experiences that point to the emergence of something new in Israel, private then public anointing from old systems of established authority move in the direction of a new thing in Israel. One who will "restrain" is anointed—in order that he might lead, but instead of leading he goes home to work in the fields. This new one does not cause conflict, does not incite violence, does not lord it over others (or ride on their shoulders). This new one does not bring retribution on detractors or rivals. And he is fully named for us, by virtue of his characterization in dialogue, by lots, by size, by relationship, we know this new one, he is Saul. And when the moment of potential conflict arises that could give way to violence and chaos like that already experienced in Gibeah and Jabesh-Gilead, the inhabitants are saved, not destroyed, and detractors are allowed to live, not killed, and no woman, no man of the Israelites, of the brothers of Israel is killed, not a one. Saul uses the threat of violence in sacrificial murder—or perhaps recalls for the people he will "restrain" the possibilities of violence. And violence is carried out in Israel only against a yoke of oxen. Then, with violence restrained and Israel maintained, is Saul inaugurated king. There is no conflict in Israel or chaos to restrain, for this new one, this inaugurated king quells the potential for violence with the memory of a murder reenacted in a way upon the yoke of oxen who help to scapegoat the possible destruction.

Indeed, in the stories of Abimelech, the Levite and the concubine, and in Saul, we move from conflict to chaos and finally to reconciliation, through different forms of violence. With Abimelech it is all against one—at least in so far as Abimelech sees it. With the Levite and the concubine the all against one, the concubine, leads to all against all in near genocidal slaughter. With Saul, conflict from outsiders leads to violence against a yoke of oxen, and reconciliation among the sons of Israel.

In the opening chapter of this study I suggested that Girard's work allows us to see beyond source-critical assumptions and perceive a unique literary and anthropological dis-ease with kingship. In the course of the stories we have studied in this narrative we have, like Israel, traversed from conflict, through chaos, to reconciliation. We witnessed reconciliation by means of Saul's violent scapegoating that brought a new thing to Israel, kingship. Taken together, these stories narrate how conflict and chaos can be quelled with sanctioned violence in the reconciling act of kingship.

Bibliography

Ackerman, Susan. "What If Judges Had Been Written by a Philistine?" *BibInt* 8 (2000) 33–41.
Ackroyd, Peter R. *The First Book of Samuel*. CBC. Cambridge: Cambridge University Press, 1971.
Ahlström, Gösta W. *The History of Ancient Palestine*. Minneapolis: Fortress, 1993.
Alison, James. *Raising Abel: The Recovery of the Eschatological Imagination*. New York: Crossroad, 1996.
Alt, Albrecht. *Essays on Old Testament History and Religion*. Translated by R. A. Wilson. Garden City, NY: Doubleday, 1968.
———. "The Formation of the Israelite State in Palestine." In *Essays on Old Testament History and Religion*, translated by R. A. Wilson, 225–309. Oxford: Blackwell, 1966.
———. "The Origins of Israelite Law." In *Essays on Old Testament History and Religion*, translated by R. A. Wilson, 88–103. Oxford: Blackwell, 1966.
Alter, Robert. *The Art of Biblical Narrative*. New York: Basic, 1981.
———. *The David Story: A Translation with Commentary of 1 and 2 Samuel*. New York: Norton, 1999.
———. *Language as Theme in the Book of Judges*. Cincinnati: University of Cincinnati, 1988.
Alter, Robert, and Frank Kermode, editors. *The Literary Guide to the Bible*. Cambridge, MA: Belknap, 1987.
Amit, Yairah. "Bochim, Bethel, and the Hidden Polemic: Judges 2:1–5." In *Studies in Historical Geography and Biblical Historiography*, edited by Gershon Galil and Moshe Weinfeld, 121–31. VTSup 81. Leiden: Brill, 2000.
———. *The Book of Judges: The Art of Editing*. Translated by Jonathan Chipman. Biblical Interpretation Series 38. Leiden: Brill, 1999.
———. "Hidden Polemic in the Conquest of Dan: Judges 17–18." *VT* 40 (1990) 4–20.
———. "A Hidden Polemic in the Story of the Rape of Dinah." *The Proceedings of the Eleventh Congress of Jewish Studies, Div A* (1994) 1–8.
———. "Literature in the Service of Politics: Studies in Judges 19–21." In *Politics and Theopolitics in the Bible and Postbiblical Literature*, edited by H. G. Reventlow, et al., 28–40. JSOTSup 171. Sheffield, UK: JSOT Press, 1994.
———. "The Story of Ehud (Judges 3:12–30) The Form and The Message." In *Signs and Wonders: Biblical Texts in Literary Focus*, edited by J. Cheryl Exum, 97–124. Semeia Studies 18. Atlanta: Scholars, 1989.
Anspach, Mark R., and René Girard. "A Response: Reflection from the Perspective of Mimetic Theory." In *Violence and the Sacred in the Modern World*, edited by Mark Juergensmeyer, 141–48. London: Cass, 1992.
Arnold, Patrick M. *Gibeah: The Search for a Biblical City*. JSOTSup 79. Sheffield, UK: JSOT Press, 1990.

Auld, A. Graeme. "Gideon: Hacking at the Heart of the Old Testament." *VT* 34 (1989) 257–67.

———. "Judges 1 and History: A Reconsideration." *VT* 25 (1975) 261–85.

———. "Reading Joshua after Kings." In *Words Remembered, Texts Renewed: Essays in Honour of John F. A. Sawyer,* edited by Jon Davies, et al., 167–81. JSOTSup 195. Sheffield, UK: Sheffield Academic, 1995.

Averbeck, Richard E. "זבח (2284)." In *NIDOTTE,* edited by Willem A. VanGemeren. 1066–73. Grand Rapids: Zondervan, 1997.

Bach, Alice. "Rereading the Body Politic: Women and Violence in Judges 21." *BibInt* 6 (1998) 1–19.

Bailie, Gil. *Violence Unveiled: Humanity at the Crossroads.* New York: Crossroad, 1995.

Bal, Mieke. "Between Altar and Wondering Rock: Toward a Feminist Philology." In *Anti-Covenant: Counter-Reading Women's Lives,* edited by Mieke Bal, 211–31. Bible and Literature Series 22. JSOTSup 81. Sheffield, UK: Sheffield Academic, 1989.

———. "A Body of Writing: Judges 19." In *A Feminist Companion to Judges,* edited by Athalya Brenner, 208–30. Sheffield, UK: Sheffield Academic, 1993.

———. *Death and Dissymmetry: The Politics of Coherence in the Book of Judges.* Chicago Studies in the History of Judaism. Chicago: University of Chicago Press, 1988.

———. *Murder and Difference: Gender, Genre, and Scholarship on Sisera's Death.* Translated by Matthew Gumpert. Indiana Studies in Biblical Literature. Bloomington: Indiana University Press, 1988.

———. "Reading as Empowerment: The Bible from a Feminist Perspective." In *Approaches to Teaching the Hebrew Bible as Literature in Translation,* edited by Barry N. Olshen and Yael S. Feldman, 87–92. New York: Modern Language Association of America, 1989.

Baloian, Bruce Edward. "Anger in the Old Testament." PhD diss., Claremont Graduate School, 1988.

Bandera, Cesáreo. *The Sacred Game: The Role of the Sacred in the Genesis of Modern Literary Fiction.* Penn State Studies in Romance Literatures. University Park: Pennsylvania State University Press, 1994.

Bar-Efrat, Shimon. "Literary Modes and Method in the Biblical Narrative: In View of 2 Samuel 10:10 and I Kings 1–2." *Imm* 8 (1978) 19–31.

———. *Narrative Art in the Bible.* Understanding the Bible and Its World. London: T. & T. Clark, 2004.

Barber, Cyril J. *Judges: A Narrative of God's Power: An Expositional Commentary.* Neptune, NJ: Loizeaux Brothers, 1990.

Bartov, Hanoch. "Son, Father, Judge: A Story." *Com* 81 (1986) 32–39.

Beal, Timothy K. "Ideology and Intertextuality: Surplus of Meaning and Controlling the Means of Production." In *Reading between Texts: Intertextuality and the Hebrew Bible,* edited by Danna Fewell, 27–39. Literary Currents in Biblical Interpretation. Louisville: Westminster John Knox, 1992.

Becker, Uwe. *Richterzeit und Königtum: Redaktionsgeschichtliche Studien zum Richterbuch.* BZAW 192. Berlin: de Gruyter, 1990.

Begg, Christopher. "Abimelech, King of Shechem according to Josephus." *ETL* 72 (1996) 146–64.

Bell, Catherine M. *Ritual: Perspectives and Dimensions.* New York: Oxford University Press, 1997.

———. *Ritual Theory, Ritual Practice.* New York: Oxford University Press, 1992.

Bellinger, Charles K. *The Genealogy of Violence: Reflections on Creation, Freedom, and Evil.* Oxford: Oxford University Press, 2001.
Belsey, Catherine. *Critical Practice.* New Accents. London: Routledge, 1980.
Besters, Andre. "Le Sanctuarire Central dans Jud 19–21." *ETL* 41 (1965) 20–41.
Beuken, Wim and Karl-Josef Kuschel, editors. *Religion as a Source of Violence.* Concilium 1997/4. London: SCM, 1997.
Beydon, France. "Violence sous Silence: A Propos Lecure Feministe de Judges 19." *Foi et Vie* 88 (1989) 81–87.
Beyerlin, Walter. "Geschichte und heilsgeschichtliche Traditionsbildung im Alten Testament: Ein Beitrag zur Traditionsgeschichte von Richter 6–8." *VT* 13 (1963) 1–25.
———. "Das Konigscharisma bei Saul." *ZAW* 73 (1961) 186–201.
Birch, Bruce C. "Choosing of Saul at Mizpah." *CBQ* 37 (1975) 447–57.
———. "The Development o the Tradition of the Anointing of Saul in 1 Sam 9:1—10:16." *JBL* 90 (1971) 55–68.
———. *The Rise of the Israelite Monarchy: The Growth and Development of 1 Samuel 7–15.* SBLDS 27. Missoula: Scholars, 1976.
Bleicher, Josef. *Contemporary Hermeneutics: Hermeneutics as Method, Philosophy, and Critique.* London: Routledge & Kegan Paul, 1980.
Bloch, Marc. *Land and Work in Mediaeval Europe: Selected Papers.* Translated by J. E. Anderson. Berkeley: University of California Press, 1967.
Block, Daniel. "Echo Narrative Technique in Hebrew Literature: A Study in Judges 19." *WTJ* 52 (1990) 325–41.
———. "The Period of the Judges: Religious Disintegration under Tribal Rule." In *Israel's Apostasy and Restoration: Essays in Honor of Roland K. Harrison,* edited by Avraham Gileadi, 39–57. Grand Rapids: Baker, 1988.
———. "Unspeakable Crimes: The Abuse of Women in the Book of Judges." *SBJT* 2 (1998) 46–55.
———. "Will the Real Gideon Please Stand Up? Narrative Style and Intention in Judges 6–9." *JETS* 40 (1997) 353–66.
Boecker, Hans Jochen. *Die Beurteilung der Anfänge des Königtums in den deuteronomistischen Abschnitten des 1. Samuelbuches; ein Beitrag zum Problem des "Deuteronomistischen Geschichtswerks.* WMANT 31. Neukirchen-Vluyn: Neukirchener, 1969.
———. *Law and the Administration of Justice in the Old Testament and Ancient East.* Minneapolis: Augsburg, 1980.
Bohmbach, Karla G. "Conventions-Contraventions: The Meanings of Public and Private for the Judges 19 Concubine." *JSOT* 83 (1999) 83–98.
Boling, Robert G. "And Who Is S-K-M? (Judges 9:28)." *VT* 13 (1963) 479–82.
———. "In Those Days There Was No King in Israel." In *A Light unto My Path: Old Testament Studies in Honor of Jacob M. Myers,* edited by Howard M. Bream, et al., 38–48. Gettysburg Theological Studies 4. Philadelphia: Temple University Press, 1974.
———. *Judges: Introduction, Translation, and Commentary.* AB 6A. Garden City, NY: Doubleday, 1975.
———. "Response." *JSOT* 1 (1976) 47–52.
———. "Some Conflated Readings in Joshua-Judges." *VT* 16 (1966) 293–98.

Boogart, Thomas A. "Stone for Stone: Retribution in the Story of Abimelech and Shechem, Judges 9." *JSOT* 32 (1985) 45–56.

Bowman, Richard G. "Narrative Criticism of Judges: Human Purpose in Conflict with Divine Presence." In *Judges and Method: New Approaches in Biblical Studies*, edited by Gale A. Yee, 17–44. Minneapolis: Fortress, 1995.

Brenner, Athalya., editor. *A Feminist Companion to Judges*. Feminist Companion to the Bible 4. Sheffield, UK: Sheffield Academic, 1993.

———, editor. *Samuel and Kings*. Feminist Companion to the Bible, Second Series 7. Sheffield, UK: Sheffield Academic, 2000.

Brensinger, Terry L. *Judges*. Believers Church Bible Commentary. Scottdale, PA: Herald, 1999.

Brettler, Marc Zvi. *The Book of Judges*. Old Testament Readings. London: Routledge, 2002.

———. "The Book of Judges: Literature as Politics." *JBL* 108 (1989) 395–418.

———. *The Creation of History in Ancient Israel*. London: Routledge, 1995.

———. *God Is King: Understanding an Israelite Metaphor*. JSOTSup 76. Sheffield, UK: JSOT Press, 1989.

Brisman, Leslie. "Sacred Butchery: Exodus 32:25–29." In *Theological Exegesis: Essays in Honor of Brevard S. Childs*, edited by Christopher R. Seitz and Kathryn Greene-McCreight, 162–81. Grand Rapids: Eerdmans, 1999.

Brooks, Simcha Shalom. "Saul and the Samson Narrative." *JSOT* 71 (1996) 19–25.

———. "Was There a Concubine at Gibeah?" *BAIAS* 15 (1996–1997) 31–40.

Brueggemann, Walter. "Kingship and Chaos: A Study in Tenth-Century Theology." *CBQ* 33 (1971) 317–32.

———. "Social Criticism and Social Vision in the Deuteronomic Formula of the Judges." In *Die Botschaft und Die Boten: Festschrift für Hans Walter Wolff zum 70. Geburtstag*, edited by Jörg Jeremias and Lothar Perlitt, 101–14. Neukirchen-Vluyn: Neukirchener, 1981.

———. "Trajectories in Old Testament Literature and the Sociology of Ancient Israel." *JBL* 98 (1979) 161–85.

Buber, Martin. *Kingship of God*. London: Allen & Unwin, 1967.

———. "The Story of Saul's Rise to Kingship." *Tarbiz* (1951) 65–86.

Burney, C. F. *The Book of Judges, with Introduction and Notes, and Notes on the Hebrew Text of the Books of Kings, with an Introduction and Appendix*. LBS. New York: Ktav, 1970.

Burrell, David B. "René Girard: Violence and Sacrifice." *CC* 38 (1988) 443–47.

Callaway, Joseph A. "The Settlement in Canaan: The Period of the Judges." In *Ancient Israel: A Short History from Abraham to the Roman Destruction of the Temple*, edited by Herschel Shanks, 53–84. Englewood Cliffs, NJ: Prentice-Hall, 1988.

Campbell, Antony F. *1 Samuel*. Forms of Old Testament Literature 7. Grand Rapids: Eerdmans, 2003.

———. "Martin Noth and the Deuteronomistic History." In *The History of Israel's Traditions: The Heritage of Martin Noth*, edited by Steven L. McKenzie and M. Patrick Graham, 31–62. JSOTSup 182. Sheffield, UK: Sheffield Academic, 1994.

Cartledge, Tony W. *Vows in the Hebrew Bible and the Ancient Near East*. JSOTSup 147. Sheffield, UK: JSOT Press, 1992.

Chalcraft, David J. "Deviance and Legitimate Action in the Book of Judges." In *The Bible in Three Dimensions: Essays in Celebration of Forty Years of Biblical Studies in the*

University of Sheffield, edited by David J. A. Clines et al., 177–201. Sheffield, UK: Sheffield Academic, 1990.

Chisholm, Robert B., Jr. "The Role of Women in the Rhetorical Strategy of the Book of Judges." In *Integrity of Heart, Skillfulness of Hands: Biblical and Leadership Studies in Honor of Donald K. Campbell*, edited by Charles H. Dyer and Roy B. Zook, 34–39. Grand Rapids: Baker, 1994.

Clements, R. E. "The Deuteronomistic Interpretation of the Founding of the Monarchy in I Sam. 7." *VT* 24 (1974) 398–410.

———, editor. *The World of Ancient Israel: Sociological, Anthropological and Political Perspectives: Essays by Members of the Society for Old Testament Study*. Cambridge: Cambridge University Press, 1989.

Cohen, Martin. "The Role of the Shilonite Priesthood in the United Monarchy of Ancient Israel." *HUCA* 36 (1965) 59–98.

Cook, Albert. "'Fiction' and History in Samuel and Kings." *JSOT* 36 (1986) 27–48.

Coote, Robert B. *Early Israel: A New Horizon*. Minneapolis: Fortress, 1990.

Coote, Robert B., and Keith W. Whitelam. *The Emergence of Early Israel in Historical Perspective*. The Social World of Biblical Antiquity Series 5. Sheffield, UK: Almond, 1987.

Cross, Frank Moore. *Canaanite Myth and Hebrew Epic; Essays in the History of the Religion of Israel*. Cambridge: Harvard University Press, 1973.

———. *From Epic to Canon: History and Literature in Ancient Israel*. Baltimore: Johns Hopkins University Press, 1998.

———. *The Structure of the Deuteronomic History*. Perspectives in Jewsih Learning 3. Chicago: College of Jewish Studies, 1968.

Crossan, John Dominic. *The Dark Interval: A Theology of Story*. Sonoma, CA: Polebridge, 1988.

Crown, A. D. "A Reinterpretation of Judges 9 in Light of Its Humour." *AbrN* 3 (1961/1962) 90–98.

Crüsemann, Frank. *Der Widerstand gegen das Königtum: die antiköniglichen Texte des Alten Testamentes und der Kampf um den frühen israelitischen Staat*. WMANT 49. Neukirchen-Vluyn: Neukirchener, 1978.

Culley, Robert C. *Studies in the Structure of Hebrew Narrative*. Semeia Supplements. Philadelphia: Fortress, 1976.

Culpepper, R. Alan. "Narrative Criticism as a Tool for Proclamation: 1 Samuel 13." *RevExp* 84 (1987) 33–40.

Cundall, A. E. "Judges—An Apology for the Monarchy?" *ET* 81 (1970) 178–81.

Daube, David. "One from among Your Brethren Shall You Set King over You." *JBL* 90 (1971) 480–81.

Davies, G. Henton. "Judges 8:22–23." *VT* 13 (1963) 151–57.

Davies, Philip R. *In Search of Ancient Israel*. JSOTSup 148. Sheffield, UK: JSOT Press, 1992.

Davis, Dale R. "Comic Literature—Tragic Theology: A Study of Judges 17–18." *WTJ* 46 (1984) 156–63.

Deeley, Mary Katharine. "The Rhetoric of Memory in the Stories of Saul and David: A Prospective Study." In *SBL Seminar Papers 1988*, edited by David L. Lull, 285–92. Missoula, MT: Scholars, 1988.

De Groot, Christiana. "The Rape of the Concubine." *Pers* (1997) 12–15.

De Wette, Wilhelm M. L. *Beitrage zur Einleitung in das Alte Testament*. Halle, 1806/1807.

———. *Dissertatio critico-exegetica qua Deuteronomium a prioribus Pentateuchi libris diversum alius cuisdam recentioris auctoris opus esse monstratur*. Jena, 1805.

Dever, William G. "The Identity of Early Israel: A Rejoinder to Keith W. Whitelam." *JSOT* 72 (1996) 3–24.

Dietrich, Walter. "History and Law: Deuteronomistic Historiography and Deuteronomic Law Exemplified in the Passage from the Period of the Judges to the Monarchial Period." in *Israel Constructs Its History: Deuteronomistic Historiography in Recent Research*, edited by Albert de Pury, et al., 315–42. JSOTSup 306. Sheffield, UK: Sheffield Academic, 2000.

———. *Prophetie und Geschichte: Eine redaktionsgeschichtliche Untersuchung zum deuternomistischen Geschichtswerk*. FRLANT 108. Göttingen: Vandenhoeck & Ruprecht, 1972.

Dhorme, P. "Les Livres de Samuel." *EB* (1910) 96–97.

Dothan, Trude. "In the Days When the Judges Ruled: Research on the Period of the Settlement and the Judges." In *Recent Archaeology in the Land of Israel*, edited by Herschel Shanks and Benjamin Mazar, 35–41. Washington DC: Biblical Archaeology Society, 1984.

Douglas, Mary. *Purity and Danger: An Analysis of Concepts of Pollution and Taboo*. Routledge Classics. London: Routledge, 2002.

Dragga, Sam. "In the Shadow of the Judges: The Failure of Saul." *JSOT* 38 (1987) 39–46.

Dumbrell, William. J. "'In Those Days There Was No King in Israel; Every Man Did What Was Right in His Own Eye.' The Purpose of the Book of Judges Reconsidered." *JSOT* 25 (1983) 23–33.

Easterly, Ellis. "A Case of Mistaken Identity: The Judges in Judges Don't Judge." *BibRev* 13 (1997) 41–47.

Edelman, Diana V. "The Deuteronomist's Story of King Saul: Narrative Art or Editorial Product?" In *Pentateuchal and Deuteronomistic Studies: Papers Read at the XIIIth IOSOT Congress, Leuven 1989*, edited by C. Brekelmans and J. Lust, 207–20. BETL 94. Leuven: Leuven University Press, 1990.

———. *King Saul in the Historiography of Judah*. JSOTSup 121. Sheffield, UK: JSOT Press, 1991.

———. "Saul's Battle against Amaleq." *JSOT* 35 (1986) 71–84.

———. "Saul's Rescue of Jabesh-Gilead." *ZAW* 96 (1984) 195–209.

Eliade, Mircea. *Images and Symbols*. Translated by Phillip Mairet. Mythos. Princeton: Princeton University Press, 1991.

———. *Myths, Rites, Symbols: A Mircea Eliade Reader*. Edited by Wendell C. Beane and William G. Doty. New York: Harper & Row, 1976.

———. *Patterns in Comparative Religion*. Translated by Rosemary Sheed. Lincoln: University of Nebraska Press, 1996.

———. *The Sacred and Profane: The Nature of Religion*. Translated by Willard. R. Trask. New York. Harcourt, 1968.

Eliot, Alexander, with contributions by Joseph Campbell and Mircea Eliade. *The Universal Myths: Heroes, Gods, Tricksters and Others*. London: Meridian, 1990.

Ellul, Jacques. *Violence: Reflections from a Christian Perspective*. Translated by Cecelia Gaul Kings. New York: Seabury, 1969.

Emerton, John A. "Gideon and Jerubbaal." *JTS* 27 (1976) 289–312.

Eslinger, Lyle M. *Kingship of God in Crisis: A Close Reading of 1 Samuel 1-12.* SBLBLS 10. Bible and Literature Series 10. Decatur, GA: Almond, 1985.

———. "Viewpoints and Point of View in 1 Samuel 8-12." *JSOT* 26 (1983) 61-76.

Evans-Pritchard, Edward. *The Divine Kingship of the Shilluk of the Nilotic Sudan.* The Frazer Lecture, 1948. Cambridge: Cambridge University Press, 1948.

Exum, J. Cheryl. "The Centre Cannot Hold: Thematic and Textual Instabilities in Judges." *CBQ* 52 (1990) 410-31.

———. *Fragmented Women: Feminist (Sub)versions of Biblical Narratives.* JSOTSup 163. Sheffield, UK: JSOT Press, 1993.

———. "The Tragic Vision and Biblical Narrative: The Case of Jephthah." In *Signs and Wonders: Biblical Texts in Literary Focus*, edited by J. Cheryl Exum, 59-84. Semeia Studies 18. Altanta: Scholars, 1989.

———, editor. *Signs and Wonders: Biblical Texts in Literary Focus.* Semeia Studies 18. Atlanta: Scholars, 1989.

Exum, J. Cheryl, and J. William Whedbee. "Isaac, Samson, and Saul: Reflections on the Comic Tragic Visions." *Semeia* 32 (1984) 5-40.

Faiman, David. "Chronology in the Book of Judges." *JBQ* 21 (1993) 31-40.

Farber, Bernard. *Conceptions in Kinship.* New York: Elsevier North Holland, 1981.

Feeley-Harnik, Gillian. "Is Historical Anthropology Possible? The Case of the Runaway Slave." In *Humanizing American's Iconic Book*, edited by Gene M. Tucker and Douglas A. Knight, 95-126. Biblical Scholarship in North America / Society of Biblical Literature. Chico, CA: Scholars, 1982.

Fewell, Danna. "Feminist Reading of the Hebrew Bible: Affirmation, Resistance, and Transformation." *JSOT* 39 (1987) 77-87.

Fields, Weston. "The Motif 'Night as Danger' Associated with Three Biblical Destruction Narratives." In *"Sha'arei Talmon": Studies in the Bible, Qumran, and the Ancient Near East Presented to Shemaryahu Talmon*, edited by Michael Fishbane and Emanuel Tov, 17-32. Winona Lake, IN: Eisenbrauns, 1992.

Flanagan, James W. *David's Social Drama: A Hologram of Israel's Early Iron Age.* Social World of Biblical Antiquity Series 7. JSOTSup 73. Sheffield, UK: Almond, 1988.

Fokkelman, Jan P. *Narrative Art and Poetry in the Books of Samuel: A Full Interpretation Based on Stylistic and Structural Analysis.* Vol. 1, *King David (II Sam. 9-20 & I Kings 1-2).* SNN 20. Assen: Van Gorcum, 1981.

———. *Narrative Art and the Poetry in the Books of Samuel.* Vol. 2, *The Crossing Fates.* SSN 23. Assen: Van Gorcum, 1993.

———. "Structural Remarks on Judges 9 and 19." In *Sha'arei Talmon: Studies in the Bible, Qumran, and the Ancient Near East Presented to Shemaryahu Talmon*, edited by Michael Fishbane and Emanuel Tov, 33-45. Winona Lake, IN: Eisenbrauns, 1992.

Foresti, Fabrizio. *The Rejection of Saul in the Perspective of the Deuteronomistic School.* Studia theologica-Teresianum 5. Rome: Teresianum, 1984.

Forher, Georg. *History of Israelite Religion.* Translated by David E. Green. Nashville: Abingdon, 1972.

Frankfort, Henri. *Kingship and the Gods, A Study of Ancient Near Eastern Religion as the Integration of Society & Nature.* Oriental Institute Essay. Chicago: University of Chicago Press, 1948.

Frear, George L., Jr. "René Girard on Mimesis, Scapegoats, and Ethics." *ASCE* (1992) 115-33.

Freedman, David Noel. "'Who Is Like Thee among the Gods?' The Religion of Early Israel." In *Ancient Israelite Religion: Essays in Honor of Frank Moore Cross*, edited by Patrick D. Miller et al., 315–35. Philadelphia: Fortress, 1987.

Fretheim, Terence E. *The Deuteronomic History*. Interpreting Biblical Texts. Nashville: Abingdon, 1983.

Frick, Frank S. *The Formation of the State in Ancient Israel: A Survey of Models and Theories*. Social World of Biblical Antiquity Series 4. Sheffield, UK: Almond, 1985.

Fritz, Volkmar. "Abimelech und Sichem in Jdc 9." *VT* 32 (1982) 129–44.

———. "Die Deutungen des Konigtums Sauls in den Uberlieferungen von seiner Entstehung I Sam 9–11." *ZAW* 88 (1976) 346–62.

Fritz, Volkmar, and Philip R. Davies, editors. *The Origins of the Ancient Israelite States*. JSOT Sup 228. Sheffield, UK: Sheffield Academic, 1996.

Gans, Eric. *Originary Thinking: Elements of Generative Anthropology*. Stanford: Stanford University Press, 1993.

———. *Signs of Paradox: Irony, Resentment, and Other Mimetic Structures*. Stanford: Stanford University Press, 1997.

Garsiel, Moshe. *The First Book of Samuel: A Literary Study of Comparative Structures, Analogies and Parallels*. Ramat-Gan, Israel: Revivim, 1985.

———. "Homiletic Name-Derivations as a Literary Device in the Gideon Narrative: Judges vi–viii." *VT* 43 (1993) 302–17.

Gerbrandt, Gerald Eddie. *Kingship according to the Deuteronomistic History*. SBLDS 87. Atlanta: Scholars, 1986.

Geertz, Clifford. *Available Light: Anthropological Reflections on Philosophical Topics*. Princeton: Princeton University Press, 2001.

———. *The Interpretation of Cultures: Selected Essays*. New York: Basic, 1973.

———. *Local Knowledge: Further Essays in Interpretive Anthropology*. New York: Basic, 1983.

Gevirtz, Stanley. "The Hapax Legomenon Tormah (Judg 9:31)." *JNES* 17 (1958) 59–60.

Girard, René. "The Bible Is Not a Myth." *LitB* 4 (1984) 7–15.

———. *Deceit, Desire and the Novel: Self and Other in Literary Structure*. Translated by Yvonne Freccero. Baltimore: John Hopkins University Press, 1965.

———. "Generative Violence and the Extinction of Social Order (Dynamics of Mimetic Rivalry Exposed by the Gospels)." *SQHSS* 63/64 (1984) 204–37.

———. "History and the Paraclete." *EcRev* 35 (1983) 3–16.

———. *I See Satan Fall Like Lightning*. Translated, with a foreword, by James G. Williams. Maryknoll, NY: Orbis, 2001.

———. *Job, The Victim of His People*. Translated by Yvonne Freccero. London: Athlone, 1987.

———. *The Scapegoat*. Translated by Yvonne Frecerro. Baltimore: Johns Hopkins University Press, 1986.

———. "Theory and Its Terrors." In *The Limits of Theory*, edited by Thomas M. Kavanagh, 225–54. Stanford: Stanford University Press, 1989.

———. *"To Double Business Bound": Essays on Literature, Mimesis, Anthropology*. Baltimore: Johns Hopkins University Press, 1978.

———. "Triangular Desire." In *Red and Black* [by Stendhal]; *A New Translation, Backgrounds and Sources, Criticism*, edited by Robert M. Adams, 503–21. A Norton Critical Edition. New York: Norton, 1969.

———. *Violence and the Sacred*. Translated by Patrick Gregory. Baltimore: Johns Hopkins University Press, 1977.
Girard René, in collaboration with Jean-Michel Oughourlian and Guy Lefort. *Things Hidden since the Foundation of the World*. Translated by Stephen Bann and Michael Metteer. Stanford: Stanford University Press, 1987.
Golsan, Richard. *René Girard and Myth: An Introduction*. Theorists of Myth 7. Garland Reference Library of the Humanities 1194. New York: Garland, 1993.
Gooart, Sandor. *Sacrificing Commentary: Reading the End of Literature*. Baltimore: Johns Hopkins University Press, 1996.
Gooding, D. W. "The Composition of the Book of Judges." *The Harry M. Orlinsky Volume*, edited by Baruch Levine and Abraham Malamat, 70–79. Eretz-Israel 16. Jerusalem: Israel Exploration Society, 1982.
Gordon, Robert P. *I & II Samuel: A Commentary*. Library of Biblical Interpretation. Grand Rapids: Regency Reference Library, 1986.
———. "Who Made the Kingmaker? Reflections on Samuel and the Institution of Monarchy." In *Faith, Tradition, and History: Old Testament Historiography in Its Near Eastern Context*, edited by A. R. Millard, et al., 255–69. Winona Lake, IN: Eisenbrauns, 1994.
Gottcent, John H. *The Bible: A Literary Study*. Twayne Masterwork Studies 2. Boston: Twayne, 1986.
Gottwald, Norman K. *The Hebrew Bible: A Socio-Literary Introduction*. Philadelphia: Fortress, 1985.
———. *A Light to the Nations: An Introduction to the Old Testament*. New York: Harper, 1959.
———. "Social Class as an Analytic and Hermeneutical Category in Biblical Studies." *JBL* 112 (1993) 3–22.
———, editor. *Social Scientific Criticism of the Hebrew Bible and Its Social World: The Israelite Monarchy*. Semeia 37. Decatur, GA: Scholars, 1986.
———. *The Tribes of Yahweh: A Sociology of the Religion of Liberated Israel: 1250–1050 BCE*. Maryknoll: Orbis, 1979.
Gottwald, Norman K., and Richard A. Horsley, editors. *The Bible and Liberation: Political and Social Hermeneutics*. Rev. ed. The Bible & Liberation Series. Maryknoll: Orbis, 1993.
Grabbe, Lester L. "Prophets, Priests, Diviners and Sages in Ancient Israel." In *Of Prophets' Visions and the Wisdom of Sages: Essays in Honour of R. Norman Whybray on His Seventieth Birthday*, edited by Heather A. McKay and David J. A. Clines, 43–62. JSOTSup 162. Sheffield, UK: JSOT Press, 1993.
Gray, John. *Joshua, Judges, Ruth*. NCB. Grand Rapids: Eerdmans, 1986.
Green, Barbara. *How Are the Mighty Fallen? A Dialogical Study of King Saul in 1 Samuel*. JSOTSup 365. London: Sheffield Academic, 2003.
———. *King Saul's Asking*. Interfaces. Collegeville, MN: Liturgical, 2003.
Greenspahn, Frederick E. "An Egyptian Parallel to Judges 17:6 and 21:25." *JBL* 101 (1982) 129–30.
———. "The Theology of the Framework of Judges." *VT* 36 (1986) 385–96.
———. *When Brothers Dwell Together: The Preeminence of Younger Siblings in the Hebrew Bible*. New York: Oxford University Press, 1994.

Gros Louis, Kenneth R. R., editor; with James S. Ackerman and Thayer S. Warshaw. *Literary Interpretations of Biblical Narratives.* 2 vols. The Bible in Literature Courses. Nashville: Abingdon, 1974–1982.

Guest, Pauline Deryn. "Can Judges Survive without Sources? Challenging the Consensus." *JSOT* 78 (1998) 43–61.

———. "Dangerous Liaisons in the Book of Judges." *SJT* 11 (1997) 241–69.

Gudemann, M. "Tendenz und Abfassungszeit der dettzten Kapitel des Buches der Richter." *MGWJ* 18 (1869) 357–58.

Gunn, David M. *The Fate of King Saul: An Interpretation of a Biblical Story.* JSOTSup 14. Sheffield, UK: JSOT Press, 1984.

———. "A Man Given Over to Trouble: The Story of King Saul." In *Images of Man and God: Old Testament Short Stories in Literary Focus,* edited by Burke O. Long, 89–112. Bible and Literature Series 1. Sheffield, UK: Almond, 1981.

———, editor. *Narrative and Novella in Samuel: Studies by Hugo Gressmann and Other Scholars 1906–1923.* Translated by David E. Orton. JSOTSup 116. Sheffield, UK: Almond, 1991.

———. "Narrative Patterns and Oral Tradition in Judges and Samuel." *VT* 24 (1974) 286–317.

———. *The Story of King David: Genre and Interpretation.* JSOTSup 6. Sheffield, UK: University of Sheffield Department of Biblical Studies, 1978.

Gunn, David M., and Danna Nolan Fewell. *Narrative in the Hebrew Bible.* Oxford Bible Series. Oxford: Oxford University Press, 1993.

Hackett, Jo Ann. "Religious Traditions in Israelite Transjordan." In *Ancient Israelite Religion: Essays in Honor of Frank Moore Cross,* edited by Patrick D. Miller et al., 25–136. Philadelphia: Fortress, 1987.

Haag, Herbert. "Gideon—Jerubbaal—Abimelek." *ZAW* 79 (1967) 305–14.

Hallo, William W. "The Origins of the Sacrificial Cult: New Evidence from Mesopotamia and Israel." In *Ancient Israelite Religion: Essays in Honor of Frank Moore Cross,* edited by Patrick D. Miller et al., 3–13. Philadelphia: Fortress, 1987.

Halpern, Baruch. *The Constitution of the Monarchy in Israel.* HSM 25. Chico, CA: Scholars, 1981.

———. "The Uneasy Compromise: Israel between League and Monarchy.'" In *Traditions in Transformation: Turning Points in Biblical Faith,* edited by Baruch Halpern and Jon D. Levenson, 59–96. Winona Lake, IN: Eisenbrauns, 1981.

Hamerton-Kelly, Robert G. "Biblical Interpretation, Mythology, and a Theory of Ethnic Violence." *Scrip* 50 (1994) 23–39.

———, editor. *Violent Origins.* Stanford: Stanford University Press, 1987.

———. *Sacred Violence: Paul's Hermeneutic of the Cross.* Minneapolis: Fortress, 1992.

Hamlin, E. John. *At Risk in the Promised Land : A Commentary on the Book of Judges.* ITC. Grand Rapids: Eerdmans, 1990.

Hardin, Richard F. "Ritual und Literaturwissenschaft." In *Ritualtheorien: Ein einfuhrendes Handbuch,* edited by Andrea Bellinger and David J. Krieger, 339–63. Opladen: Westdetscher, 1998.

Harris, J. Gordon, et al. *Joshua, Judges, Ruth.* NIBC: Old Testament Series 5. Peabody, MA: Hendrickson, 2000.

Hauer, Christian E. "Does 1 Samuel 9:1—11:15 Reflect the Extension of Saul's Dominions?" *JBL* 86 (1967) 306–10.

Hauser, Alan J. "Unity and Diversity in Early Israel before Samuel." *JETS* 22 (1979) 289-304.

Hawk, L. Daniel. *Every Promise Fulfilled: Contesting Plots in Joshua.* Literary Currents in Biblical Interpretation. Louisville: Westminster John Knox, 1991.

Hayes, John H. *An Introduction to Old Testament Study.* Nashville: Abingdon, 1980.

Herion, Gary A. "The Impact of Modern and Social Science Assumptions on the Reconstruction of Israelite History." *JSOT* 34 (1986) 3-33.

Hertzberg, Hans Wilhelm. *I & II Samuel: A Commentary.* Translated by J. S. Bowden. OTL. Philadelphia: Westminster, 1964.

Hillers, Delbert R. "A Note on Some Treaty Terminology in the Old Testament." *BASOR* 176 (1964) 46-47.

Hinson, David F. *History of Israel.* Rev. ed. Old Testament Introduction 1. TEF Study Guide 7. London: SPCK, 1990.

Hobson, Theo. "Faith and Rhetorical Violence: A Response to Girard." *MB* 40 (1999) 34-41.

Holloday, John S., Jr. "Religion in Israel and Judah under the Monarchy: An Explicitly Archaeological Approach." In *Ancient Israelite Religion: Essays in Honor of Frank Moore Cross*, edited by Patrick D. Miller, et al., 249-99. Philadelphia: Fortress, 1987.

Honeyman, A. M. "The Salting of Shechem." *VT* 3 (1953) 192-95.

Howard, David M., Jr. "The Case for Kingship in Deuteronomy and the Former Prophets." *WTJ* 52 (1990) 101-15.

Humphreys, W. Lee. "From Tragic Hero to Villain: A Study of the Figure of Saul and the Development of 1 Samuel." *JSOT* 22 (1982) 95-117.

———. "The Story of Jephthah and the Tragic Vision: A Response to J. Cheryl Exum." In *Signs and Wonders: Biblical Texts in Literary Focus*, edited by J. Cheryl Exum, 85-95. Semeia Studies 18. Atlanta: Scholars, 1989.

———. "The Tragedy of King Saul: A Study of the Structure of 1 Samuel 9-31." *JSOT* 6 (1978) 18-27.

Hudson, Don Michael. "Living in a Land of Epithets: Anonymity in Judges 19-21." *JSOT* (1994) 49-66.

Ishida, Tomoo. *History and Historical Writing in Ancient Israel: Studies in Biblical Historiography.* Studies in the History and Culture of the Ancient Near East 16. Leiden: Brill, 1999.

———. "The Leaders of the Tribal League 'Israel' in the Pre-Monarchic Period." *RB* 80 (1973) 514-30.

———. *The Royal Dynasties in Ancient Israel: A Study on the Formation and Development of Royal-Dynastic Ideology.* BZAW 142. Berlin: de Gruyter, 1977.

———, editor. *Studies in the Period of David and Solomon and Other Essays: Papers Read at the International Symposium for Biblical Studies, Tokyo, December 1979.* Winona Lake, IN: Eisenbrauns, 1982.

Janzen, J. Gerald. "A Certain Woman in the Rhetoric of Judges 9." *JSOT* 38 (1987) 33-37.

———. "'Samuel Opened the Doors of the House of Yahweh' (1 Samuel 3.15)." *JSOT* 26 (1983) 89-96.

Jay, Nancy. *Throughout Your Generations Forever: Sacrifice, Religion, and Paternity.* Chicago: University of Chicago Press, 1992.

Jensen, Hans J. L. "Desire, Rivalry and Collective Violence in the 'Succession Narrative.'" *JSOT* 55 (1992) 39–59.

Jobling, David. *1 Samuel*. Berit Olam. Collegeville, MN: Liturgical, 2000.

———. "What, If Anything, Is 1 Samuel?" *SJOT* 7 (1993) 17–31.

Johnson, Aubrey, R. *Sacral Kingship in Ancient Israel*. 2nd ed. Cardiff: University of Wales Press, 1967.

———. *The Vitality of the Individual in the Thought of Ancient Israel*. 2nd ed. Cardiff: University of Wales Press, 1964.

Jones-Warsaw, Koala. "Toward a Womanist Hermeneutic: A Reading of Judges 19–21." *JITC* 22 (1994) 18–35.

Jüngling, Hans-Winfried. *Richter 19—Ein Plädoyer für das Königtum: Stilistische Analyse der Tendenxerzählung Ri 19, 1–30a; 21,25*. Analecta Biblica 84 Rome: Pontifical Biblical Institute Press, 1981.

Kahn, Sholom J. "The Samuel-Saul Story as Drama" *Jud* 4 (1955) 3–12.

Keefe, Alice A. "Rapes of Women/Wars of Men." *Semeia* 61 (1993) 79–97.

Keim, Paul. "Reading Ancient Near Eastern Literature from the Perspective of René Girard's Scapegoat Theory." In *Violence Renounced: René Girard, Biblical Studies, and Peacemaking*, edited by Willard M. Swartley, 157–77. Studies in Peace and Scripture 4. Telford, PA: Pandora, 2000.

Kerr, Fergus. "Rescuing Girard's Argument?" *ModT* 8 (1992) 385–99.

———. "Revealing the Scapegoat Mechanism: Christianity after Girard." In *Philosophy, Religion and the Spiritual Life*, edited by Michael McGhee, 161–75. Cambridge: Cambridge University Press, 1992.

Kim, Jichan. *The Structure of the Samson Cycle*. Kampen: Kok Pharos, 1993.

Klein, Lillian R. *The Triumph of Irony in the Book of Judges*. Bible and Literature Series 14. JSOTSup 68. Sheffield, UK: Almond, 1988.

Klein, Ralph W. *1 Samuel*. WBC 10. Waco, TX: Word, 1983.

Knight, Douglas A., editor. *Ethics and Politics in the Hebrew Bible."* Semeia 66. Atlanta: Scholars, 1994.

Krondorfer, Bjorn. "Response to James G. Williams: Re-Mythologizing Scriptural Authority; On Reading 'Sacrifice and the Beginning of Kingship'" *Semeia* 67 (1995) 93–107.

Kuenen, Abraham. *Historisch-kritische Einleitung in die Bucher des Alten Testaments*. Vol. 1, bk. 2, *Stück. Historischen Bücher des alten Testaments*. Leipzig: Schulze, 1890.

Lambert, Wilfred G. "Kingship in Ancient Mesopotamia." In *King and Messiah in Israel and the Ancient Near East: Proceedings of the Oxford Old Testament Seminar*, edited by John Day, 55–70. JSOTSup 270. Sheffield, UK: Sheffield Academic, 1998.

Langlamet, F. "Lés récits dé l'institution dé la royauté israélité (1 Sam VII–XII)." *RB* 77 (1970) 161–200.

Lasine, Stuart. "Guest and Host in Judges 19: Lot's Hospitality in an Inverted World." *JSOT* 29 (1984) 37–59.

Latvus, Kari. *God, Anger, and Ideology: The Anger of God in Joshua and Judges in Relation to Deuteronomy and the Priestly Writings*. JSOTSup 279. Sheffield, UK: Sheffield Academic, 1998.

Lefebure, Leo D. "Beyond Scapegoating: A Conversation with René Girard and Ewert Cousins." *ChrCent* 115 (1998) 372–75.

———."Victims, Violence and the Sacred: The Thought of René Girard." *ChrCent* 113 (1996) 1226–29.

LeMaire, Andre. "The United Monarchy: Saul, David and Solomon." In *Ancient Israel: A Short History from Abraham to the Roman Destruction of the Temple*, edited by Herschel Shanks, 91–128. Englewood Cliffs, NJ: Prentice-Hall, 1988.

Lemche, Niels Peter. *Ancient Israel: A New History of Israelite Society*. Biblical Seminar 5. Sheffield, UK: JSOT Press, 1988.

———. *The Canaanites and Their Land: The Tradition of the Canaanites*. JSOTSup 110. Sheffield, UK: JSOT Press, 1991.

———. *Early Israel: Anthropological and Historical Studies on the Israelite Society before the Monarchy*. VTSup 37. Leiden: Brill, 1985.

———. "The Greek 'Amphictyony': Could It Be a Prototype for the Israelite Society in the Period of the Judges?" *JSOT* 4 (1977) 48–59.

———. "Israel in the Period of the Judges: The Tribal League in Recent Research." *ST* 38 (1984) 1–28.

———. "The Judges—Once More." *BN* 20 (1983) 47–55.

Lévi-Strauss, Claude. *The Raw and the Cooked*. Translated by John and Doreen Weightman. New York: Harper & Row, 1969.

———. *The Savage Mind*. The Nature of Human Society Series. London: Weidenfeld & Nicolson, 1966.

———. *Totemism*. Translated by Rodney Needham. Boston: Beacon, 1963.

Levinson, Bernard M. "The Reconceptualization of Kingship in Deuteronomy and the Deuteronomistic History's Transformation of Torah." *VT* 51 (2001) 511–30.

Lewis, I. M. *Religion in Context: Cults and Charisma*. Cambridge: Cambridge University Press, 1986.

Lilley, J. P. U. "A Literary Appreciation of the Book of Judges." *TynB* 18 (1967) 94–102.

Lindars, Barnabas. "Gideon and Kingship." *JTS* 16 (1965) 315–26.

———. "Jotham's Fable: A New Form-Critical Analysis." *JTS* 24 (1973) 355–66.

———. *Judges 1–5: A New Translation and Commentary*. Edited by A. D. H. Mayes. Edinburgh: T. & T. Clark, 1995.

———. "The Israelite Tribes in Judges." In *Studies in the Historical Books of the Old Testament*, edited by J. A. Emerton, 95–112. VTSup 30. Leiden: Brill, 1979.

Lindblom, J. "Lot-Casting in the Old Testament." *VT* 12 (1962) 164–78.

Linden, Nico ter. *The Stories of Judges and Kings*. Translated by John Bowden. The Story Goes 3. London: SCM, 2000.

Liss, Hanna. "Die Fabel des Yotam in Ri 9,8-15—Versuch Einer Strukturellen Deutung." *BN* 89 (1997) 12–18.

Long, Burke O. "Historical Narrative and the Fictionalizing Imagination." *VT* 35 (1985) 405–16.

———, editor. *Images of Man and God: Old Testament Short Stories in Literary Focus*. Bible and Literature Series 1. Sheffield, UK: Almond, 1981.

Long V. Philips. "How Did Saul Become King? Literary Reading and Historical Reconstruction." In *Faith, Tradition, and History: Old Testament Historiography in Its Near Eastern Context*, edited by A. R. Millard, et al., 271–84. Winona Lake, IN: Eisenbrauns, 1994.

———. *The Reign and Rejection of King Saul: A Case for Literary and Theological Coherence*. SBLDS 118. Atlanta: Scholars, 1989.

Mabee, Charles. "Judicial Instrumentality in the Abimelech Story." In *Early Jewish and Christian Exegesis: Studies in Memory of William Hugh Brownlee*, edited by

Craig Evans and W. Stinespring, 17–32. Scholars Press Homage Series 10. Atlanta: Scholars, 1987.

———. "Text as Peacemaker: Deuteronomic Innovations in Violence Detoxification." In *Violence Renounced: René Girard, Biblical Studies, and Peacemaking*, edited by Willard M. Swartley, 70–84. Telford, PA: Pandora, 2000.

Macintosh, Andrew Alexander. "The Meaning of *Mklym* in Judges 18:7." *VT* 35 (1985) 68–77.

Malamat, Abraham. "The Danite Migration and the Pan-Israelite Exodus-Conquest: A Biblical Narrative Pattern." *Bib* 51 (1970) 1–16.

———. "The Period of the Judges." In *Judges*, edited by Benjamin Mazar, 162–165. The World History of the Jewish People: Ancient Times, 1st series 3. London: Allen, 1971.

Maly, Eugene H. "The Jotham Fable—Anti-Monarchical?" *CBQ* 22 (1960) 299–305.

Mandell, Sara R. "Reading Samuel as Saul and Vice Versa." In *Approaches to Ancient Judaism*, edited by Jacob Neusner, 13–32. South Florida Studies in the History of Judaism 7. Atlanta: Scholars, 1996.

March, Eugene W. "II Samuel 7:1–17." *Int* 35 (1981) 397–401.

Marr, Andrew. "Violence and the Kingdom of God: Introducing the Anthropology of René Girard." *ATR* 80 (1998) 590–603.

Martin, John A. "The Literary Quality of 1 and 2 Samuel." *BSac* (1984) 131–45.

Matthews, Victor H. "Hospitality and Hostility in Genesis 19 and Judges 19." *BTB* 22 (1992) 3–11.

Matties, Gordon H. "Can Girard Help Us to Read Joshua?" In *Violence Renounced: René Girard, Biblical Studies, and Peacemaking*, edited by Willard M. Swartley, 85–102. Telford, PA: Pandora, 2000.

Mauchline, John. *1 and 2 Samuel*. NCB. London: Oliphants, 1971.

Mayes, A. D. H. "Deuteronomistic Ideology and the Theology of the Old Testament." In *Israel Constructs Its History: Deuteronomistic Historiography in Recent Research*, edited by Albert de Pury et al., 456–80. JSOTSup 306. Sheffield, UK: Sheffield Academic, 2000.

———. "Israel in the Pre-Monarchy Period." *VT* 23 (1973) 151–70.

———. *Israel in the Period of the Judges*. Studies in Biblical Theology, Second Series 2. London: SCM, 1974.

———. *Judges*. OTG 3. Sheffield, UK: JSOT Press, 1985.

———. "The Period of the Judges and the Rise of the Monarchy." In *Israelite and Judaean History*, edited by John H. Hayes and J. Maxwell Miller, 285–331. OTL. Philadelphia: Westminster, 1977.

———. *The Story of Israel between Settlement and Exile: A Redactional Study of the Deuteronomistic History*. London: SCM, 1983.

McCarter, P. Kyle, Jr. *1 Samuel: A New Translation*. AB 8. Garden City, NY: Doubleday, 1980.

McCarthy, Dennis J. "Compact and Kingship: Stimuli for Hebrew Covenant Thinking." In *Studies in the Period of David and Solomon and Other Essays*, edited by Tomoo Ishida, 75–92. Winona Lake, IN: Eisenbrauns. 1979.

———. "The Inauguration of Monarchy in Israel: A Form-Critical Study of 1 Samuel 8–12." *Int* 27 (1973) 401–12.

McGinnis, Claire Mathews. "Swimming with the Divine Tide: An Ignatian Reading of 1 Samuel." In *Theological Exegesis: Essays in Honor of Brevard S. Childs*, edited

by Christopher Seitz and Kathryn Greene-McCreight, 240-70. Grand Rapids: Eerdmans, 1999.
McKenna, Andrew J. "René Girard and Biblical Studies." *Semeia* 33 (1985) 1-11.
———. *Violence and Difference: Girard, Derrida, and Deconstruction.* Urbana: University of Illinois Press, 1992.
McKenzie, John L. "Royal Messianism." *CBQ* 19 (1957) 25-52.
McKenzie, Steven L. "The Trouble with Kingship." In *Israel Constructs Its History: Deuteronomistic Historiography in Recent Research*, edited by Albert de Pury, et al., 286-314. JSOTSup 306. Sheffield, UK: Sheffield Academic Press, 2000.
McKenzie, Steven L., and M. Patrick Graham, editors. *The History of Israel's Traditions: The Heritage of Martin Noth.* JSOTSup 182. Sheffield, UK: Sheffield Academic, 1994.
Meier, Sam. "The King as Warrior in Samuel-Kings." *HAR* 13 (1991) 63-76.
Mendelsohn, Isaac. "Samuel's Denunciation of Kingship in the Light of the Akkadian Documents from Ugarit." *BASOR* 143 (1956) 17-22.
Merrill, Eugene H. "The Demand for Kingship." In *Kingdom of Priests: A History of Old Testament Israel*, edited by Eugene H. Merrill, 189-92. Grand Rapids: Baker, 1987.
Mettinger, Tryggve N. D. *King and Messiah: The Civil and Sacral Legitimation of the Israelite Kings.* ConBOT 8. Lund: Gleerup, 1976.
Milbank, John. "Stories of Sacrifice." *ModT* 12 (1996) 27-56.
Miller, Geoffrey P. "Verbal Feud in the Hebrew Bible: Judges 3:12-30 and 19-21." *JNES* 55 (1996) 105-17.
Miller. J. M. "Saul's Rise to Power: Some Observations Concerning 1 Sam 9:1—10.16; 10:26—11:15; and 13:2—14:46." *CBQ* 36 (1974) 157-74.
Miller, Patrick D., and J. J. M. Roberts. *The Hand of the Lord: A Reassessment of the Ark Narrative of 1 Samuel.* Johns Hopkins Near Eastern Studies. Baltimore: Johns Hopkins University Press, 1977.
Mills, Mary E. *Historical Israel, Biblical Israel: Joshua to 2 Kings.* The Cassell Biblical Studies Series. London: Cassell, 1999.
Mommer, Peter. *Samuel: Geschichte und Überlieferung.* WMANT 65. Neukirchen-Vluyn: Neukirchener, 1991.
Moore, Johannes de, and Harry van Rooy, editors. *Past, Present, Future: The Deuteronomistic History and the Prophets.* OtSt 44. Leiden: Brill 2000.
Mullen, E. Theodore, Jr. "Judges 1:1-36: The Deuteronomistic Reintroduction of the Book of Judges." *HTR* 77 (1984) 33-54.
"The 'Minor Judges': Some Literary and Historical Considerations." *CBQ* 44 (1982) 185-201.
———. *Narrative History and Ethnic Boundaries: The Deuteronomistic Historian and the Creation of Israelite National Identity.* Semeia Studies. Atlanta: Scholars, 1993.
Munk, Linda. "The Design of Violence [Girard on mimetic doubling and 'design']." *LT* 4 (1990) 251-62.
Na'aman, Nadav. "The Pre-Deuteronomistic Story of King Saul and Its Historical Significance." *CBQ* 54 (1992) 638-58.
Nelson, Richard D. *The Double Redaction of the Deuteronomistic History.* JSOTSup 18. Sheffield, UK: JSOT Press, 1981.
———. "Josiah in the Book of Joshua." *JBL* 100 (1981) 531-40.
Neuchterlein, Paul J. "The Work of René Girard as a New Key to Biblical Hermeneutics." *CurTM* 26 (1999) 196-209.

Nicholson, Sarah. *Three Faces of Saul: An Intertextual Approach to Biblical Tragedy.* JSOTSup 339. Sheffield, UK: Sheffield Academic, 2002.

Niditch, Susan, editor. *Text and Tradition: The Hebrew Bible and Folklore.* Semeia Studies. Atlanta: Scholars, 1990.

———. "The 'Sodomite' Theme in Judges 19–20: Family, Community, and Social Disintegration." *CBQ* 44 (1982) 365–78.

North, Robert. "Violence and the Bible: The Girard Connection." *CBQ* 47 (1985) 1–27.

Noth, Martin. "Background of Judges 17–18." In *Israel's Prophetic Heritage: Essays in Honor of James Muilenburg,* edited by Bernhard W. Anderson et al., 68–85. New York: Harper, 1962.

———. *The Deuteronomistic History.* JSOTSup 15. Sheffield, UK: University of Sheffield Department of Biblical Studies, 1981.

———. *The History of Israel.* 2nd ed. Translated by P. R. Ackroyd. London: Black, 1960.

———. *Überlieferungsgeschichtliche Studien: Die sammelnden und bearbeitenden Geschichtswerke im Alten Testament.* 3rd ed. Tubingen: Niemeyer, 1967.

O'Brien, Mark A. *The Deuteronomistic History Hypothesis: A Reassessment.* OBO 92. Freiburg, Schweiz: Universitatsverlag, 1989.

———. "Judges and the Deuteronomistic History." In *The History of Israel's Traditions: The Heritage of Martin Noth,* edited by Steven L. McKenzie and M. Patrick Graham, 235–59. JSOTSup 182. Sheffield, UK: Sheffield Academic, 1994.

O'Connell, Robert H. *The Rhetoric of the Book of Judges.* VTSup 63. Leiden: Brill, 1996.

Ogden, Graham S. "Jotham's Fable: Its Structure and Function in Judges 9." *BT* 46 (1995) 301–8.

Olson, Dennis T. *Deuteronomy and the Death of Moses: A Theological Reading.* OBT. Minneapolis: Fortress, 1994.

Omason, Roger L., and John E. Ellington. *A Handbook on the First and Second Books of Samuel.* Helps for Translators. UBS Handbook Series. New York: United Bible Societies, 2001.

Page, Hugh R., Jr. "Boundaries: A Case Study Using the Bible Book of Judges." *RSSSR* 10 (1999) 37–55.

Pattison, George. "Violence, Kingship and Cultus." *ET 102* (1991) 135–40.

Patton, Corrine L. "From Heroic Individual to Nameless Victim: Women in the Social World of the Judges." In *Biblical and Humane: A Festschrift for John F. Priest,* edited by Linda Bennett-Elder and David Barr, 33–46. Scholars Press Homage Series 20. Atlanta: Scholars, 1996.

Penchansky, David. "Staying the Night: Intertextuality in Genesis and Judges." In *Reading between Texts: Intertextuality and the Hebrew Bible,* edited by Danna Nollan Fewell, 77–88. Literary Currents in Biblical Interpretation. Louisville: Westminster John Knox, 1992.

Perry, Menahem, and Meir Sternberg. "The King through Ironic Eyes: Biblical Narrative and the Literary Reading Process." *PT* 7 (1986) 275–322.

Phillips, Anthony. *Ancient Israel's Criminal Law: A New Approach to the Decalogue.* Oxford: Blackwell, 1970.

———. "*Nebalah*: A Term for Serious Disorderly and Unruly Conduct." *VT* 25 (1975) 237–41.

Pitt-Rivers, Julian. "The Stranger, the Guest, and the Hostile Host: Introduction to the Study of the Laws of Hospitality." In *Contributions to Mediterranean Sociology,* edited by J. G. Peristiany, 13–30. Paris: Mouton, 1968.

Polzin, Robert. *Moses and the Deuteronomist: A Literary Study of the Deuteronomic History*. San Francisco: Seabury, 1980.

———. "On Taking Renewal Seriously: 1 Sam 11:1–15." In *Ascribe to the Lord: Biblical & Other Studies in Memory of Peter C. Craigie*, edited by Lyle M. Eslinger and Glen Taylor, 493–507. JSOTSup 67. Sheffield, UK: Sheffield Academic, 1988.

———. *Samuel and the Deuteronomist: A Literary Study of the Deuteronomic History: Part Two; 1 Samuel*. San Francisco: Harper & Row, 1989.

———. "'HWQY and Covenantal Institutions in Early Israel." *HTR* 62 (1969) 227–40.

Preston, Thomas R. "The Heroism of Saul: Patterns of Meaning in the Narrative of the Early Kingship." *JSOT* 24 (1982) 27–46.

Provan, Iain W. *Hezekiah and the Books of Kings: A Contribution to the Debate about the Composition of the Deuteronomistic History*. BZAW 172. Berlin: de Gruyter, 1988.

———. "Ideologies, Literary and Critical: Reflections on Recent Writing on the History of Israel." *JBL* 114 (1995) 283–300.

Provan, Iain, et al. *A Biblical History of Israel*. Louisville: Westminster John Knox, 2003.

Pury, Albert de et al., editors. *Israel Construit Son Histoire: L'historiographie Deuteronomiste a la Lumiere des Recherches Recentes*. Le monde de la Bible 34. Geneva: Labor et Fides, 1996.

Quinn-Miscall, Peter D. *1 Samuel: A Literary Reading*. Indiana Studies in Biblical Literature. Bloomington: Indiana University Press, 1986.

Rabin, Chaim. "The Origin of the Hebrew Word *Pilegesh*." *JJS* 24 (1974) 353–64.

Radday, Yehuda T. "The Book of Judges Examined by Statistical Linguistics." *Bib* 58 (1977) 469–99.

Revell, John E. "The Battle with Benjamin (Judges 20:29–48) and Hebrew Narrative Techniques." *VT* 35 (1985) 417–33.

Reviv, Hanoch. "The Government of Shechem in the El-Amarna Period and in the Days of Abimelech." *IEJ* 16 (1966) 252–57.

Richter, Wolfgang. "Die nāgīd Formel." *BZ* 9 (1965) 71–84.

———. *Traditionsgeschichtliche Untersuchungen zum Richterbuch*. 2nd ed. Bonn: BBB 18. Bonn: Hanstein, 1966.

Ricoeur, Paul. "The Narrative Function." *Semeia* 13 (1978) 177–202.

Ridout, Samuel. *King Saul: The Man after the Flesh: Being Notes on 1 Samuel*. New York: Loizeaux, 1930.

Roberts, J. J. M. "In Defense of the Monarchy: The Contribution of Israelite Kingship to Biblical Theology." In *Ancient Israelite Religion: Essays in Honor of Frank Moore Cross*, edited by Patrick D. Miller et al., 377–96. Philadelphia: Fortress, 1987.

Rofé, A. "The Acts of Nahash according to 4QSam^a." *IEJ* 32 (1982) 129–33.

Römer Thomas, editor. *The Future of the Deuteronomistic History*. BETL 147. Leuven: Leuven University Press, 2000.

Rosel, Hartmut N. "Uberlegungen zu Abimelech und Sichem in Jdc 9." *VT* 33 (1983) 500–503.

Rowlett, Lori L. *Joshua and the Rhetoric of Violence: A New Historicist Analysis*. JSOTSup 226. Sheffield, UK: Sheffield Academic, 1996.

Salmon, John Mellersh. "Judicial Authority in Early Israel: An Historical investigation of Old Testament Institutions." ThD diss., Princeton Theological Seminary, 1968.

Sanford, John A. *King Saul, the Tragic Hero: A Study in Individuation*. New York: Paulist, 1985.

Satterthwaite, Philip E. "Narrative Artistry in the Composition of Judges XX 29ff." *VT* 42, (1992) 80–89.

———. "'No King in Israel': Narrative Criticism and Judges 17–21." *TynB* 44 (1993) 75–88.

———. "Some Septuagintal Pluses in Judges 20 and 21." *BIOSCS* 24 (1991) 25–35.

Scarry, Elaine. *The Body in Pain: The Making and Unmaking of the World*. New York: Oxford University Press, 1985.

Scheffler, Eben H. "Saving Saul from the Deuteronomist." In *Past, Present, Future: The Deuteronomistic History and the Prophets*, edited by Johannes de Moore and Harry van Rooy, 263–71. OtSt 44. Leiden: Brill 2000.

Schmidt, Ludwig. *Menschlicher Erfolg und Jahwes Initiative: Studien zu Tradition, Interpretation und Historie in Überlieferungen von Gideon, Saul und David*. WMANT 38. Neukirchen-Vluyn: Neukirchener, 1970.

Schneider, David M., and Kathleen Gough., editors. *Matrilineal Kinship*. Berkeley: University of California Press, 1961.

Schneider, Tammi. *Judges*. Berit Olam. Collegeville, MN: Liturgical, 2000.

Schwager, Raymund. *Must There Be Scapegoats? Violence and Redemption in the Bible*. Translated by Maria L. Assad. San Francisco: Harper & Row, 1987.

Seebass, Horst. "Die Vorgeschichte der Konigserhebung Sauls: I Sam 10–11." *ZAW* 79 (1967) 155–71.

Seitz, Christopher, and Kathryn Greene-McCreight, editors. *Theological Exegesis: Essays in Honor of Brevard S. Childs*. Grand Rapids: Eerdmans, 1999.

Sharkansky, Ira. *Israel and Its Bible: A Political Analysis*. Garland Reference Library of Social Science 1031. New York: Garland, 1996.

Simons, Louise. "'An Immortality Rather Than a Life': Milton and the Concubine of Judges 19–21." In *Old Testament Women in Western Literature*, edited by Raymond-Jean Frontain and Jan Wojcik, 153–67. Conway, AR: UCA, 1991.

Simonse, Simon. *Kings of Disaster: Dualism, Centralism and the Scapegoat King in the Southeastern Sudan*. Studies in Human Society 5. Leiden: Brill, 1992.

Smend, Rudolf. *Die Entsehung des Alten Testaments*. TW 1. 2nd rev. ed. Stuttgart: Kohlhammer, 1981.

———. "Das Gesetz und die Völker: Ein Beitrag zur deuteronomistischen Redakionsgeschichte." In *Probleme Biblischer Theologie: Gerhard von Rad zum 70. Geburtstag*, edited by by Hans Walter Wolff, 494–509. Munich: Kaiser, 1971.

Smith, Jonathan Z. *To Take Place: Toward Theory in Ritual*. Chicago Studies in the History of Judaism. Chicago: University of Chicago Press, 1992.

Snyman, S. D. "Trends in the History of Research on the Problem of Violence in the Old Testament." *SK* 18 (1997) 127–45.

Soggin, J. Alberto. *Das Königtum in Israel: Ursprünge, Spannungen, Entwicklung*. BZAW 104. Berlin: Töpelmann, 1967.

———. *Joshua: A Commentary*. Translated by R. A. Wilson OTL. Philadelphia: Westminster, 1972.

———. *Judges: A Commentary*. Translated by John Bowden. OTL. Philadelphia: Westminster, 1981.

Speiser, E. A. "'Coming' and 'Going' at the City Gate." *BASOR* 144 (1956) 20–23.

Spina, Frank Anthony. "Eli's Seat: The Transition from Priest to Prophet in 1 Samuel 1–4." *JSOT* 62 (1994) 67–75.

Steinberg, Naomi. "Social Scientific Criticism: Judges 9 and Issues of Kinship." In *Judges and Method: New Approaches in Biblical Studies* edited by Gale A. Yee, 45–64. Philadelphia: Fortress, 1995.

Sternberg, Meir. *The Poetics of Biblical Narrative: Ideological Literature and the Drama of Reading.* Indiana Literary Biblical Series. Bloomington: Indiana University Press, 1987.

Stirling, Mack C. "Violent Religion: René Girard's Theory of Culture." In *Religion, Psychology and Violence,* edited by J. Harold Ellens, 11–50. The Destructive Power of Religion: Violence in Judaism, Christianity, and Islam 2. Westport, CT: Praeger, 2003.

Stoebe, Hans Joachim. *Das erste Buch Samuelis.* KAT 8/1. Gütersloh: Mohn, 1973.

———. *Das zweite Buch Samuelis.* KAT 8/2. Gütersloh: Mohn, 1994.

———. "Noch Einmal: Die Eselinnen Des Kīš (1 Sam IX)." *VT* 7 (1957) 362–70.

Stone, Kenneth Alan. "Gender and Homosexuality in Judges 19: Subject-Honor, Object-Shame?" *JSOT* 67 (1995) 87–107.

———. *Sex, Honor, and Power in the Deuteronomistic History.* JSOTSup 234. Sheffield, UK: JOST Press, 1996.

Sturdy, John. "The Original Meaning of 'Is Saul Also among the Prophets?' (1 Samuel 10:11, 12; 19:24)." *VT* 20 (1970) 206–13.

Sweeney, Marvin A. "Davidic Polemics in the Book of Judges." *VT* 47 (1997) 517–29.

Tanner, J. Paul. "The Gideon Narrative as the Focal Point of Judges." *BSac* 149 (1992) 146–61.

Toorn, Karel van der. "Saul and the Rise of Israelite State Religion." *VT* 43 (1993) 519–42.

Tapp, Anne Michele. "An Ideology of Expendability: Virgin Daughter Sacrifice in Genesis 19:1–11, Judges 11:30–39 and 19:22–26." In *Anti-Covenant: Counter-Reading Women's Lives,* edited by Mieke Bal, 157–74. Bible and Literature Series 22. JSOTSup 81. Sheffield, UK: Sheffield Academic, 1989.

Trible, Phyllis. *Texts of Terror: Literary-Feminist Readings of Biblical Narratives.* OBT 13. Philadelphia, Fortress, 1984.

Turner, Victor Witter. *The Forest of Symbols; Aspects of Ndembu Ritual.* Ithaca: Cornell University Press, 1973.

———. *The Ritual Process: Structure and Anti-Structure.* The Lewis Henry Morgan Lectures, 1966. Chicago: Aldine, 1969.

Ushedo, Benedict O. "'Unloading Guilt: The Innocent Victim as Illustrated by James Baldwin and René Girard.'" *JRT* 53 (1997) 131–48.

Van der Hart, Rob. "The Camp of Dan and the Camp of Yahweh." *VT* 25 (1975) 720–28.

Van Seters, John. "Histories and Historians of the Ancient Near East: The Israelites." *Or* 50 (1981) 137–85.

———. *In Search of History: Historiography in the Ancient World and the Origins of Biblical History.* New Haven: Yale University Press, 1983.

———. "Problems in the Literary Analysis of the Court History of David." *JSOT* 1 (1976) 22–29.

Vaux, Roland de. *Ancient Israel: Its Life and Institutions.* Translated by John McHugh. New York: McGraw-Hill, 1961.

Veijola, Timo. *Die ewige Dynastie: David und die Entstehung seiner Dynastie nach der deuteronomistischen Darstellung.* Suomalaisen Tiedeakatemian toimituksia. Sarja B. nide 193. Helsinki: Suomalainen Tiedeakatemia, 1975.

Vonk, C. "Ume'ah in Judges 20:35." In *The Law and the Prophets: Old Testament Studies Prepared in Honor of Oswald Thompson Allis*, edited by John H. Skilton, 277–82. Nutley, NJ: Presbyterian & Reformed, 1974.

Waard, Jan de. "Jotham's Fable: An Exercise in Clearing Away the Unclear." In *Wissenschaft und Kirche*, edited by Kurt Aland and Siegfried Meurer, 362–70. Texte und Arbeiten zur Bibel 4. Bielefeld: Luther, 1989.

Wadsworth, Michael, editor. *Ways of Reading the Bible*. Brighton, UK: Harvester, 1981.

Warner, Sean M. "Dating of the Period of the Judges." *VT* 28 (1978) 455–63.

———. "The Period of the Judges within the Structure of Early Israel." *HUCA* 47 (1976) 57–79.

Washburn, David L. "The Chronology of Judges: Another Look." *BSac* (1990) 414–24.

Wallace, Mark I. "Postmodern Biblicism: The Challenge of René Girard for Contemporary Theology." *ModT* 5 (1989) 309–25.

Wallace, Mark I., and Theophus H. Smith., editors. *Curing Violence*. Forum Fascicles 3. Sonoma, CA: Polebridge, 1994.

Wallis, Gerhard. "Eine Parallele zu Richter 19, 29ff. und 1 Sam 11,5ff. aus dem Briefarchiv von Mari." *ZAW* 64 (1952) 57–61.

Webb, Barry. G. *The Book of Judges: An Integrated Reading*. JSOTSup 46. Sheffield, UK: JSOT Press, 1987.

Weiser, Artur. *The Old Testament: Its Formation and Development*. Translated by D. M. Barton. New York: Association, 1961.

———. *Samuel; seine geschichtliche Aufgabe und religiose Bedeutung. Traditionsgeschichtliche Untersuchungen zu 1 Samuel 7–12*. FRLANT 81. Gottingen: Vandenhoeck & Ruprecht, 1962.

Wellhausen, Julius. *Die Composition des Hexateuchs und der historischen Bucher des Alten Testaments*. 3rd ed. Skizzen und Vorarbeiten Wellhausen 2. Berlin: Reimer, 1899.

———. *History of Israel*. Translation of *Prolegomena zur Geschichte Israels*. Edinburgh: Black, 1885.

———. *Der Text der Bücher Samuelis*. Göttingen: Vandenhoeck & Ruprecht, 1871.

———. *Prolegomena to the History of Ancient Israel*. New York: World 1957.

Westermann, D. Claus. "Was ist Frieden—Eine Anfrage an die Bibel." *CSF* (1982) 21–28.

White, Hayden V. "The Historical Text as Literary Artifact." In *Tropics of Discourse: Essays in Cultural Criticism*, edited by Hayden V. White, 81–100. Baltimore: Johns Hopkins University Press, 1985.

White, Marsha. "The History of Saul's Rise: Saulide State Propaganda in 1 Samuel 1–14." *BJS* 325 (2000) 271–92.

Whitelam, Keith W. *The Just King: Monarchical Judicial Authority in Ancient Israel*. JSOTSup 12. Sheffield, UK: JSOT Press, 1979.

Whybray, R. N. *The Succession Narrative: A Study of II Samuel 9–20 and I Kings 1 and 2*. Studies in Biblical Theology 2/9. Naperville, IL: Allenson, 1968.

Wildberger, H. "Samuel und die Enstehung des israelitischen Konigtums." *TZ* 13 (1957) 442–69.

Williams, James G., and René Girard. "Epilogue: The Anthropology of the Cross: A Dialogue with René Girard." In *The Girard Reader*, edited by James G. Williams, 289–94. New York: Crossroad, 2003.

Williams, James G. *The Bible, Violence, and the Sacred: Liberation from the Myth of Sanctioned Violence*. San Francisco: HarperSanFrancisco, 1991.

———. "History-Writing as Protest: Kingship and the Beginning of Historical Narrative." *CJVMC* 1 (1994) 91–110.
———, editor. *The Girard Reader*. New York: Crossroad, 1996.
———. "King as Servant, Sacrifice as Service: Gospel Transformations." In *Violence Renounced: René Girard, Biblical Studies, and Peacemaking*, edited by Willard M. Swartley, 178–99. Telford, PA: Pandora, 2000.
———. "René Girard without the Cross? Religion and the Mimetic Theory." *Anthropoetics* 2 (1996). Online: http://www.anthropoetics.ucla.edu/ap0201/girardw.htm/.
———. "Sacrifice and the Beginning Kingship: Ritual and Sacrifice in Biblical Studies." *Semeia* 67 (1995) 73–92.
———. "The Structure of Judges 2:6—16:31." *JSOT* 49 (1991) 77–85.
Williams, Rowan. *Violence, Society and the Sacred*. OPPS Paper 14. Oxford: Oxford Project for Peace Studies, 1989.
Wilson, Michael K. "'As You Like It': The Idolatry of Micah and the Danites (Judges 17–18)." *RTR* 54 (1995) 73–85.
Wilson, Robert R. "Israel's Judicial System in the Pre-Exilic Period." *JQR* 74 (1983) 229–48.
Wimbush, Vincent L., editor. *The Bible and the American Myth: A Symposium on the Bible and Constructions of Meaning*. Studies in American Biblical Hermeneutics 16. Macon, GA: Mercer University Press, 1999.
Wink, Walter. *Engaging the Powers: Discernment and Resistance in a World of Domination*. The Powers 3. Minneapolis: Fortress, 1992.
Wolff, Hans Walter. "The Kerygma of the Deuteronomic Historical Work." In *The Vitality of Old Testament Traditions*, Walter Brueggemann and Hans Walter Wolff, 83–100. Translated by Frederick C. Prussner. Atlanta: John Knox, 1975.
Van Wyk, W. C. "The Fable of Jotham in Its Ancient Near Eastern Setting (Judg 9:8–15)." In *Studies in Wisdom Literature*, edited by W. C. van Wyk, 89–95. OTWSA Series 15 and 16. Potchefstroom, South Africa: Pro Rege-Pers Beperk, 1976.
Yee, Gale A. "Ideological Criticism: Judges 17–21 and the Dismembered Body." In *Judges and Method: New Approaches in Biblical Studies*, edited by Gale A. Yee, 146–70. Minneapolis: Fortress, 1995.
———, editor. *Judges and Method : New Approaches in Biblical Studies*. Minneapolis: Fortress, 1995.
Yonick, Stephen. *Rejection of Saul as King of Israel according to 1 Sm. 15: Stylistic Study in Theology*. Jerusalem: Franciscan Printing, 1970.
Younger, K. Lawson, Jr. "Judges 1 in Its Near Eastern Literary Context." In *Faith, Tradition, and History: Old Testament Historiography in Its Near Eastern Context*, edited by A. R. Millard, et al., 207–27. Winona Lake, IN: Eisenbrauns, 1994.
Zeligs, Dorothy F. *Psychoanalysis and the Bible: A Study in Depth of Seven Leaders*. New York: Human Sciences, 1974.

Subject Index

Abel, 111, 163, 186
Abraham, 53, 92
Abram, 145
Acquisitive, 158
Ambivalent, 3, 9, 39, 45, 60, 85, 124, 138, 151, 155, 194
Ambivalence, 3, 10, 12, 13, 49, 56, 57, 111, 118, 154, 181, 194
Amphictyony, 26, 27
Anarchy, 2, 72, 73, 81, 87, 106, 144, 154, 163, 164, 167, 176, 181, 185, 187, 189, 197
Anonymity, 12, 47, 75, 83, 110, 111, 124, 126, 182
Anonymous, 6, 74, 75, 77, 98, 110, 111, 125, 127, 172, 186
Anti-kingship/ Anti-monarchy, 3, 4, 11, 12, 18–20, 30–32, 35, 36, 39, 114, 117, 127, 151, 181, 194, 195
Ark, 35, 105
Asses, 87, 123–25, 128, 133–35, 189
Assyria, 18, 21, 25
Atrocity/ Atrocities, 93, 111, 125, 188

Baal, 48, 49, 52, 54, 75
Babylon/ Babylonians, 2, 18, 21
Baggage, 139, 140
Barak, 69, 104
Belial, 91–95, 102, 145, 185, 195, 196
Benevolence, 62, 109
Benjamin, 84, 89, 93, 103–9, 111, 120, 122, 124, 129, 131, 134, 137, 138, 141, 142, 172, 173, 185, 186, 189, 196, 197
Bethlehem, 76, 82, 84–86, 89, 182
Beth-Millo, 56
Bone (and flesh), 50–52, 54, 100

Cain, 111, 163
Cathartic, 166
Chaos, 2, 15, 70, 72, 81, 101, 103, 111, 112, 118, 124, 141, 150–52, 164, 165, 170, 181, 186, 187, 198, 200, 201
Contagious, 8, 180
Corpse, 64, 98, 99, 143, 148, 192
Crowned/ Crowning, 64, 141, 187

Darkness, 88, 90, 96, 97, 105
Deborah, 28, 41, 71, 104, 171
Difference-maker, 67, 93, 149, 193

Ehud, 41, 71, 132
Ephod, 44, 54, 75, 77, 79, 103, 178, 179, 181, 183, 184
Escalates/ Escalating/ Escalation, 2, 7, 62, 92, 143, 154, 162, 178, 179, 185, 187, 189, 192
Exploitation, 109, 110

Fratricide, 1, 8, 13, 54, 107, 144, 176, 177, 200

Gaal, 62, 63, 64, 66, 69, 109, 110, 147, 162, 179, 180, 194, 199
Gerizim, 57

Gibeah, 76, 87, 89, 91–93, 97, 99, 102, 104–6, 121, 131, 133, 134, 136–38, 141–43, 151, 189, 191, 200
Gilgal, 123, 148, 149
Girls (unnamed), 109, 123, 124, 126, 129, 130, 136
Gore, 108, 110

Herem, 107
Holocaust, 107
Horror, 8, 68, 98, 108, 192

Imitation, 9, 43, 52, 54, 158, 160, 163, 164, 170
Inaugurate/Inaugurated/Inaugurating/Inauguration, 6, 10, 13, 15, 19, 20, 28, 31, 33, 35, 43, 45, 54, 56, 60, 62, 68, 87, 100, 101, 104, 108, 116–18, 122, 125, 126, 138–40, 144, 146–50, 152, 154, 155, 180, 189, 198, 200
Insider, 12, 47, 48, 49, 52, 57, 62, 63, 124, 125, 165, 172, 174, 177, 188

Jabesh-Gilead, 6, 13, 63, 103, 104, 108, 141, 142, 144–46, 148, 189, 191, 197, 200
Jebusites, 88, 136
Jepthah, 10, 71, 112, 171, 172

Kinsfolk, 106, 107, 192
Kinship, 5, 48, 59, 62, 68, 108, 117, 150
Kish, 120–22, 125, 139

Laish, 77, 78, 80, 81, 83, 183, 184, 195
Lamech, 163
Lots (cast), 29, 35, 103, 104, 138–40, 200

Mediator, 160–63
Midianites, 42–44
Mimesis, 2, 8, 9, 11, 43, 50, 148, 156–58, 160, 162, 163, 194, 199
Mizpah, 34, 101, 102, 108, 109, 123, 138, 141, 147

Nagid, 129, 130, 133
Nebalah, 94, 95

Outsider, 12, 45, 47–50, 52, 53, 59, 60, 62, 63, 76, 83, 124, 125, 151, 165, 172, 174, 177, 178, 201
Oxen, 9, 13, 100, 101, 118, 126, 143, 144, 146, 147, 148, 150, 151, 187, 189, 190, 191, 192, 193, 197, 200, 201

Peace, 12, 62, 77–79, 90, 109, 113, 141, 144, 151, 152, 154, 156, 164–68, 178–81, 186, 194–97
Pilegesh, 47, 83, 84, 87, 115
Prince , 6, 130, 138
Pro-kingship/Pro-monarchy, 3, 11, 12, 18–20, 31, 32, 35, 36, 39, 73, 87, 117, 127, 151, 152, 181, 194

Ramah, 123, 124, 189
Rape, 1, 92–95, 97, 98, 105, 109, 110, 142–45, 147, 173, 176, 182, 188, 196, 199, 200
Ravish, 95, 97
Reconciliation, 10, 39, 107, 108, 118, 129, 141, 150–52, 168, 169, 174, 187, 197, 201
Reign, 22, 23, 27, 34, 41, 60, 118, 120, 150, 151, 178, 180
Renewal, 6, 13, 149
Resolution, 2, 8–10, 12, 13, 110–12, 156, 157, 162–64, 166–68, 188

Ritual, 7, 8, 48, 129, 132, 157, 163, 166–69, 176, 181, 186, 192, 195, 196
Rival, 9, 62, 63, 159–61, 164, 194, 195
Ruler, 46, 50, 51, 53, 54, 62, 63, 78, 115, 129, 130, 133

Sacerdotal, 37, 39, 75, 89, 175
Sacrificial , 9, 12, 28, 30, 76, 82, 99, 107, 115, 116, 128–30, 143, 146, 150, 151, 163, 188–90, 193–95, 200
Salt, 65, 67, 195
Seventy, 43, 45, 48, 50, 51, 54–57, 59, 61, 63, 67, 75, 91, 177, 178
Shiloh, 93, 108–10, 125, 147, 186, 188
Shoulder(s), 56, 66, 67, 121, 132, 159, 199, 200
Silver, 54, 62, 81, 125, 182
Stone (one), 55, 56, 59, 67–69, 91, 178, 180, 195
Sword, 43, 44, 68, 69, 80, 107, 108

Thebez, 12, 66, 67, 69, 147, 162, 180, 199
Theocracy, 35
Thigh, 45, 131, 132, 134
Tower, 43, 60, 65–67, 107, 198
Triangular, 162, 180

Unification, 2, 166, 170, 195

Vengeance, 55, 65, 163, 188
Vile, 94

Warfare, 1, 192, 196
Warriors, 54, 104, 108, 195

Yoke of oxen, 9, 100, 143, 146, 151, 200, 201

Zuph, 124

Scripture Index

Genesis
18–19   92, 95, 96, 145, 151, 173

Exodus
29:17   193

Leviticus
1:6   193
1:12   193
8:20   193

Deuteronomy
3, 17, 18, 24, 53, 57, 91, 115

Joshua
5:10   149
10:43   149
22   116

Judges
1:1   106
2:5   116
6–8   37, 42, 44
6   116, 123
8:6   114
8:22   30, 43, 103
8:23   48, 50, 115
8:28   44
8:29—9:56   2, 10, 12
8:31   47, 48, 84, 116
9:2   50, 52
9:6   48
9:20   66
9:21   60, 131
9:22   60, 61, 129
9:23   61
9:26   62
9:27   63, 109
9:28   62, 63
9:29   63
11   102, 108
17–21   9–12, 35, 37, 46, 52, 68, 71–78, 110, 116, 131, 133, 170, 182, 183, 185–87, 194, 195
17–18   74, 82, 87, 181, 182, 184, 185, 195
17:1   2, 10, 75, 81
17:6   72, 181
17:12   76
18:5   77, 81
18:19   79, 184
18:20   79, 81, 87, 182
18:31   181, 182
19–21   13, 29, 47, 69, 74, 82, 86, 87, 96, 110, 133, 134, 136, 137, 141, 143, 144, 146, 147, 155, 181, 182, 184–86, 189, 193, 195, 197
19:1   9, 72, 76, 181, 182
19:3   84, 86, 97, 125
19:11   88, 136
19:13   125
19:14   89
19:15   89
19:16   142

229

19:17	89	9:24	131
19:28	70, 97, 98	10:1	129, 131, 132
20:1	100, 102, 142	10:6	61, 133
20:3	102, 138	10:7	124, 134, 135
20:5	61, 102	10:12	132
20:7	100, 102	10:16	30, 119, 205
20:10	103, 104	10:17	30, 34, 120, 136, 138
20:11	104	10:22	140
20:13	104, 147	10:24	139
20:23	106	10:26	30, 54, 104, 133, 140, 217
20:31	129, 137	11:1	30, 138, 141, 189, 219
20:34	107	11:2	154
20:39	137	11:4	106, 133, 142
20:40	107	11:5	106
21:3	185	11:6	61, 135, 145
21:4	185	11:7	100, 146, 193
21:6	185	11:9	135
21:10	108	11:10	144
21:25	2, 7, 10, 13, 72, 106, 112, 186	11:12	147
		11:13	147, 148
		12	4, 5, 33, 117
		31	148

1 Samuel

1–12	35
1	143
2	106
3	106
7–15	5, 6, 34, 205
7–12	5, 6, 222
7–8	30, 33
7	127
8–12	4, 5, 19, 32, 33, 35
8	4, 32, 114, 117, 129, 131, 132, 150
8:1	114
9–11	4, 5, 6, 9, 10, 11, 13, 19, 46, 73, 117–19, 138, 150, 170, 176, 182, 188, 194
9:1	2, 7, 10, 30, 50, 119, 120, 122, 123, 140, 212
9:4	124
9:6	125
9:9	125
9:16	48, 106, 129, 130, 135
9:23	129

2 Samuel

2, 4, 5, 6, 11, 38, 52, 69, 87, 103, 106, 190, 203, 204

1 Kings

1–8	38
18:23, 33	193

2 Kings

3, 4, 6, 16, 22, 23, 30, 38, 87